DATE DUE

Demco, Inc. 38-293

Applied Quantitative
Methods for
Health Services Management

Applied Quantitative Methods for Health Services Management

by

Lee F. Seidel, Ph.D.
Robin D. Gorsky, Ph.D.

and

James B. Lewis, Sc.D.

Department of Health Management and Policy
University of New Hampshire
Durham, New Hampshire

 HEALTH
PROFESSIONS
PRESS

Baltimore • London • Toronto • Sydney

#32016012

1-28-03

Health Professions Press, Inc.
P.O. Box 10624
Baltimore, MD 21285-0624

Typeset by Brushwood Graphics, Inc., Baltimore, Maryland.
Manufactured in the United States of America by
The Maple Press Company, Binghamton, New York.

Library of Congress Cataloging-in-Publication Data
Seidel, Lee F.
  Applied quantitative methods for health services management / by Lee F. Seidel,
  Robin D. Gorsky, and James B. Lewis.
      p.   cm.
  Includes bibliographical references and index.
  ISBN 1-878812-24-6
  1. Health services administration—Statistical methods.   2. Health services
  administration—Mathematical models.   I. Gorsky, Robin D.
  II. Lewis, James B. (James Bradley), 1950–   .   III. Title.
  [DNLM: 1. Statistics—methods.   2. Health Services—organization & adminis-
  tration.   3. Health Policy.   WA 950 S458a 1995]
RA394.S43   1995
362.1′068–dc20
DNLM/DLC
for Library of Congress   95-3855
                                                                        CIP

British Library Cataloguing-in-Publication data are available from the British
Library.

Contents

About the Authors

Lee F. Seidel, Ph.D., Department of Health Management and Policy, University of New Hampshire, Durham, New Hampshire 03824

Lee F. Seidel joined the faculty at the University of New Hampshire from Arthur Andersen & Co., an accounting and management consulting firm. While there, he specialized in providing management services to medical centers and voluntary health agencies. He has also served as Director of Institutional Development for Frisbie Memorial Hospital (Rochester, New Hampshire) and its related corporations, and was a project manager in the City of New York's Medicaid Reform Program during the Lindsay administration. He is a past chair of the Association of University Programs in Health Administration (AUPHA) and the senior author of *Strategic Management for Health Care Organizations* (AUPHA Press/National Health Publishing, Baltimore, MD: 1989). At the University of New Hampshire, Professor Seidel teaches baccalaureate and graduate courses on the management of hospitals and health care organizations and is Director of the Teaching Excellence Program. He is a faculty member in the American College of Healthcare Executives, has served on committees and task forces of the leading professional societies in his field, and is a recipient of the University of New Hampshire Faculty Award for Excellence in Public Service. Professor Seidel earned a baccalaureate degree from Hobart College, and a Master of Public Administration with concentration in hospital and health services administration and a doctoral degree in health systems planning and development from The Pennsylvania State University.

Robin D. Gorsky, Ph.D., Department of Health Management and Policy, University of New Hampshire, Durham, New Hampshire 03824

Robin D. Gorsky joined the faculty at the University of New Hampshire from the graduate faculty in health administration at the School of Public Health at the University of California at Berkeley. Her research has specialized in developing and applying quantitative models to epidemiological problems and analyzing the costs of preventing specific diseases. She is actively affiliated with the Centers for Disease Control and Prevention (CDC) as a cost-effectiveness consultant, providing technical assistance to many programs seeking to determine the costs and effectiveness of prevention interventions. Her research has appeared in many scholarly journals. She is an active member of the Operations Research Society of America, the American Public Health Association, the Society for Epidemiologic Research, and the American Association for the Advancement of Science. She has held visiting faculty appointments at the Harvard School of Public Health and the Emory University School of Medicine. At the University of New Hampshire, Professor Gorsky teaches courses in epidemiology and quantitative methods. She earned a baccalaureate degree from the University of California at San Diego, a Master of Business Administration from the University of Houston, and a doctoral degree in systems analysis and health policy from the University of California at Berkeley.

James B. Lewis, Sc.D., Department of Health Management and Policy, University of New Hampshire, Durham, New Hampshire 03824

James B. Lewis joined the faculty at the University of New Hampshire after 13 years as a management consultant, most recently as a principal for William M. Mercer, Inc. His consulting clients included some of the nation's largest health care delivery systems, academic medical centers, large employers and unions, community hospitals, physician groups, managed care organizations, and several state and local governments. At the University of New Hampshire, Professor Lewis teaches courses in health care finance and reimbursement, managed care, and marketing. His writings have appeared in *Topics in Health Care Financing, Healthcare Financial Management, Compensation and Benefits Management, Best of Healthcare Marketing,* and the *Journal of Health Administration Education.* His research focuses on the behavioral impact of various reimbursement strategies on providers. He also has served as a Fellow for the Accrediting Commission on Education for Health Services Administration (ACEHSA), and was named a Health Insurance Faculty Fellow by the Health Insurance Association of America and the Association of University Programs in Health Administration. In 1994 Professor Lewis was honored as the Outstanding Assistant Professor at the University of New Hampshire. He earned a baccalaureate degree from the University of Pittsburgh, a Master in Management with concentration in hospital and health services management from Northwestern University, and a Doctor of Science degree in health policy and management from the Johns Hopkins University.

Preface

Our purpose in writing this book is to enhance the ability of students of health administration to manage health care services. This book is designed to bring numerous quantitative methods drawn from many other fields into the field of health services management. Its sole intent is to ensure that these skills are included in the repertoire of the professional manager employed by health care organizations.

This book assumes a general understanding of algebra, statistics, and financial and managerial accounting, as well as a general understanding of economics, health care organizations, and health services management. Based on these foundation competencies, quantitative methods are presented within the context of health services administration. Some methods are highly quantitative, others are not. Every effort has been made to avoid obscuring these methods behind algebraic or quantitative curtains. Where doubt exists, we have simplified our presentation.

Methods are limited to those that have broad application to the management of health care organizations. In some instances, presentation of methods has been limited to only those aspects of a specific quantitative method that has broad application in health services management, leaving more advanced and more specialized applications for advanced study. We have attempted to avoid quantitative methods that are not used by health services managers. Similarly, this book is not intended to expand a student's ability to perform health services research. It includes only those quantitative methods we believe are actually used by health services managers.

An important competency of a health services administrator is to know when to use a specific skill or quantitative method, as well as how to use that specific skill or method. The first competency requires judgment and wisdom; the second requires practice and understanding. As you proceed through this book, remember the first as well as the second. Being able to match a management situation with the appropriate quantitative methods is an important aspect of this topic. Professional health service administrators know when as well as how to use a specific quantitative method. Knowing when a technique is not appropriate is an important corollary.

The eclectic array of methods presented may surprise many. Some methods appear basic—so basic, in fact, that they are generally not included in other collections with similar purposes. These basic methods of analysis are included here to ensure that all students have a solid grasp of both basic and more advanced methods of analysis. Our experience with students at the University of New Hampshire, both baccalaureate and graduate, suggests that learning and being able to use quantitative methods requires learning experiences designed as loops, not straight lines. Basic points, terms, and calculations must be repeated to be incorporated effectively in the student's repertoire. Assuming that a student possesses complete recall of an earlier course in statistics, for example, is an instructional blunder that jeopardizes the effectiveness of a professor as well as the ability of students to learn.

In other aspects this book resembles texts used throughout the management and administrative sciences. Whenever appropriate, supporting bibliographies have been included. Material contained in this work has been drawn from many fields, including industrial engineering, operations research, finance, and general systems analysis. In some instances, included material has been designed to meet specific competency requirements for health services managers. Many of the quantitative methods and applications stress basic, in contrast to advanced, understanding, knowledge, and skills. Knowing the basics provides the student the foundation necessary for competent professional practice as well as to advance as needed. Above all, it is a book written for the field of health services management.

Many of the quantitative methods included in this work can be used with general spreadsheet programs. In some instances, specific software exists to apply specific methods. We have, however, avoided specific software applications and specific instructions on how to use specific spreadsheet programs. Students need to be encouraged to use the power of computers and available software whenever possible to complete assigned exercises.

This volume was originally designed and developed for health management and policy students at the University of New Hampshire. It emerged from the authors' search for a more effective approach to teaching students how to use quantitative methods as health services managers. Recent students deserve special recognition for helping us appreciate the difference between teaching and learning quantitative methods, for critically evaluating earlier drafts, and for assisting in determining effective teaching and learning strategies. However, we take full responsibility for our efforts. Throughout this book, practice as well as understanding is stressed. It is our conclusion that students are better able to incorporate these methods into their professional repertoires when they have had the opportunity to experience and apply these methods in a context related to their professional interests. Exercises have been incorporated into each chapter for students to use to try out a particular method. When we use this book, students are often required to turn in assigned exercises as their ticket into a specific course. Reading about a quantitative method is not the same as using the method to solve a realistic health services management problem.

Developing the comprehensive repertoire of skills needed to be a professional manager of health services is a student's responsibility. It is a complex, ambiguous, and challenging endeavor that spans a career. No one collection of quantitative methods is sufficient to meet this challenge. We hope, however, that this collection will assist many in developing their basic repertoire.

Applied Quantitative
Methods for
Health Services Management

I

FOUNDATION COMPETENCIES

A foundation competency is a skill or insight considered essential for subsequent success. Chapter 1, "The Role and Function of Quantitative Methods in Health Services Management," presents a conceptual statement concerning this subfield in the overall field of health services management. Knowing the role and function of quantitative methods in health services management is a fundamental skill and should lead to the reasoned use of these methods. It links specific methods to the professional fields and, in the process, establishes the basis for the application of specific methods. It also provides a general overview of this book.

The proficient use of quantitative methods requires the ability to construct and solve mathematical equations and use basic statistics. Chapter 2, "Working With Numbers," reviews basic algebra and statistics to ensure a common understanding. It cannot replace formal study in these areas but is designed to refresh and sharpen memories and skills.

Chapter 3, "Presenting Data," indicates the rules and conventions to follow when tables and charts are used to report analyses. Too often, expert analysis is clouded behind incompetent presentations. Chapter 3 indicates that presentation is a management competency inseparable from the professional use of quantitative methods.

Chapter 4, "General Systems Flow Charting," presents a very basic and robust method of describing and analyzing systems. Even though it involves no mathematics or statistics, general systems flow charting is an analytical method. Like methods rooted in mathematics and statistics, it uses a type of symbolic logic to provide the health services manager with the ability to describe current operations as well as to design needed revisions.

Students traditionally approach resource valuation concepts and methods with some trepidation. Chapter 5, "The Present and Future Value of Money," provides a clear and systematic review of techniques needed to value resources within the appropriate time periods used in an analysis.

Each of these chapters discusses a fundamental competency needed as part of the repertoire of the health services manager. Although other fundamental competencies exist, this section includes only subjects directly related to methods presented in subsequent parts. Some students may approach this part with expert knowledge in these areas. If this is the case, Part I can be used to solidify knowledge. Others may need to use this section to become proficient in the foundations skills and insights. All users are advised to complete all exercises included in this part.

1

The Role and Function of Quantitative Methods in Health Services Management

Chapter Objectives

1. To describe how quantitative methods fit into the repertoire of the health services manager
2. To define and explain efficiency as a managerial interest
3. To examine how health services managers analyze, design, and implement in a systems context

Key Terms and Concepts

Analysis	Implementation
Capacity	Inputs
Conversion processes	Outputs or outcomes
Design	Suboptimization
Effectiveness	System modifiers
Efficiency	Utilization
Feedback	Value added

Health administration, as a profession, deals with management of human, fiscal, physical, and information resources to meet the goals and objectives of health care organizations. Survival of the health care organization in a competitive environment, as well as characteristics of this survival, involve multiple factors, including the abilities of managers. The challenge in health administration is to provide health care organizations, and the communities, patients, and clients they serve, with competent individuals able to perform the robust and challenging role of manager.

Being a competent manager in a health care organization means fundamentally different things depending on specific role expectations, perspectives, and circumstances. Within a health care organization, managers are assigned very different functions, each with potentially different definitions of core competency. Managers in the human resources department of a hospital face different management challenges than do managers in the hospital's planning and marketing department. Different types of health care organizations may require different types of managers. The types of skills and values required to manage a nursing home may be different from those required to manage an ambulatory care clinic. Health care organizations also may shift their definition of desired or needed management competency as a result of a shift in their objectives, in characteristics in their environment, or in both. A hospital in the process of affiliating with a regionally integrated health care system may require different management talents than would a hospital intending to remain a solo institution. Horizontally integrated health care corporations may require different types of managers than do vertically integrated health care corporations. Definitions of management competency also may change based on perceived or real changes in the field of management. The competencies expected of a professional health services manager encompass a substantial breadth and depth of potential responsibilities, values, interests, and abilities. Health administrators need a large repertoire of skills to function in this dynamic situation. Being able to use specific formal quantitative methods designed to assist managers in making decisions is one essential part of this repertoire—a common denominator that transcends the many roles and functions performed by the health services manager.

THE MANAGER'S ROLE AND FUNCTION

Multiple perspectives abound concerning the role and function of the health administrator in contemporary health care organizations. Multiple perspectives also exist concerning what the manager should be able to do. Figure 1-1 shows one framework for integrating many of these perspectives, based on the simple recognition that all managers need the abilities to analyze, to design, and to implement. Although they are general management competencies, these abilities must be adapted to the challenges faced by the health administrator in a health care organization.

Analyzing, as a core managerial competency, is the ability to discover what is. It involves, for example, discovering the current market share of an organization. It involves discovering the actual total cost of a specific service rendered by the organization. It involves discovering who does what with what resources in order to provide a specific service. It involves using forecasting to discover the logical or reasonable future of the organization. The key and defining aspect of analysis is discovery. Sometimes discoveries shift the organization's goals and objectives. Other times, discovery is used to determine whether and how the organization is meeting its goals and objectives. To facilitate discovery, quantitative methods provide the man-

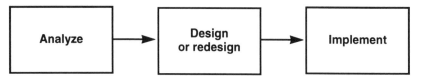

Figure 1-1.   General management competencies.

ager with an analytical road map. Each quantitative method has a unique analytical ability. For example, a method such as queuing theory can be used only to analyze specific types of waiting lines. When incorporated into the manager's repertoire, quantitative methods provide the manager with useful and robust tools.

Designing, as a core management competency, is the ability to identify and arrange resources in a manner commensurate with goals and objectives. If the goal is to provide a specific service, managers need to be able to design (or redesign) the mix of resources required to provide the service. The goal of operating a short-stay surgical unit in a hospital requires that a manager identify and arrange the resources needed to realize the goal, such as specialized equipment and staff. The goal of retaining specific information within the organization requires the manager to be able to design work processes to capture, report, and store the desired information. Design as a managerial competency often involves industrial engineering because it encompasses the ability to break down desired capabilities, such as an organization's goals and objectives, into requisite components or parts. Managers must be able to analyze existing services and then design the changes and additions needed to meet changing expectations. If the organization desires a new service, it is the manager's responsibility to design the service by first determining the different mix of human, fiscal, physical, and informational resources needed to provide the service and then specifying exactly how much of each will be needed to provide the service. Design of new work processes, or the redesign of existing ones, involves developing detailed plans so that, when the plans are executed, the desired capability has been incorporated into the organization. Design also involves determining how the necessary resources should be used. Design is performance oriented; the new or revised design must establish the desired performance capability.

Implementing, as a core management competency, is the ability to change the organization. The process of implementation may require the manager to change the behavior of specific employees. It also may involve the ability of the manager to accumulate and operationalize the resources necessary to achieve desired goals and objectives. Whereas design determines what is needed, implementation is the process that installs new or revised elements in the organization. The manager's repertoire must include quantitative methods to assist him or her in implementing change within the organization. These methods include, for example, *program evaluation review technique (PERT)*. PERT is a formal method used by managers to plan and control projects. It informs managers of the desired order and schedule of activities that must be accomplished to realize the overall completion of a project or change within the organization, such as the opening of a new short-stay surgical unit in a hospital.

MANAGING IN THE HEALTH CARE ORGANIZATION

A health care organization is any organization that provides health and medical services to patients, residents, and clients, such as an acute care or specialty hospital, a nursing home, an ambulatory care clinic (e.g., university health services), or a home health agency. The defining characteristic in this definition of a health care organization is patient care: care provided by physicians, nurses, and therapists to prevent and treat disease or infirmity. The mission of these organizations serves to distinguish them as health care organizations.

Services provided to patients could include a surgical procedure, a diagnostic examination, a specialized treatment, or a disease prevention or screening program. These services could also be an appropriate meal, a safe and comfortable environment, or an accurate and timely bill for service. All health care organizations provide a range of services and specialize in providing individual patients with a particularized array of services based on each patient's needs or diagnosis. The central and defining element of all health care organizations is the provision of a personal and personalized, high-quality health or medical service. Therefore, a central expectation shared by all health administrators is that management practice will lead to the *efficient* provision of *effective* services to people in need of service.

Efficiency and Effectiveness as Management Interests

The interests of managers and the interests of the health care organizations that employ health administrators as managers are difficult to distinguish. Both interests emphasize that patients receive needed services and that services are provided in an *efficient* manner. Health care organizations and health administrators rely on physicians, nurses, and therapists to determine or diagnose the needs of a patient accurately and to plan and execute an intervention or treatment that has some probability of success in maintaining or improving the health status of the patient. Clinical interests stress the needs of individual patients and the identification of appropriate service interventions. Decisions made by clinicians are based on what they consider to be *effective* approaches, interventions that have some probability of clinical or medical success. The physician, nurse, or therapist has been educated and trained to select and apply current knowledge to assist patients. Clinical interests and perspectives are focused on the effectiveness of a service—the ability of a service to accomplish its predetermined objective. Although clinicians are not necessarily oblivious or insensitive to efficiency, their unique role and function stems from their commitment to provide effective service to patients. They alone have the expertise to determine a patient's needs (i.e., diagnosis) and to meet them (i.e., treatment), and they are judged by their peers, specific systems, and patients based on their ability to provide an effective, but not necessarily an efficient, service.

Efficiency as a Management Interest

Efficiency is the ratio measure of input to output. High efficiency is achieved when a service is rendered using the least amount of resources. Inefficient clinical practice, such as requiring more clinical tests than necessary to make an accurate diagnosis, if rampant throughout the health care organization, can lead to a highly inefficient health care organization. Other examples of operational inefficiency are using more medical supplies than needed or even stocking more medical supplies than needed. Using an excess number of people to prepare a meal or render a bill is inefficient; an excess amount of input resources are being used to produce a specific output. Unlike operational effectiveness, which is primarily the province of the clinician, operational efficiency lies within the dual province of both clinicians and managers. Health administrators are retained to analyze, design, and implement work processes in the health care organization that lead to desired levels of operational efficiency.

Inefficient work processes waste scarce resources. Efficient work processes provide services that maximize the opportunities created by the mix of resources used to produce the service. Managers are employed by organizations to ensure that desired levels of efficiency are attained not by accident, but by design. Being interested in efficiency differentiates the health services manager from the health services clinician. Striving for maximum appropriate efficiency is a management value that requires a specific repertoire of skills—the ability to analyze current levels of efficiency, the ability to design and redesign services to achieved desired levels of efficiency, and the ability to implement new or revised services.

Effectiveness as a Management Interest

Effectiveness is the ability to accomplish a defined task. For example, if a specific drug is able to cure a specific infection, then that drug is effective. If a specific medical procedure or therapy is able to cure or alleviate a specific disease or infirmity, then the procedure or therapy is effective. To be effective, then, a procedure or drug must accomplish its intended purpose. Multiple factors may influence the effectiveness of a planned intervention or treatment. For example, some patients may respond differently to the same drug. Sometimes the effectiveness of a procedure or treatment is influenced by the behavior of the patient, something not totally controllable by the clinician. Effective treatments are those treatments that have a probability of success; sometimes these probabilities may be 5%, 50%, or 95% depending on the state of clinical and scientific knowledge, the existing health status of the patient, or both.

Health care organizations rely on clinically trained professionals to select the appropriate clinical services or treatments for specific patients from the array of services offered by the organization. Clinical professionals are expected to select appropriate services and, if these services are not available in the health care organization, to refer the patient to another organization. In the health care organization, managers are not empowered to override or veto clinical judgments involving a patient's diagnosis or treatment. Clinical protocols are established by clinical professionals, not managers. At the operational level, the clinical staff determine how effective the organization will be in accomplishing its mission to provide a high-quality personal and personalized health or medical service to specific patients (in order to treat disease or infirmity).

At the strategic or macro level of organizational decision making and action, however, managerial interests involving organizational effectiveness emerge. For example, the costs and benefits of investing in a new technology must be identified and examined from both a clinical and an organizational perspective before the decision is made by the organization to acquire and implement it. Even though a new technology may enhance the effectiveness of the clinicians affiliated with the organization and thereby increase the organization's effectiveness, its acquisition and/or operational cost to the organization may prevent the organization from acquiring it. Managerial involvement in these types of strategic decisions is one example of how managers influence the effectiveness of the health care organization. Health administrators are also trained to use epidemiology and are expected to use it to analyze the health and medical needs of the communities and groups of individuals served or potentially served by the health care organization.

Efficiency and Managerial Competence

Just as clinical operational effectiveness is the responsibility of the clinical professional, operational and organizational efficiency is the primary responsibility of the health administrator as manager. As stated, efficiency means providing a needed service using no more resources than necessary; it is a ratio measure of input to output. Health administrators are employed in part to ensure that any service provided by the health care organization is provided in an efficient manner. Being able to determine current levels of efficiency is an example of analysis as a managerial competency. Being able to design or redesign how the organization does something in order to enhance efficiency is an example of design as a managerial competency. Being able to change how the organization provides a service in order to enhance operational efficiency is an example of implementation as a managerial competency.

Striving to make the health care organization efficient is a dominating, unique, and defining value associated with management and managers in the field of health administration. Whereas the credit for effective clinical practice must be given to the clinical sciences and professions and the technologies they use, credit for efficient operations and the efficient use of resources must be given to health administrators and their abilities to analyze, design, and implement.

QUANTITATIVE METHODS AS MANAGEMENT SKILLS

Health administrators as managers have unique repertoires. Health services managers know how to do things other people do not. Health services management is a profession based on a unique body of knowledge, values, and skills. As part of their defining repertoire, managers employed by a health care organization need to know how to design efficient systems of health and medical care and how to improve the efficiency of existing systems of care. In other words, efficiency is important to health services managers. Tools, techniques, and models to use to improve the efficiency of health and medical care systems are essential elements in the repertoire of health services managers. Most methods are related to "efficiency." This should not be misinterpreted to mean, however, that health services management is only interested in or trained to improve efficiency. Efficiency as well as effectiveness are central values for the professional manager of health services.

Like many other fields, management can be thought of as reasoned judgment. In making a reasoned judgment, managers need formal methods to assist them to define and resolve problems. Just as master chefs need recipes to govern their culinary creations, the health services manager needs formal methods to analyze and improve complex systems. Using quantitative methods, however, does not absolve the manager from the responsibility of being a manager; they merely aid the manager in making reasoned judgments. These methods, many of which come from operations research, applied statistics, and industrial engineering, provide managers with specific protocols to analyze current levels of efficiency, design new services or redesign existing services to enhance efficiency, and implement change efficiently.

Most of the quantitative methods used by health services managers are based on the fundamental ability of health care organizations and health administrators to count. For example, to determine service efficiency, health care organizations count or account for their resources and services. Health care organizations count:

The number of laboratory tests performed
The number of patient visits to an emergency room
The number of meals served to nursing home residents

The number and type of surgical operations
The number and type of employees used to provide specific services
The costs associated with each service

Management actions designed to assess and improve the efficiency and effectiveness of a health care organization always begin by counting what is being done currently.

Although basic, counting may not be simple. Every health care organization provides a broad array of services, and not everything done in the health care organization can or should be counted. Health care organizations count those aspects of their operation necessary to assess service effectiveness and/or efficiency. For example, hospitals count the number of patients discharged and the number of days patients spend in a hospital in order to calculate the average length of stay (ALOS) of their patients. ALOS is a traditional measure of hospital activity. Some hospitals compare themselves with other similar institutions to determine whether they are adhering to similar patterns of utilization. All hospitals generally compare their ALOS with national trends and take national trends into consideration when forecasting service utilization. When ALOS is calculated by specific medical diagnosis, comparing results by attending physicians may also yield important information concerning the effectiveness and efficiency of clinical practice. Calculating the ALOS of a hospital, like so many similar calculations, begins with counting.

Ambulatory care clinics also count. For example, they count the number of patient visits per day, usually by time of day. This information can assist the manager in determining whether the staffing in the clinic is appropriate for the demand for service. This information can also be used to design efficient staffing levels based on demand levels that change according to the hour of the day, the day of the week, and the month of the year.

Other examples of counting include dietary departments in hospitals and nursing homes counting the number of meals prepared and served. Custodial services in all types of health care organizations usually count the number of square feet cleaned and the number of staff hours used to clean. Because efficiency is a ratio measure of input (e.g., staff hours used to clean) to output (square feet cleaned), counting enables the manager to analyze current levels of efficiency, design new approaches to enhance efficiency, and implement any needed changes. Being more efficient requires knowing the amount of work accomplished as a measure of output and the amount of resources used to accomplish the work as a measure of input. Knowing input and output levels is a prerequisite for analysis and design or redesign.

Still other examples can be found throughout health care organizations. For example, medical laboratories count the number and type of medical tests processed. This provides a statement of the laboratory's output. It also provides a statement of the tests physicians ordered to accomplish their diagnoses. Both can be used to assess efficiency and effectiveness. Business offices in hospitals count the number and type of health insurance claims processed, pharmacies count the number and type of prescriptions filled, and hospitals count the number of live births. Counting is the universal common attribute of each of these activities and a prerequisite to assessing and improving service efficiency and effectiveness.

To count appropriately often requires using a unique classification or counting system. Diagnosis-related groups (DRGs) help hospitals count appropriately the number and type of patients discharged. The classification system objectively assigns each discharged patient to a specific category. The number of patients in each category can then be counted by day, week, or year to yield an accurate listing of hospital actions by discharge diagnosis. Although they are currently used as a basis for reimbursement, DRGs were developed as an output measurement system for hospitals.

Health care organizations also count mistakes, such as mistakes made in administering medications and blood transfusions and mistakes made in surgery. Surgical deaths are counted. Postoperative infections are counted. Pathology reports that indicate an unnecessary surgical extraction are counted. Patient complaints are counted. Inaccurate patient bills are counted. Meals served cold are counted. Patients inappropriately transported to another health care organization are counted. Stock-out conditions in inventory are counted. Single mistakes and/or patterns of mistakes can be used to determine where change (i.e., redesign) is needed in the health care organization.

The services provided by the health care organization create a record that can be counted. Once services are counted, the information expands the manager's ability to analyze the effectiveness and efficiency of the organization or a part of the organization. Service counts are a product of what services were offered by the organization (i.e., capacity) and the frequency with which these services were used (i.e., utilization). The difference between capacity and utilization is an important distinction.

Every health care organization offers a unique array of services and has a finite or limited service capacity. For example, a 100-bed hospital has the capacity to generate no more than 36,500 patient days in a typical year (i.e., 365 days $\times$ 100 beds). Some health care organizations have the capacity to perform surgery and others do not. For example, not all hospitals have the capacity to perform neurosurgery and therefore would not create any service counts involving this type of surgical operation. Not all hospitals have the capacity to offer patients certain cancer treatments. To assess efficiency requires knowing the capacity of the health care organization as well as how the capacity is used.

Utilization is the amount of capacity actually used and is usually reported for a specific period of time, such as an hour, shift, day, week, month, or year. The frequency of a service being rendered, aside from being dependent on its availability, also reflects the need (and demand) for the available service. Often this need is a decision made by a clinician. A count of laboratory tests by type of test indicates the contribution a medical laboratory makes to the effective operation of the health care organization and effective medical care. This same count also can be used to assess service efficiency when combined with counts of the number and type of supplies used and the number and type of staff used in the laboratory as input measures. When combined with measures of capacity, counts that indicate utilization provide the ability to determine the amount and percentage of capacity being used.

Improving the operation of any health care organization through the application of quantitative methods begins with improving its ability to count, something usually performed by an information system. What is counted and how it is counted is important because these counts establish the data library managers rely on as they analyze and design. Formal analytical methods, techniques, and models designed to assess efficiency and effectiveness can be used only in conjunction with an adequate data library. Some quantitative methods have very specialized demands in terms of what must be counted in order to use the specific method. Therefore, what is placed in a data library will influence the manager's ability to perform expected functions, namely, the improvement of the efficiency of the health care organization using an appropriate method, technique, or model.

THE GENERAL SYSTEMS MODEL

Management, as a profession and field, has long searched for specific methods to assist managers in analyzing, designing, and implementing change as organizations strive to enhance their efficiency and effectiveness. Some methods still in use today trace their birth to the era of scientific management and the needs of large-scale production lines designed to produce physical products, such as automobiles, efficiently. In that era, the complex organization was conceptualized as a machine, with the pieces of the organization thought of as cogs in the machine. Workers were considered cogs. Equipment was considered cogs. Managers were retained to design organizations as machines and ensure that the cogs did what they were supposed to do in the most efficient manner possible. Managers wrote procedures to tell human cogs how to do their specific job. Specific methods also were developed to determine the efficiency of individual cogs and assist managers in designing or redesigning cogs and machines. Organizations that produced the best for least were considered survivors.

In that earlier era, division of labor was a new concept; workers were retained to perform one set of tasks necessary for the finished product, not as craftsmen held individually responsible for an entire product. The need for people as managers also was new. Managers were expected to coordinate the cogs in the machine to ensure efficiency. More efficient machines were understood to be more desirable than less efficient machines, workers were considered nothing more than extensions of the machine, and science or engineering professionals were called upon to analyze operations and design or redesign work processes. Some of the quantitative methods used today by health administrators trace their conceptual roots to this era. Techniques drawn from industrial engineering, operations research, and operations management emphasize the production characteristics of the organization. Although the era of managers looking to classical bureaucratic theory and the principles of scientific management is over, many quantitative techniques remain available for health administrators to use to analyze, design, and implement within the health care organization.

Today, managers in general, and health administrators in particular, are more likely to rely on general systems theory (Figure 1-2) for concepts and direction. This theory suggests that health care organizations are one example of goal-directed systems with identifiable inputs, work processes that convert inputs into outputs (outcomes), identifiable outputs, and feedback loops that serve to direct and control the system. To understand the complexity of activity within any organization, the general systems model provides the ability to assign activities or features of the organization to one of four categories: inputs or resources, conversion processes (i.e., what is done with the inputs), outcomes (what is desired), and feedback.

Organizations are considered open systems that are influenced by events and circumstances external to the organization. Organizations as open systems draw resources from their dynamic environment and provide back to their environment

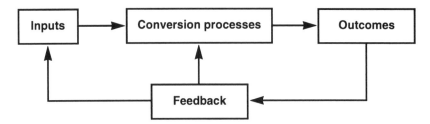

Figure 1-2.   The general systems model.

some valued product or service. In spite of this fundamental change in the way managers think about organizations and management, quantitative methods originally developed during the era of scientific management are still used and considered central in the repertoire of methods that defines the unique abilities of the manager.

Elements of the General Systems Model

Using general systems theory to improve the efficiency and effectiveness of the health care organization requires appreciation of the defining elements of the general systems model.

Organizational Goals

Any system strives to attain its goals by accumulating sufficient resources and converting these resources into desired products or services. Goals express the intent of the system. Organizations, however, have multiple and sometimes conflicting goals. For example, maximizing organizational profit and providing services to anyone regardless of his or her ability to pay are potentially conflicting goals for any private health care corporation. Therefore, the use of the general systems model may be limited by the type and amount of goal ambiguity or conflict that exists in the health care organization. The first and most important analytical challenge faced in the quest for improved efficiency and effectiveness is to identify system goals.

Inputs

Inputs are the resources needed to achieve a desired goal, often expressed as a desired output or outcome. Inputs are what is needed to accomplish the desired goal of the system. Inputs can be referred to as the organization's resources. Examples include:

People, each with a skill deemed to be needed by the organization
Time
Supplies and materials
Capital assets, such as buildings and equipment

Based on this definition, it is reasonable to expect that, because of their different goals, different types of health care organizations have different input resources. For example the input resources needed by a nursing home are different from the input resources needed by an acute care hospital or a clinic. An organization's wealth may also determine its inputs. Many inputs can be purchased, so the amount and type of input resources held by the organization may be a product of the financial position of the organization.

As they are used, most input resources are counted. Financial accounting counts expenses and revenues by category. Other processes count the number and types of workers employed and the numbers of hours worked. Still other systems count the supplies used.

Conversion Processes

Conversion processes convert inputs into outputs or outcomes. A surgical procedure is a conversion process. It takes a specific array of inputs (e.g., people such as a surgeon and nurses, plus capital assets and equipment) and converts them into a desired outcome, such as the removal of a diseased gallbladder. Conversion adds value. A conversion process takes inputs and produces an outcome. In the process, value is added. Working with clinicians, health administrators strive for efficient as well as effective conversion processes.

System Modifiers

System modifiers influence inputs and conversion processes. A system modifier is a something that influences a conversion process but is outside the direct control of the system. Examples of modifiers include needs, demands, desires, social values, and physical climate. For example, how a hospital converts resources into patient days is influenced by the "need" for medical care. As "need" changes, such as with the advent of HIV infection, conversion processes are changed (e.g., blood is transfused using different procedures/universal precautions). Laws and regulations also modify and influence conversion processes.

System modifiers can be as bold as a fundamental change in reimbursement policies or as subtle as a specific health profession striving for the autonomy, status, and income historically reserved for the physician. A system modifier also can be the cultural attributes of the specific organization when these attributes either cannot or will not be changed.

Outcomes and Outputs

Outcomes or outputs are the results created by the system. It is hoped that these results are the desired, intended, or expected goals of the system (or subsystem) under study. If results match expectations, the system is accomplishing its goals. If results do not match expectations, change may be required. Examples of outcomes include the improved health status of the population, the organization's financial position, the number and type of hospital patient days or discharges, the number and type of clinic visits, or the number of meals served. Outcomes or outputs are the units of service produced by the organization. Many outcomes or outputs are counted by organizations. For example, outcomes involving the worth of an organization are counted using financial accounting. Statistics are generated by organizations that report their outputs and outcomes.

Subsystems and Suboptimization

For purposes of analysis, design, and implementation, large complex systems are usually conceptualized as having multiple layers or subsystems. For example, a human body as a system has one subsystem for circulation and another to control its nerve functions. Subsystems serve systems. For example, the dietary, imaging, medical information, and patient processing subsystems serve the acute care system, called a hospital, created by the interplay of numerous subsystems.

Within the hierarchical and interdependent arrangement created by subsystems within a system, suboptimization may occur. Suboptimization reflects the recognition that the ultimate goal of any subsystem is to meet the requirements of its larger system, and that meeting these larger and more important system requirements may mean that any individual subsystem may need to operate at less than its highest level of efficiency. Because expectations placed on subsystems come from system goals and objectives, managers expect to have inefficient subsystems so that the organization as a system can be efficient. Suboptimization occurs when subsystems perform below their potential so that the overall organization as a system meets its goals and objectives. In some instances, managers design subsystems to perform below their potential. In other words, suboptimization can be a design parameter used in designing subsystems.

A classic example of suboptimization is a hospital's emergency room. By definition, the emergency room is intended to be very inefficient. Staff are retained to be available and provide services when they are needed. Service is expected to be available, but not necessarily used, 24 hours per day, 7 days per week. From this perspective, the utilization of an emergency room typically is only a small percentage of its capacity. In most emergency rooms, input levels are high and output levels relatively low.

Feedback

Feedback is typically information the organization generates to adjust inputs and/or conversion processes in order to change the desired outcome or make the actual outcome resemble more closely the organization's goals. Health care organizations produce multiple forms of feedback. Patient outcomes are feedback. Patient opinions about their service encounters are feedback. Market share is feedback. The balance sheet and statement of income and expenses are feedback, just as conversation between employees is a form of feedback. Generally, feedback is system or subsystem output information that is used to monitor, evaluate, adjust, or change the system or subsystem so that the organization is better able to achieve its stated goals and objectives.

Quantitative Analysis and the General Systems Model

The general systems model provides the framework for an examination of specific quantitative methods. This model focuses attention on inputs, conversion processes, outputs, feedback loops, and modifiers. It is sufficiently robust to capture the essence of all types of health care organizations and tells managers to analyze and design health care organizations as systems and subsystems. Efficiency and effectiveness are the two primary performance measures used in health care organizations. To be an effective health care manager requires the ability to view the health care organization as a system and to make the organization perform better on both performance measures. Quantitative methods exist to assist managers to analyze and design systems and facilitate implementation of change within the organization not as ends, but as means to enhance organizational effectiveness and efficiency.

A quantitative method is a specific tool, technique, or model that can be used by health services managers to help solve specific situations or problems. Frequently, quantitative methods involve collecting information (or using information collected by others) and manipulating it using mathematics and statistics. Examples include economic analysis, queuing theory, PERT, and general systems flow charting. Many quantitative methods involve using specific mathematical models to analyze systems. Some methods have very specific applications and specific rules governing these applications. Methods included in this book have been drawn from many fields, including industrial engineering, operations research, and general management analysis. Selected methods have the ability to assist managers in analyzing systems, designing or redesigning systems, and implementing desired change in systems.

Another way to explain quantitative methods for health services managers involves applicability. To be considered a quantitative method in this context, the tool, technique, or model must have broad application in the health care organization and serve the needs of managers. The method must be something that the health administrator working in the hospital, nursing home, or ambulatory clinic needs to use or needs to know about.

Not all quantitative methods have applications in health services management. Also, some quantitative methods are not purely mathematical. For example, in statistics students learn the rudiments of testing a hypothesis using t and F tests. These tests are statistical methods used under specific conditions to test a hypothesis based on a sample. They are not quantitative methods for health services management, and their use in health services management situations is very limited. In contrast, often in the same statistics course, students learn basic linear regression. Linear regression is a professionally recognized technique used in forecasting, which is a quantitative method often used in health services management. General systems flow charting is a specific method to analyze settings. It is not mathematical or statistical. However, in certain applications throughout health care, this type of method also meets the criterion of being a quantitative method for health services management.

A REPERTOIRE OF QUANTITATIVE METHODS: OVERVIEW

This book expands a health services manager's abilities to analyze, design, and implement. It provides methods to analyze systems and complex work processes. It also provides methods to design and implement new or revised work processes or subsystems in health care organizations. Frequently, the tools, models, and techniques involve using mathematical approaches. The book is organized by area of application.

The remainder of Part I, "Foundation Competencies," describes basic skills needed to use the quantitative methods included in subsequent sections. For some students, it will be well-known material. For others, it provides a needed review.

Part II, "Forecasting Models," addresses many approaches that can be used to forecast. Chapter 6, "The Art and Science of Forecasting," examines forecasting as a management concept. Chapter 7, "Trend Extrapolation Techniques," covers specific mathematical models to detect and extend trends for purposes of forecasting. Chapter 8, "The Regression Model," covers the application of this statistical model to forecasting. Overall, this section establishes the health services manager's ability to understand and use basic analytical forecasting to construct logical and reasoned forecasts. Forecasting is presented as a core competency associated with the role of the health services manager. Basic algebraic and statistical competencies are needed to complete this section of the book.

Section III, "Project Analysis," covers four types of applied quantitative methods related to projects. A project is defined as a one-time activity or significant modification to an existing service. Chapter 9, "Decision Analysis," formalizes the decision-making process regarding a choice among projects. Chapter 10, "Economic Analysis," is presented as one form of cost–benefit–effectiveness analysis used by managers to select among different projects or different project approaches to achieve similar results. Chapter 11, "Program Evaluation Review Technique (PERT)," describes a technique to define a new project and to establish an appropriate time schedule and project implementation control system. Chapter 12, "Financial Evaluation of Projects," covers methods used to assess the financial implications of projects and includes specific methods related to the cost of capital and project risk. Overall, this section establishes the manager's ability to analyze, design, and implement projects within the health care organization. A basic understanding of economic concepts, financial accounting, statistics, and algebra are needed to complete this section.

Section IV, "Designing and Analyzing Systems," provides health services managers with the ability to apply specific quantitative methods to specific types of service systems. Chapter 13, "Analyzing Waiting Lines," addresses the application of single- and multiple-channel queuing theory as a method to describe waiting lines. Chapter 14, "Analyzing Capacity and Resources," includes methods to estimate the capacity of service systems given certain levels of resources. These chapters require basic abilities in algebra and statistics. The last chapter, Chapter 15, "The Business Plan," covers the information contained in and format of the formal document used in many health care organizations to report recommendations involving significant changes. Unlike other chapters presented to expand the health services manager's ability to use formal methods to analyze, design, and implement, this chapter reviews the issues that must be addressed as proposals for change are considered by the decision-making structure in the health care organization.

Also included are two appendices. Appendix A, "Management Communications," presents conventions to govern written and oral reports prepared by managers. The importance of this appendix cannot be overstated. The ability to describe and explain the methods used in any analysis, as well as the results and recommendations, is a fundamental managerial competency. Individuals lacking the ability to communicate effectively are not competent managers, regardless of their ability to solve equations and use statistics. Appendix B, "Probability Distributions Used in Queuing Theory," provides additional detail on the application of the Poisson and exponential data distributions. A list of suggested readings is also included in the book.

This book expands the repertoire of the health services manager to analyze complex systems, and to be able to design and implement changes in systems. Applications are drawn from hospitals, nursing homes, and ambulatory care clinics. Traditional quantitative methods with limited management applications in these settings have been reserved for more advanced presentations. Application is of paramount importance. Throughout the book, repeated reference is made to the importance of the ability to communicate results effectively. No matter how perfect or insightful the analysis or design, if it cannot be or is not effectively communicated to decision makers in the health care organization, the health services manager has failed. Quantitative methods are a robust tool in the skill repertoire of the health services manager and need to be used skillfully.

EXERCISES

1-1. The hospital's admitting office needs a new copying machine. One model costs $2,400 and can make 720 copies per hour. The other machine costs $4,800 and can make 3,600 copies per hour. Both have the same operational costs and produce copies of equal quality. Which copier should be purchased, and why? Which is more efficient? What other information do you want before you make your recommendation?

1-2. For each of the following types of health care organizations, indicate three performance measures related to efficiency and effectiveness:

Acute care hospital
Nursing home
Ambulatory care clinic
Home health agency

1-3. The ambulatory care clinic provides routine physical examinations. The examination includes a review of the patient's medical history, gross physical examination, chest x-ray, EKG, and urine and blood tests. Using a list, identify the input resources needed to perform the physical. Write an action-oriented task list (e.g., patient completes medical history form) of the conversion processes that must be performed to provide the physical. Next to each task, identify who would perform the task (e.g., registered nurse, physician, patient, medical laboratory). Identify feedback.

1-4. The Mountain View Nursing Home, a typical 100-bed nursing home, provides 3 meals per day to each resident. Last year, Mountain View Hospital, a typical 100-bed acute care hospital, provided 3.4 meals per day to each inpatient. Which institution needs the higher capacity to produce and deliver meals, and why? Identify the assumptions used in your analysis.

1-5. Consider the following data from two adjacent home health agencies. Which is more efficient, and why? Identify all assumptions.

	A	B
Number of nursing staff hours devoted to home care, including travel time	80	125
Number of home visits	56	87
Number of miles traveled	212	174

2

Working with Numbers_____

This chapter reviews algebra and statistics as a foundation for developing and using mathematical models to analyze and design work processes and systems in health care organizations. Its principal purpose is to ensure a common understanding. Its other purpose is to build the ability to construct models.

ALGEBRAIC RELATIONSHIPS

Algebra is a branch of mathematics that provides relationships and rules for determining the value of variables in an algebraic relationship. An algebraic relationship is expressed as an equation. For example, the equation:

$$y = 2x + 1 \qquad \text{(Eq. 2-1)}$$

indicates that the value of y (the dependent variable) will always be twice the value of x (the independent variable) plus 1. Even though the value of x may change, the relationship described in the equation remains. Algebra specializes in presenting relationships between dependent and independent variables. Equations provide the ability to examine such a relationship over the range of values of one or more independent (i.e., x) variables.

19

Establishing and solving algebraic equations that describe the operation of the health care organization are essential aspects of analysis as a management competency. Often these equations are simple. For example, the equation:

$$y = 3.1x \qquad \text{(Eq. 2-2)}$$

where

y = the number of meals served in a hospital
x = the number of patient days

indicates that, for every 1 patient day (the x variable), the hospital will serve 3.1 meals (the y variable). If the hospital generates 100 patient days in a week, then the number of meals served will be 310. If the hospital generates 1,000 patient days in a month, then the number of meals served will be 3,100. Although algebra provides the rules necessary to construct and solve this equation, it does not provide guidelines concerning the specific relationships between the independent (i.e., y) variable, patient days, and the dependent (i.e., x) variable, meals served.

Analysis is used to determine the relationship between variables. In this case, analysis was used to determine that 3.1, not 2.7 or 3.6, meals were served for every patient day generated by this hospital. Perhaps the analysis was as simple as counting the number of meals served to inpatients and dividing that number by the number of inpatient days generated over the last year. Regardless of how 3.1 was arrived at, 3.1 provides the relationship between the variables and has nothing to do with algebra; it is the product of analysis.

Equation 2-2 is a production function. It indicates how many meals will be produced by the hospital at different levels of patient day production. As a production function, it provides the ability to estimate future meal production needs based on estimates or forecasts of inpatient days.

This equation indicates that the hospital will produce 3.1 meals for every 1 patient day. In this form, the equation is a quantitative model—it replicates and describes the reality experienced in this specific hospital. A model is a representation of reality. A quantitative model is a mathematical expression, such as an equation, that represents a reality, such as the relationship between the number of meals served and the number of inpatient patient days in a hospital.

However, what if last week's count indicated that the hospital was producing 3.9 meals per patient day? This deviation or variance from the original model could suggest that either too many meals are being served or that something has occurred to alter the historic 3.1 relationship between meals served and patient days. Numerous possibilities exist, each worth examining given a manager's orientation to efficiency:

Because the dietary department reports the count of meals served, perhaps nurses on the floor are having to reorder meals in order to get a sufficient number of hot meals.
Perhaps staff are ordering patient meals for themselves.
Perhaps a higher percentage of patients are being discharged later in the day and being served lunch prior to discharge, even as new patients are being admitted early in the day and also being provided with lunch.

Determining why the 3.1 relationship between meals and patient days has changed is appropriate analysis. Either inefficient practice must be changed or the original model must be changed so that the hospital retains an accurate model of the demand for meals as a production function.

The implications of this model can be considered from a design perspective. It would not be logical to design and staff a dietary department so that it had the capacity to produce significantly more than 3.1 meals per patient day. As a service department in a hospital, the capacity of the dietary department must be determined by its expected demand.

The relationship between meals served and patient days, as presented in Equation 2-2, is also a deterministic model—it indicates an exact answer to one situation, not an answer couched in probabilities. If 100 patient days are forecast, for example, then this formula or model indicates that the hospital will serve 310, not 311 or 309, meals. As expressed, 310 meals is the only right answer to the situation of 100 patient days. However, if the equation indicated its answer in terms of probabilities, then the model would be a probabilistic, not a deterministic, model.

The Equation for a Straight Line

Often models or equations used in analysis take on the general algebraic form of a straight line or linear relationship. The general algebraic notation for the equation for a straight line is:

$$y = mx + b \qquad \text{(Eq. 2-3)}$$

where

m = the slope of the line
b (a specific number) = the y intercept

The y intercept is that value of y obtained when x is zero and refers to where on a graph the line would cross the y axis.

For example, the equation:

$$y = 4x + 7 \qquad \text{(Eq. 2-4)}$$

describes a straight line with a slope of 4 and a y intercept of 7. The equation can be plotted on a graph by selecting values for x and solving the equation for corresponding values of y. Table 2-1 contains a list of various x and y values that represent the equation $y = 4x + 7$. Plotting these data points yields the graph contained in Figure 2-1.

Table 2-1. Data representing the equation $y = 4x+7$

x	y
5	27
4	23
3	19
2	15
1	11
0	7
−1	3
−2	−1
−3	−5
−4	−9
−5	−13

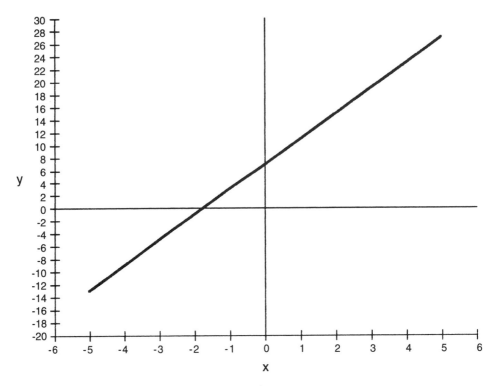

Figure 2-1.   Data plot of the equation $y = 4x + 7$.

The slope of a line is defined as the change in y divided by the change in x. Using the data in Table 2-1, one can calculate the slope of the line described by Equation 2-4. By definition, the slope must be 4. Slope indicates in this case that, for each 1-unit change in the independent variable x, y (the dependent variable) changes by 4 units. Table 2-2 contains the slope calculations for the data presented in Table 2-1.

The equation for a straight line or linear relationship can take on many different forms:

$$y = 3x - 5 \qquad \text{(Eq. 2-5)}$$

$$2y = 9x + 17 \qquad \text{(Eq. 2-6)}$$

In contrast, the following equation is a curvilinear relationship:

$$y = 3x^2 + x - 17 \qquad \text{(Eq. 2-7)}$$

In this equation, y does not change in a constant fashion as x changes; therefore, y is not in a linear relationship to x.

In subsequent chapters, linear regression analysis is presented as a method to forecast and develop algebraic models. Basic familiarity with the algebraic model of y as the dependent variable and x as the independent variable and the general equation $y = mx + b$ is essential for such methods.

Solving Algebraic Equations

When solving algebraic equations, the rules of precedence must be followed:

1. Exponents take precedence over multiplication/division.
2. Multiplication/division takes precedence over addition/subtraction.
3. Parenthetical expressions (operations contained in parentheses) take precedence over operations not in parentheses.

In other words, starting at the innermost bracketed operands, the equation is first cleared of all exponential functions (e.g., squaring, square roots). Then the multiplication and division are done, and, finally, the addition and subtraction.

For example, the equation:

$$y = 23x + 2x(4 - x)^2 \qquad \text{(Eq. 2-8)}$$

can be solved for $x = 2$ and $x = 28$ by using the rules of precedence. The solution if $x = 2$ is:

$$
\begin{aligned}
y &= 23x + 2x (4 - x)^2 \\
&= 23x + 2x(4 - 2)^2 \\
&= 23x + 2x(2)^2 \\
&= 23x + 2x \times (4) \\
&= (23 \times 2) + (2 \times 2) \times (4) \\
&= (46) + (4 \times 4) \\
&= 46 + 16 \\
&= 62
\end{aligned}
$$

The solution if $x = 28$ is:

$$
\begin{aligned}
y &= 23x + 2x(4 - x)^2 \\
&= 23x + 2x(4 - 28)^2 \\
&= 23x + 2x(-24)^2 \\
&= 23x + 2x \times (576) \\
&= (23 \times 28) + (2 \times 28) \times (576) \\
&= 644 + (56) \times (576) \\
&= 644 + 32{,}256 \\
&= 32{,}900
\end{aligned}
$$

As the above calculations illustrate, precedence is important. In the following problem:

$$3 + 4 \times 5 = ?$$

Table 2-2. Slope calculations for the equation $y = 4x+7$

x	y	Change in x	Change in y	Slope
5	27			
4	23	1	4	4
3	19	1	4	4
2	15	1	4	4
1	11	1	4	4
0	7	1	4	4
−1	3	1	4	4
−2	−1	1	4	4
−3	−5	1	4	4
−4	−9	1	4	4
−5	−13	1	4	4

correctly following the rules of precedence yields the (correct) answer of $3 + 20 = 23$. However, if incorrect precedence is used, so that the addition is done before the multiplication, then the (incorrect) answer is $7 \times 5 = 35$. Following the rules of precedence is essential to obtaining accurate answers. To avoid confusion concerning precedence, parentheses should be used when presenting equations: $3 + (4 \times 5)$.

STATISTICS REVISITED

Statistics is not mathematics. Instead, statistics uses mathematics and algebraic equations to describe data and help managers to draw logical conclusions about the data. Data are defined as a series of numbers that represent the values of one or more specific measurements or variables.

Measures of Central Tendency and the Standard Deviation

All data can be described based on measures of central tendency. These measures describe the center of the data distribution; they include:

* The mean, or average of all the data. Some refer to the mean as the center of gravity in the data distribution.
* The median, or value at the midpoint of the data points in the data distribution.
* The mode, or most frequently appearing value in the data distribution.

However, measures of central tendency describe nothing about the distribution of the data.

The dispersion of the data is described by their variance—a measure of how widely or tightly the data are grouped or dispersed around the mean. The standard deviation (s) is the square root of the variance. The standard deviation provides an estimate approximating the average distance of most data points away from the mean value based on characteristics of the data distribution.

The standard normal data distribution (i.e., bell-shaped curve) is the most common theoretical distribution used in statistics and the management sciences. The standard normal curve is perfectly symmetrical: exactly half of the curve is above the mean and excatly half is below the mean. In situations in which actual data do not fit this symmetrical representation, statistics provides alternative data distributions. (Unless indicated otherwise, the standard normal data distribution and the formulas for standard deviations will be used here. The central limit theorem from statistics allows the use of the standard normal distribution in almost all cases where the sample size is greater than 30.)

By definition, the standard normal distribution has the mean in the middle and has *95% of all data within $+1.96$ and -1.96 standard deviations of the mean.* In other words, $+1.96$ and -1.96 standard deviations represent 95% of the area under the standard normal distribution curve. Calculating the standard deviation provides the ability to apply the statistical properties of this distribution to many situations.

For example, estimating how many staff to assign to a clinic is a complex decision. If a clinic is overstaffed, it will be inefficient. However, if it is understaffed, patients may experience unusually long waits, not be able to be seen, and/or leave out of frustration without being seen by the physician. Knowing how to use the standard deviation provides the ability to estimate (within levels of probability) phenomena that fluctuate, such as clinic visits per day.

If a clinic has an average (mean) number of visits per day of 25.3, with a standard deviation (s) of 7.89 visits, using the standard normal distribution and the standard deviation provides the ability to estimate that, 95% of the time, the number of clinic visits per day will be between the mean minus $1.96s$ and the mean plus $1.96s$. This range is called a confidence interval. Managers can be confident that, 95% of the time, the true mean will be in this interval. In the clinic example, the 95% confidence interval would be between *a high of* mean $+ 1.96s = 25.3 + (1.96 \times 7.89)$, or 40.76 visits per day, and *a low of* mean $- 1.96s = 25.3 - (1.96 \times 7.89)$, or 9.84 visits per day.

The 95% confidence interval is a very important management calculation. In the clinic example, knowing that the 95% confidence interval for clinic visits per day is from 40.76 to 9.84 does not rule out the possibility that, on any given day, the clinic could experience 50 visits or 2 visits. Knowing the 95% confidence interval indicates that 50 or 2 visits per day, however, should be rare events. Visit levels should be between 40.76 and 9.84 visits per day 95% of the time.

Here lies the critical difference between using a point estimate and an interval estimate in management decision making. Point estimates provide an exact answer that almost always will be incorrect. In the clinic example, using just the average provides a point estimate, indicating that, on average, the number of clinic visits per day will be 25.3. Adding the standard deviation and the 95% confidence interval changes the model into an interval estimate—on 95% of the days, the number of clinic visits will be between 40.76 and 9.84 per day.

Given this example, the appropriate staffing level for this clinic can be determined. If staffed at the average (25.3 visits per day), sufficient staff would be available for 50% or fewer of the clinic days because volume varies, and, on 50% of the days, utilization will be higher than the average. (By definition, the average is the exact middle of a symmetrical data distribution, and 50% of the values lie at or below the mean and 50% of the values lie at or above the mean.) If staffed at the level of 40.76, or 41, visits per day (the upper limit of the confidence interval), sufficient staff should be available 95% of the days. (Staffing at the high end of the 95% confidence interval covers 97.5% of the data distribution—that is, 95% plus the 2.5% between 0 and 9.84 visits per day.)

Deciding on the appropriate level of staffing involves management, not statistics. Before statistics can be used to help make the staffing decision, "management" must decide whether efficiency or service is more important. If they are equally important, then the clinic should staff at the average. However, if service is more important than efficiency, then the clinic should staff at an expected daily volume above the average. Knowing the 95% confidence interval and the standard deviation provides the ability to staff based on these types of decisions.

Standard normal data distributions and the 95% confidence interval are based on two-tailed probability distributions. The standard normal distribution includes 100% of all data under the curve. Knowing the mean establishes the center of the distribution. Knowing the variance and standard deviation establishes the width of the curve. Knowing the standard deviation provides the ability to determine those values that occur within 1.96 standard deviations above and below the mean and to be certain that these values represent 95% of the area under the curve. The other

5% of values are above and below the limits established by the 95% confidence interval.

Using the standard normal distribution enables the manager to extend his or her knowledge about the number of visits per day in the clinic example. By definition, 95% of all data are +1.96 and −1.96 standard deviations away from the mean. Also by definition, the standard normal curve is perfectly symmetrical, with half of the distribution above the mean and half below the mean. Half of 95% is 47.5%. Therefore, by definition, the limits of the 95% confidence interval establish the data range at 47.5% on either side of the mean. This means that 2.5% of the data are expected to be below the lower limit and 2.5% to be above the upper limit of the 95% confidence interval. In the clinic example, the lower limit of the confidence interval is 9.84, and the upper limit is 40.76 visits per day. Therefore, 1) on 2.5% of all days there will be between 0 and 9.84 visits per day, and 2) on 2.5% of all days there will be more than 40.76 visits per day.

Calculating the Standard Deviation

The standard deviation is the single most important mathematical calculation used in management today. Unlike means, averages, medians, or modes, which describe the center point of a data distribution, the standard deviation provides a measure of the variation of the data. In other words, the standard deviation describes the scope of the data distribution. Variation may be more significant to management efficiency than the average value, so it is important to be familiar with this common measure of the amount of variation in a data set.

Before calculating the standard deviation, the manager must determine whether the data being analyzed are a sample of all data potentially available (n) or are all the data (i.e., a population; N). If sample data are used, then the denominator for the equation is $n − 1$. If a population or all data are being used, the equation uses N (not $n − 1$), where N is the number of data observations.

The equation for the population standard deviation (σ) is written as:

$$\sqrt{\sigma^2} = \text{the square root of the variance of a data point away from the mean}$$

or

$$\sigma = \text{the square root of the sum of (each data point minus the mean)}^2$$
$$\text{divided by the number of data points}$$

$$= \sqrt{\frac{\Sigma (x_i - \mu)^2}{N}} \qquad \text{(Eq. 2-9)}$$

The equation for the sample standard deviation (s) is written as:

$$\sqrt{s^2}$$

or

$$s = \sqrt{\frac{\Sigma (x_i - \bar{x})^2}{n - 1}} \qquad \text{(Eq. 2-10)}$$

where $\bar{x}$ = the mean
  n = the number of observations

The observations contained in Table 2-3 can be used to calculate the standard deviation for the number of visits per day to the sample clinic. It must be remembered that, when working with a complicated equation, exponents are done first, then multiplication and division, and finally addition and subtraction. The calculation proceeds according to the following steps (Table 2-4):

Step 1:   Calculate the mean (μ).
Step 2:   Subtract the mean from each observation (= deviation).
Step 3:   Square each deviation.
Step 4:   Sum the squared deviations (Σ).
Step 5:   Divide the sum of the squared deviations (i.e., 1,246.11) by the number of data points or observations (i.e., N = 20) (= variance).
Step 6:   Calculate the square root of the variance. This is the *standard deviation* (σ).

Correlation Coefficient

Building algebraic models often requires being able to describe the association or associative relationship between two variables or phenomena, such as x-rays and emergency room visits. Statistics provides a measure that can describe the parallel rate of change in any two factors. Determining the linear correlation coefficient (r)

Table 2-3.   Number of clinic visits per day observed over 20 days

Day	x^a
1	23
2	23
3	45
4	23
5	26
6	15
7	19
8	18
9	28
10	26
11	35
12	38
13	7
14	23
15	26
16	26
17	28
18	27
19	20
20	30
Total	506

[a]x = clinic visits per day; N = 20 days.

Table 2-4.   Calculation of standard deviation for clinic visits per day

Day	x	Mean[a] (Step 1)	Deviation (Step 2)	Squared deviation (Step 3)
1	23	25.3	−2.3	5.29
2	23	25.3	−2.3	5.29
3	45	25.3	19.7	388.09
4	23	25.3	−2.3	5.29
5	26	25.3	0.7	0.49
6	15	25.3	−10.3	106.09
7	19	25.3	−6.3	39.69
8	18	25.3	−7.3	53.29
9	28	25.3	2.7	7.29
10	26	25.3	0.7	0.49
11	35	25.3	9.7	94.09
12	38	25.3	12.7	161.29
13	7	25.3	−18.3	334.89
14	23	25.3	−2.3	5.29
15	26	25.3	0.7	0.49
16	26	25.3	0.7	0.49
17	28	25.3	2.7	7.29
18	27	25.3	1.7	2.89
19	20	25.3	−5.3	28.09
20	30	25.3	4.7	22.09
Total	506			
Sum of squared deviations (Step 4)				$\Sigma = 1246.11$
Sum of squares divided by N (Step 5)				62.3055
Standard deviation (Step 6)			7.89	

[a]Mean = total x divided by N = 506/20 = 25.3.

will indicate (with a certain degree of probability) whether a linear associative relationship exists between, for example, the number of x-rays taken in an emergency room and the number of visits per day. The correlation coefficient also will indicate the strength of the linear association between the two variables. Strength is the absolute distance away from zero; therefore, a correlation coefficient of -0.97 indicates a stronger relationship than does a correlation coefficient of $+0.45$.

Correlation coefficients DO NOT indicate either the existence of a causal relationship (i.e., x causes y) or the direction of the mathematical relationship (e.g., a change in x then changes y). The correlation coefficient indicates only whether an associative relationship exists between two variables and, if so, whether it is positive or negative and the strength of the relationship.

Statistics indicates that a correlation coefficient (r) in the range of 0 to $+1.00$ indicates a positive correlation (an increase in x is always associated with a parallel increase in y) and that a correlation coefficient in the range of 0 to -1.00 indicates that for every increase in x, y always decreases. By definition, correlation coefficients can only range from $+1.00$ to -1.00 because two variables cannot associate more than 100%. Therefore, whenever a correlation coefficient is calculated, it should be verified to ensure that the value is between $+1.00$ and -1.00.

The equation for the sample correlation coefficient (r) is:

$$r_{xy} = \frac{n\Sigma x_i y_i - \Sigma x_i \Sigma y_i}{\text{SQRT}\left\{\left[n\Sigma x_i^2 - \left(\Sigma x_i\right)^2\right] \times \left[n\Sigma y_i^2 - \left(\Sigma y_i\right)^2\right]\right\}}$$

(Eq. 2-11)

where n = the number of (paired) data points in the sample
SQRT = the notation used to signify the square root function

Table 2-5 presents data on x-rays taken in (x) and patient visits to (y) an emergency room. Initial calculations have been made for x times y, x^2, and y^2. Given this data set, the correlation coefficient can be calculated as follows:

$$r_{xy} = \frac{(10)\,(12{,}978) - (339)\,(365)}{\text{SQRT}\left\{\left[(10)\,(12{,}481) - (339)^2\right]\left[10(14{,}171) - (365)^2\right]\right\}}$$

(Eq. 2-12)

$$= \frac{129{,}780 - 123{,}735}{\text{SQRT}\,\{(9{,}889)\,(8{,}485)\}}$$

$$= \frac{6{,}045}{99.44 \times 92.11}$$

$$= 0.66$$

This means that, 66% of the time, x and y associate positively—that is, they move in the same direction. In other words, the calculated correlation coefficient of .66 indicates that the relationship between x-rays (x) and emergency room visits (y) is potentially a positive relationship. In a positive relationship:

An increase in x is associated with an increase in y.
An increase in y is associated with an increase in x.
A decrease in x is associated with a decrease in y.
A decrease in y is associated with a decrease in x.

If the calculated correlation coefficient had been a negative number, then this would indicate a potentially negative relationship. In a negative relationship:

An increase in x is associated with a decrease in y.
An increase in y is associated with a decrease in x.
A decrease in x is associated with an increase in y.
A decrease in y is associated with an increase in x.

Similar to testing a hypothesis, before one can conclude that a strong relationship exists between x and y as expressed by the correlation coefficient, the correlation coefficient must be examined based on the size of the data set or sample used to generate it. If the calculated r is higher than the critical r value for the given sample size, then one can conclude (with 95% confidence) that a true association exists between x and y. When this is the case, one can conclude that:

1. A linear relationships exists between x and y.
2. The strength of the relationship is expressed in the value of the correlation coefficient.

In the clinic example, given that the r value calculated from the data on emergency room visits and x-rays (Table 2-5) was .66, which is above the critical value for

Table 2-5.   Observational data and initial calculations for correlation between x-rays taken and patient visits in an emergency room

Day	Number of x-rays (x)	Number of patient visits (y)	xy	x^2	y^2
Aug. 8	27	30	810	729	900
Aug. 9	22	26	572	484	676
Aug. 10	15	25	375	225	625
Aug. 11	35	36	1,260	1,225	1,296
Aug. 12	33	33	1,089	1,089	1,089
Aug. 13	52	36	1,872	2,704	1,296
Aug. 14	35	32	1,120	1,225	1,024
Aug. 15	40	54	2,160	1,600	2,916
Aug. 16	40	50	2,000	1,600	2,500
Aug. 17	40	43	1,720	1,600	1,849
Σ	339	365	12,978	12,481	14,171
$N =$	10	10			
Mean	33.9	36.5			

r with a sample of 10 (i.e., critical value = .632, from Table 2-6), it can be concluded that a true association exists between emergency room visits and x-rays.

Assessing Differences Between Averages (t Test)

On occasion, a manager may need to evaluate an average value against another average value to determine whether, from a statistical perspective, a difference exists. For example, one manager may need to decide whether the average length of stay (ALOS) at a specific hospital (a single average) is similar to or different from that at all other hospitals in the same community or region (a group average). Another manager may want to know whether the average number of clinic visits per day in clinic A is similar to or different from that at other clinics.

Statistics can help answer these types of questions. Specifically, the t test can be used to assess the similarity or difference between two observed averages. An ALOS of 4.53 days at a given hospital may or may not be significantly different from a community-wide ALOS of 4.67 days given patterns of variation as measured by the standard deviation. Although these two average values are numerically different by 0.14 days, whether the ALOS of one hospital is significantly different from the ALOS of all other hospitals in the community is a decision that must be made recognizing the pattern of variation.

To assess the similarity and difference between two averages or means appropriately, the manager must determine how many standard deviations separate the two values. The t test provides the calculations to determine this. Managers can use the t test to determine the similarity or difference between two averages at a level of statistical confidence (e.g., 95% confidence). The t test employs the standard difference to assess the difference between the two averages or means.

The standard difference is defined as the difference between the two mean values divided by the standard deviation of the mean (i.e., the standard error). This calculation expresses the number of standard errors between a given average value and the standard value. If this number of standard errors represents more than 95% of the area toward the tail of the standard normal distribution (i.e., bell-shaped curve), then the difference between the two means is significant at a level

Table 2-6. Critical values of r for various sample sizes (n)

n	r
5	0.878
6	0.811
7	0.754
8	0.707
9	0.666
10	0.632
11	0.602
12	0.576
13	0.553
14	0.532
15	0.514
16	0.497
17	0.482
18	0.468
19	0.456
20	0.444
22	0.423
24	0.404
26	0.388
28	0.374
30	0.361
40	0.312
50	0.279
60	0.254
80	0.220
100	0.196

of 95% confidence. However, if the standard difference is not that extreme, then, although the calculated averages may be different, the overall difference between the two groups represented by the average values cannot be expressed at the level of 95% confidence.

The equation for the t test is:

$$t = \frac{(\bar{x}_o - \bar{x}_s)}{\sqrt{\dfrac{s_o^2}{N}}}$$

where $\bar{x}_o$ = observed mean
$\bar{x}_s$ = standard mean
s_o = standard deviation of observed mean
N = number of observations used to calculate $\bar{x}_o$

Using the t test, if the standard difference is greater than 1.96 there is less than a 5% chance that the means are the same. Conversely, if the standard difference is 1.96 or less the means can be considered similar at the 95% confidence level.

For example, over a span of 20 days ($N = 20$), clinic A had an average number of visits per day of 25.3, with a standard deviation (s) of 7.89 visits. All other similar clinics in the community experienced an average of 26.5 visits per day. Using these data, the two averages can be assessed with the t test:

$$t = \frac{(25.3 - 26.5)}{\sqrt{\dfrac{7.89^2}{20}}}$$

$$= \frac{-1.2}{\sqrt{3.11}}$$

$$= -0.68$$

Given that the calculated t value (-0.68) is less than 1.96 (the reference standard at 95% confidence), the manager *cannot* conclude with 95% confidence that the observed mean (i.e., 25.3 visits per day, with a standard deviation of 7.89 visits) is significantly different from the overall community average of 26.5 clinic visits per day. If the calculated t value were above 1.96, then the manager could conclude that the number of visits experienced at clinic A were significantly different from the number of visits experienced at other clinics. Using this approach, 1.96 is the threshold used to evaluate the t statistic and yields an answer at the level of 95% statistical confidence.

Assessing Difference Between Proportions (Z Statistic)

If the data used in an analysis are not discrete numbers, such as the ALOS, but proportions, such as a rate, a different form of the t test applies. This is true only when the data come from binomial distributions—that is, when only two answers are possible.

For example, occupancy rate represents a binomial variable. Either a hospital bed is occupied or it is not; there is no such thing as partial occupancy of a hospital bed. To test whether one hospital's occupancy rate is different from that of another (or from a peer group rate), the following equation expressing a Z statistic is used:

$$Z = \frac{P_2 - P_1}{\text{SQRT}\left(\dfrac{P_1 Q_1}{N_1} + \dfrac{P_2 Q_2}{N_2}\right)}$$

where P_1 = proportion with attribute in group 1
$\quad\ P_2$ = proportion with attribute in group 2
$\quad\ Q_1$ = proprtion without attribute in group 1
$\quad\ Q_2$ = proportion without attribute in group 2
$\quad\ N_1$ = number of observations in group 1
$\quad\ N_2$ = number of observations in group 2

For example, analysis indicates that for the last 20 years, Mercy Hospital's average occupancy rate was 73%. All other hospitals of similar size in the same state had an average hospital occupancy rate of 85%. To determine whether Mercy Hospital's occupancy rate was the same as or different from this peer group's rate, the Z statistic is calculated as follows:

$$Z = \frac{0.73 - 0.85}{\text{SQRT}\left(\dfrac{(0.73)(0.27)}{20} + \dfrac{(0.85)(0.15)}{20}\right)}$$

$$= \frac{-0.12}{\text{SQRT}(0.00986 + 0.00638)}$$

$$= \frac{-0.12}{0.1274}$$

$$= -0.94$$

To conclude with 95% confidence that a difference exists, the calculated Z statistic must be equal to or greater than $+1.96$ or -1.96. Therefore, given this example, even though the two rates are different (73% for Mercy Hospital and 85% for the peer group—a mathematical difference of 12%), the rates are not significantly different because 12%, or a difference of 0.12, leads to a calculated Z statistic of -0.94, which is less than 1.96 standard errors away from zero. Conversely, if the calculated Z statistic was greater than or equal to $+1.96$ or less than or equal to -1.96, the rates would be considered different.

This application of the Z statistic is reserved for those situations involving a binomial variable. It is presented to ensure that managers select the appropriate statistical test based on data characteristics.

BUILDING MODELS

Management analysis often involves developing mathematical models that describe or portray the relationship among two or more variables. A model provides the ability to describe complex systems and can be used with desired performance parameters to design new or revised systems. Models can be production functions. For example, if a linear relationship exists between the number of patient days generated per month in a hospital and the number of meals served, a forecast of patient days plus the model provides the ability to estimate the number of meals that will be required. This chapter contains sufficient tools to develop linear models with two variables:

Step 1:   Calculate the mean and standard deviation for each variable.
Step 2:   Determine the 95% confidence interval for each variable.
Step 3:   Test for and describe the linear relationship between the two variables using a linear correlation coefficient.
Step 4:   If warranted by Step 3, present the model in either a deterministic or probabilistic form.

EXERCISES

2-1.   If x is 34, calculate y in the following equation:

$$y = 15x^3 + 12x^2 + 14x(x - x^2)^2$$

2-2.   Calculate the linear correlation coefficient between patient deaths (x) and emergency admissions (y) for the data in Table 2-7.

2-3.   Using appropriate statistics, analyze the data in Table 2-8. Present a model.

2-4. Using the data in Table 2-8, what is the 95% confidence interval for laboratory tests and clinic visits?

2-5. Based on its most recent 100 patients, hospital A has an ALOS of 5.25 days, with a standard deviation of 1.2 days. The ALOS for all other 100- to 150-bed hospitals in the state is 5.00 days. Is hospital A's ALOS similar to or different from the ALOS for all other 100- to 150-bed hospitals in the state? Base your answer on a level of 95% confidence.

2-6. Based on last year's births in Durham Hospital, the rate of infants needing neonatal intensive care was 5 per 1,000 births. The regional average is 7.5 per 1,000 births. Is Durham Hospital doing better than the regional average? (*Hint:* Use the Z statistic on proportions where N_1 and $N_2 = 1,000$).

Table 2-7. Observations of patient deaths (x) and emergency admissions (y) during a 10-week period

Week	Number of patient deaths (x)	Number of admissions (y)
1	7	28
2	9	31
3	12	40
4	4	18
5	12	42
6	3	13
7	8	33
8	3	10
9	7	27
10	6	25

Table 2-8. Observations of number of lab tests and clinic visits during a 20-week period

Week	Number of lab tests	Number of clinic visits
1	72	125
2	80	140
3	56	112
4	89	145
5	101	159
6	67	101
7	78	134
8	83	134
9	40	70
10	98	140
11	91	140
12	83	130
13	73	125
14	87	137
15	59	101
16	90	145
17	66	115
18	69	116
19	76	132
20	98	137

3
Presenting Data

Chapter Objectives

1. To describe the appropriate use of tables and charts in management presentations
2. To illustrate numerous examples of tables and charts to help users select appropriate forms to present data

Key Terms and Concepts

Bar chart
Charts as data pictures
Line chart

Pie chart
Scatter plot
Tables as data lists

Being able to present data effectively and use data presentations as part of oral and written analyses is a competency expected of all health services managers. Too often, the results of highly competent analysis are obscured in an incompetent data presentation. Data become useful to the manager when they have been arranged, categorized, and analyzed to assist the manager to make decisions. Raw data usually help no one. For data to be useful in management, they must be presented in a systematic manner that lends itself to reasonable and reasoned conclusions. The data must be easy to use. This chapter presents rules and conventions related to presenting data.

OVERVIEW OF DATA PRESENTATION

Data, usually in the form of numbers, are presented in both written and oral presentations. Data are the substance and rationale for the argument and recommendations contained in a report. When poorly organized or presented, the data detract from the overall logic of the report. In contrast, when presented well, data are the logical theme that unites the entire presentation.

Presenting data is a managerial art. The presentation must appear simple and attract receiver or viewer attention. Intended messages must be easy to discern. At the same time, few precise rules exist governing data presentations, leaving much discretion to the designer and preparer. As long as the data presentation fulfills the following general rules and conventions, it should satisfy basic requirements and expectations.

The primary rule in presenting data is to make the data "user friendly." The data presentation should be designed to meet the needs of the viewer, not the preparer or the spreadsheet program used to prepare the table or chart. It is essential that the data presentation be audience specific. To be useful to the viewer, the data presentation also must be simple and easy to read. The tendency to "squeeze" too much data into one table or chart must be resisted. Such practices typically make the presentation "user hostile" and convey many confusing messages.

The presentation must attract viewer interest and be able to be read and interpreted quickly. Every table or chart must be designed so it can be understood quickly by someone who is unfamiliar with the data. A table that takes 5 minutes to understand benefits no one. A chart that only makes sense to its creator also benefits no one. Little things like the size of the print on the table or chart mean a great deal to any viewer, especially the viewer of an oral presentation. Making a chart or table useful to the viewer also assumes some knowledge on the part of the designer of the viewer's expectations. The table or chart must be designed to meet these expectations.

As essential building blocks in written and oral presentation, tables and charts must be designed to convey predefined messages efficiently and contribute to the overall objective of the report. Every data presentation, such as a specific table, figure, or chart, must have at least one primary message. Data are never presented merely to show data. They are presented to convey one or more messages deemed important. Every table or chart included in either a written or oral presentation must pass the test of being an important, in contrast to a peripheral, building block in the overall presentation. Every table or chart requires a specific reason for being included in a report.

TABLES

Tables, either in written reports or as visual aids in oral presentations, are used to list data. The key term is "list." A table is nothing more than a data list, even though other information is sometimes added to make the data presentation more analytical. In presenting tables, certain conventions must be considered:

1. Every table needs an accurate title—for example, "Table 45: Hospital Admissions for the Month of May, 199X." In some cases, abbreviations used in the table are explained in the title.
2. Every table should be numbered consecutively in the presentation. In long written reports, tables should be numbered within chapters or sections (e.g., Table 2-1, Table 2-2, Table 3-1, Table 3-2). In this style, the first number is the section or chapter number, and the second number is the table number in that specific chapter or section. In long written reports, it is customary to include, after the table of contents, a list of all tables and charts by name, with corresponding page numbers. When this approach is used, the list is divided into categories of tables, charts, and figures (figures are diagrams).
3. Data sources (bibliographic citations) must be included on every table and chart. The source can be incorporated into the title or column headings or

placed at the bottom of the table—for example, "(SOURCE: *AHA Guide*, Issue, 199X)."

4. Column headings and row labels should be worded clearly. The convention is to document everything. Use a key or legend placed at the bottom of the table to explain abbreviations and specific terms—for example, KEY: ADC = average daily census, ALOS = average length of stay, PDs = patient days. Usually, column headings are types of data and row labels are individual data names.

5. Significant figures are important. All numbers included in tables should contain the same number of digits after the decimal point.

6. Generally, data should be presented vertically. Categories of data should be listed horizontally; data is then listed vertically under each category. Tables are usually longer than their width.

Consider Table 3-1. If the only purpose were to list data, Table 3-1 would be acceptable. However, if the purpose were to report a potential relationship between bed size and average length of stay (ALOS), rearranging the data by bed size would create a more useful presentation. Table 3-2 rearranges the order in which the data are presented and conveys a different message than Table 3-1.

Table 3-1 reports the raw data as described in its heading. Table 3-2, by arranging the row data in descending order based on bed size, enables the viewer to examine the relationship between hospital bed size and ALOS quickly and easily. Table 3-2 presents the same data included in Table 3-1 but adds meaning by arranging the row data to accomplish a specific purpose.

It is often helpful to the viewer to add to a table a specific reference point or summary calculations, such as the average or mean and the standard deviation.

Table 3.1.   Average length of stay (ALOS) in days in selected hospitals by hospital (199X data)

Hospital	Bed size	ALOS
A	100	6.3
B	123	7.1
C	44	4.6
D	87	6.7
E	57	5.9
F	145	7.9
G	103	6.4

Source: *AHA Guide, 7*, 199X.

Table 3.2.   Average length of stay (ALOS) in days in selected hospitals by hospital bed size (199X data)

Hospital	Bed size	ALOS
F	145	7.9
B	123	7.1
G	103	6.4
A	100	6.3
D	87	6.7
E	57	5.9
C	44	4.6

Source: *AHA Guide, 7*, 199X.

Table 3-3 adds descriptive statistics to the data list for bed size and ALOS. These statistics can help the viewer consider individual data points in relation to general characteristics of the data as presented by the descriptive statistics.

Tables are located throughout a report, whether written or oral. There is no standard location. Options and strategies do exist, however. Primary tables establish a specific point or conclusion and are embedded in the text of a written report. Secondary tables are used to simplify a point previously made or to list all data. They are included in appendices and referenced in the text. Primary tables establish a specific point or conclusion; secondary tables either list all data or are used to simplify a point previously made. A statement such as "(see Table A-4: Hospital Size and Average Daily Census for additional information)" directs the reader to secondary tables.

When preparing a draft of a report, it is common to include in the text a location statement for a specific table. This is done in recognition of the difficulty of placing a table in an exact location in a preliminary document. Statements such as "(INCLUDE TABLE 23 HERE)" are commonly used when preparing the initial drafts of written reports. When the final draft is prepared, such statements should be replaced by appropriate text citations, renumbering if necessary. With newer versions of popular word-processing programs, tables can easily be made part of a text document.

In today's business environment, most tables and charts are generated using specific spreadsheet programs. For example, this chapter was prepared using ClarisWorks, a fully integrated word-processing, spreadsheet, and data entry program for a Macintosh. Spreadsheet programs such as LOTUS and EXCEL usually also provide the ability to make tables. Some, like ClarisWorks, provide the ability to embed tables in text and move them as necessary. Using a spreadsheet program to create tables is recommended.

In oral presentations, tables are one way to present relevant data. Especially long tables, however, are very hard for viewers to understand quickly. When data are viewed as a table, the viewer must consider every piece of data and then make some conclusions. The controlled pace of the oral presentation usually makes tables of data inappropriate.

In either context, it is important that the table be a simple representation of the data. When in doubt, use two tables instead of one and do not try to make one table do the job of multiple tables. Keep the data presentation focused on its objec-

Table 3.3. Average length of stay (ALOS) in days in selected hospitals by hospital bed size (199X data)

Hospital	Bed size	ALOS
F	145	7.9
B	123	7.1
G	103	6.4
A	100	6.3
D	87	6.7
E	57	5.9
C	44	4.6
Average	94.1	6.4
Standard deviation	32.7	0.95

Source: *AHA Guide, 7,* 199X.

tives, simple, and straightforward. It is the responsibility of the preparer to design an effective presentation.

CHARTS AND FIGURES

Unlike tables, which are used to list data, charts are intended to arrange data and present them so that they take on a special, new, or unique meaning. Charts are data pictures, not data lists. Charts create a visual image of the data to convey a specific message. Different types of charts, such as the pie chart, the bar chart, the line chart, and the scatter plot, are used to present different types of information and messages.

Presenting data in a chart is similar to presenting data in a table. The presentation must be useful to the viewer, must simplify the task of the receiver, and must be constructed to deliver a specific message. One chart should never be used to do the job of many. All rules and conventions presented above for tables also govern charts and figures.

In addition, a reasonable and appropriate scale must be used for all charts because the scale will influence the picture created by the chart. When two or more charts will be compared by the viewer, it is essential that the same scale be used for each. Any hints of attempting to falsify the findings associated with the data by manipulating the scale or using different scales to make points not really associated with the data are grounds for a viewer to consider the entire presentation to be without merit.

Charts are based on data. Therefore, when a chart is used in a written report, the data used to construct the chart must be included in the report as a table or tables, even if they are included in appendices. The data included in Table 3-4 are used to illustrate different types of charts.

The Pie Chart

The pie chart provides a pictorial representation of both the whole and what constitutes the whole. As can be seen in Figure 3-1, the pie chart provides an easy way to depict a whole (e.g., a week) and its pieces (e.g., the days of the week). However, if the pie were to be divided into too many pieces, the message would be confused. If Figure 3-1 included all 31 days in the month, any intended message would be lost because the pie had too many "slices" to present a coherent picture. Pie charts are used most often when the data comprise a small number of elements, and the intended message involves illustrating the relative relationships between data elements and the whole.

Table 3.4.   Clinic visits for week 12, 199X

Day	Visits
Monday	55
Tuesday	34
Wednesday	45
Thursday	67
Friday	34

Source: Clinic records.

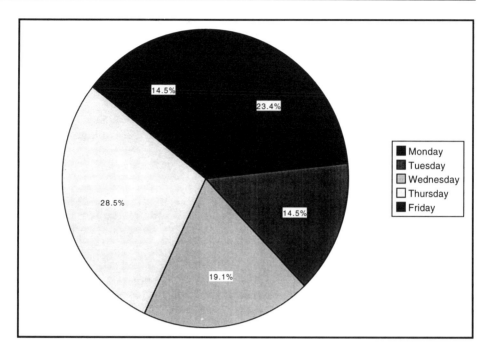

Figure 3-1.   Example of pie chart.

The Bar Chart

The bar chart (also known as a histogram) provides a data picture that compares and contrasts individual data elements. Unlike the pie chart, which provides a sense of the whole, the bar chart enables the viewer to compare two or more quantities visually. Vertical (Figure 3-2) or horizontal (Figure 3-3) bars can be used.

Another version of the bar chart is the stacked bar chart. This version stacks data elements for purposes of comparison. For example, Figure 3-4 stacks the data by day of the week. This type of bar chart is usually used when comparing a series of data elements with each other.

The Line Chart

The line chart is best used to illustrate how values change over time. The vertical and horizontal movement—or lack of it—in the line conveys a message concerning the variability of the data. A line chart is typically the best type of chart to use to illustrate a trend, especially a trend over a period of time. Figure 3-5 is a line chart of the data included in Table 3-4. The line visually demonstrates the amount of variability in the number of clinic visits for each of the days included in the 1 week of data.

Table 3-5 expands the data originally presented in Table 3-4 to include multiple weeks of data. Figures 3-6 and 3-7 use this expanded data to demonstrate other aspects of the line chart. Figure 3-6 is a line chart that illustrates the variability in the number of clinic visits by day of the week. One message is that Thursday is the peak day in terms of demand. In contrast, Figure 3-7 presents the same data using a different format to illustrate the amount of variability in the number of clinic visits

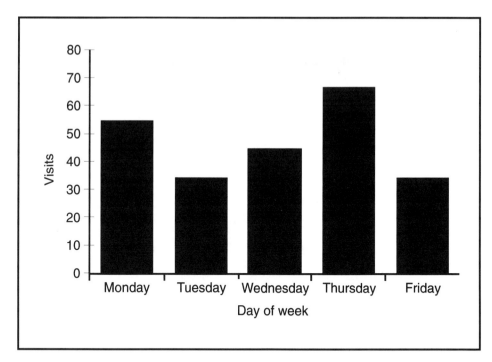

Figure 3-2.   Example of vertical bar chart.

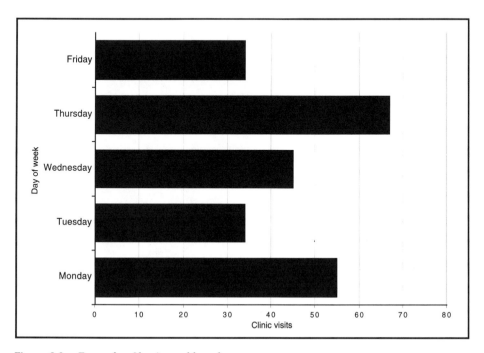

Figure 3-3.   Example of horizontal bar chart.

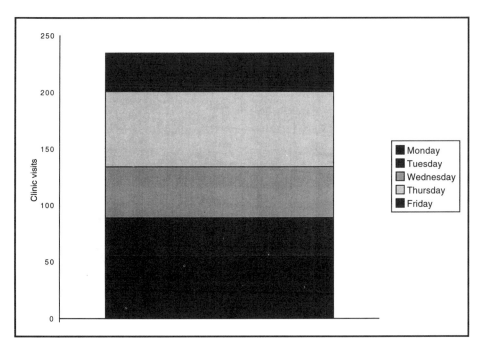

Figure 3-4.   Example of stacked bar chart.

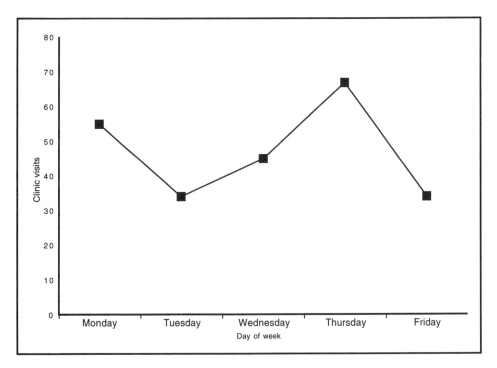

Figure 3-5.   Example of line chart for 1 week of data.

Table 3.5.   Clinic visits by day of week for 5-week period beginning July 1, 199X

	Clinic visits				
	Week 1	Week 2	Week 3	Week 4	Week 5
Mon	55	59	50	61	54
Tue	34	40	46	30	36
Wed	45	49	49	53	46
Thur	67	60	62	79	56
Fri	34	45	39	50	36

Source: Clinic records.

by day of the week. One message is that Wednesdays tend to experience the least amount of variation in the number of clinic visits.

These two examples of line charts demonstrate how the line, in contrast to individual data points, tends to dominate the picture. The line chart provides the opportunity to present a large volume of data, with the primary message being the degree of variability in the data (e.g., by week or by day of week). The line chart is used to indicate a potential trend.

The line chart should be used when the relationship between two continuous variables (x and y) is of interest. When used in this form, the slope of the line indicates characteristics of the relationship. Using a line chart to display a frequency distribution can distort the data picture. Frequency distributions are best illustrated using bar charts or scatter plots. Line charts should be reserved to display trends.

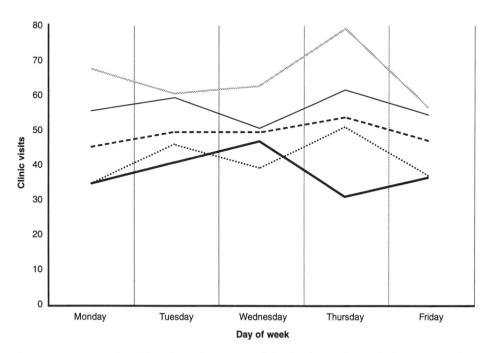

Figure 3-6.   Example of line chart showing variability by day of the week. (——— = Monday; ▬▬ = Tuesday; - - - - = Wednesday; ∿∿∿ = Thursday; ⋯⋯⋯ = Friday)

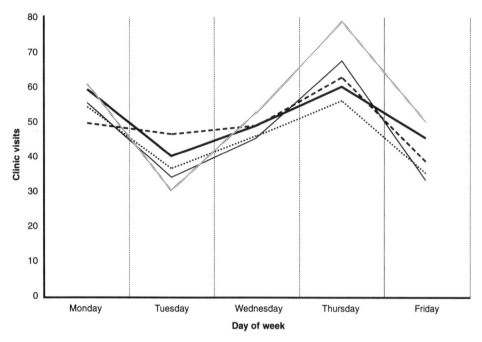

Figure 3-7. Example of line chart showing variability by week. (——— = week 1; ▬▬ = week 2; - - - - = week 3; ▬▬▬▬ =week 4; ⋯⋯ = week 5)

The Scatter Plot

The scatter plot illustrates discrete points of data. Sometimes these types of charts are referred to as "clouds of data." The scatter plot merely presents the data plotted on a scale. Scatter plots call the viewer's attention to the degree of dispersion or clustering in the data and the degree of association between two variables. Figure 3-8 is a scatter plot of the data presented in Table 3-5.

Incorporating additional data (Table 3-6) further demonstrates the utility of the scatter plot to create a cloud of data. Figure 3-9 plots the number of clinic visits per day with the number of laboratory tests also done on that day. A highly dispersed cloud of data would suggest no relationship between these two phenomena. In contrast, a tightly clustered cloud, especially a cloud that points toward the left or right, may indicate a relationship. Figure 3-9, for example, suggests the existence of a positive linear correlation between clinic visits and laboratory tests; that is, as clinic visits increase, the number of laboratory tests also increases. Although the scatter plot does not provide a definitive basis to make such a conclusion without appropriate statistical analysis, it is an appropriate visual presentation of the relationship.

Choice of Chart Type

Other variations of each of these basic types of charts exist. Overall, it is important that managers use the appropriate style of chart to convey the intended message. The choice of the type of chart is not random; the chart selected must conform with the purpose of the illustration and the question to be answered. If a frequency distribution is needed, do not use a line chart. If a relationship must be displayed, use a line chart. Examine all finished charts from the perspective of the viewer. Be

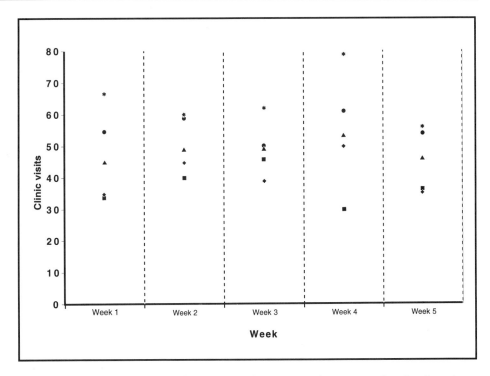

Figure 3-8. Example of scatter plot. (• = Monday; ■ = Tuesday; ▲ = Wednesday; * = Thursday; ♦ = Friday)

Table 3.6. Clinic visits and laboratory tests for 20-day period beginning July 1, 199X

Days	Clinic visits	Lab tests
1	55	59
2	34	45
3	45	32
4	67	57
5	34	50
6	59	65
7	40	47
8	49	56
9	60	67
10	45	32
11	50	57
12	46	49
13	49	43
14	62	60
15	39	47
16	61	69
17	30	45
18	53	59
19	79	88
20	50	60

Source: Clinic records.

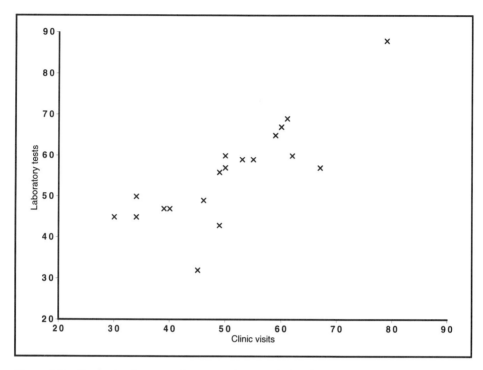

Figure 3-9. Example of scatter plot suggesting association between variables.

sure that all charts convey the intended message. Label everything so that a historian 50 years from now can understand what the chart presents.

CONCLUSION

In the managerial world of health care organizations, effective communications are essential. Being able to use a specific quantitative method is of little value to the professional manager if he or she lacks the ability to present findings and recommendations to others. In presentations, tables are used to list data, and charts help to transform data into information. Tables and charts are used to tell a story—a management story. If they are of no or little utility to the manager as decision maker, then they were not worth preparing. It is important to stress that the only good table or chart is the table or chart that helps the manager manage.

This chapter establishes general rules and conventions associated with presenting data either in written reports or as part of oral presentations. The primary rule is to make all presentations "user friendly." The manager should keep the presentation simple, adhere to conventions, and not attempt to accomplish multiple objectives with one table or chart. It is important to use as many tables and charts as necessary to make the critical points needed for the presentation. The manager must be sensitive to the perspective of the viewer and design tables and charts that are aids, not roadblocks, to understanding. Additional guidelines and conventions concerning management communications are included in Appendix A at the end of this book.

EXERCISES

The following data on licensed nursing home beds and full-time therapists were gathered in eight nursing homes. Each row of data lists the nursing home identification letter, number of licensed beds, number of occupied beds as of April 15, 199X, and number of full-time therapists employed. Data are as of September 1, 199X, from "The State Report on Nursing Homes."

A, 120, 115, 3
B, 155, 138, 3
C, 100, 98, 2
D, 85, 80, 2
E, 190, 178, 4
F, 130, 129, 4
G, 103, 100, 1
H, 50, 40, 2

3-1. Display each data field (e.g., number of licensed beds) in a table.

3-2. Use a table to examine the relationship between two appropriate data elements.

3-3. Present a pie chart, bar chart, line chart, and scatter plot using all or part of the data set. Indicate the question addressed by each chart.

3-4. Present tables and charts that describe the relationship between number of occupied beds as of April 15, 199X, and number of full-time therapists employed.

4

General Systems Flow Charting

Chapter Objectives

1. To understand how general systems flow charts can assist health services managers to improve the efficiency and effectiveness of systems, subsystems, and specific work processes
2. To be able to construct a general systems flow chart

Key Terms and Concepts

Coordination   Sequence
Division of labor   Task list
Flow

General systems flow charting is used to create a descriptive picture of an operational system. Once described using general systems flow charting, the system can be analyzed and redesigned as necessary. General systems flow charting also is used to design new systems. This chapter establishes the general rules and conventions associated with general systems flow charting.

CONCEPTS OF SYSTEMS

Operations and processes within the health care organization are complex. Any operation, such as preparing a meal, sending a letter, admitting a patient to the hospital, or developing a budget, is a complex process that requires the systematic interplay of numerous people doing different things in some predetermined order or sequence. The fact that a process is complex, however, does not mean it is chaotic. Consider the example of sending a letter:

1. Someone must write or compose the letter.
2. Someone must type the letter.
3. Someone must make sufficient copies of the letter for retention in the organization's memory (the files).
4. Someone must proofread the letter and sign it.
5. Someone must address the envelope.

6. Someone must put the letter into the envelope.
7. Someone must affix sufficient postage to the envelope to pay for the mailing.
8. Someone must take the letter/envelope to an appropriate place to be mailed.
9. Someone must file the copy of the letter in a place so that it can be located if necessary.
10. Someone must decide whether and when the copy of the letter can be withdrawn from the file and destroyed so that, over the long term, the files only retain copies of important correspondence.

Sending a letter is a complex (and routine) process in any organization. Because it is a commonly done process, the steps may seem a natural and implicit sequence of events performed by specific people. Duties and responsibilities are usually set by job descriptions and traditions—for example, secretaries generally do all the steps except 1 and 4.

Efficient systems are orderly. They seek routine. They seek stability. They adhere to precedents. How a process or operation was done yesterday is a very good predictor of how that operation or process will be done tomorrow. When systems and the people who function in them confront uncertainty and ambiguous expectations, they attempt to drive out uncertainty and replace it with explicit (or implicit) direction.

Managers make systems more efficient by establishing explicit expectations. For example, using the process referred to as "division of labor," they decide who in the organization does what tasks and they establish the qualifications needed to perform the tasks. Similarly, using the management process referred to as "coordination," managers establish formal and informal mechanisms so that different parts of systems act in a predetermined, efficient, and effective manner. Organizational and system efficiency and effectiveness are not accidental. Efficiency and effectiveness are central management concerns, not peripheral by-products.

To create order and routine and drive out as much uncertainty as possible, managers need a technique able to describe current operations as well as design new or revised operations. The technique must encompass the macro elements of the system (i.e., goals and objectives) and the micro elements, such as who does what and in what order. General systems flow charting provides the health services manager with a technique able to capture both the micro and macro elements of a system. It is used to describe and analyze the processes used to convert inputs into outcomes at the system and subsystem levels.

FLOW CHARTS AS A MANAGERIAL TOOL

Two conditions must be satisfied to warrant use of a general systems flow chart. First, the work process should be complex. It should involve at least two or more people engaged in at least two or more steps to accomplish some predetermined objective, such as sending a letter or admitting a patient to a hospital. Second, the work process must have a formal start point and stop point. General systems flow charting requires the ability to define when a complex process starts and stops, even if the process or operation is continuous. For example, a hospital admits patients continuously. Even though the complex process of admitting patients may be continuous, it can be defined as a process with a formal beginning (e.g., when a specific patient arrives at the door) and end (e.g., when that patient is formally admitted into the hospital).

When these two conditions are met, general systems flow charting provides health services managers with the basis to describe a complex work process and then to use the descriptions to analyze, improve, and/or change the process. As implied by the name of the technique, two general properties are included in general systems flow charts—systems and flows. A flow chart depicts a system or subsystem (i.e., inputs, conversion processes, outcomes, and feedback loops) as well as the flow or sequence of inputs and conversion processes and feedback loops.

A general systems flow chart should be developed for any new complex work process in a health care organization. After a new system is designed using general systems flow charting, written work procedures can be developed and work tasks grouped into new or revised job descriptions to support the new system.

For many health care organizations, general systems flow charts are a new method, even though they originally became popular decades ago in production line settings. The technique was initially developed by industrial engineers and then used by systems analysts when they designed computer-based information systems. Today, interest in total quality management (TQM) has made the technique relevant again and served to introduce the method into health care organizations. The technique forces examination of the micro work process used to convert inputs into outcomes. It provides a systematic approach to determine how things are done and to change processes to achieve higher levels of efficiency and effectiveness. General systems flow charting is a technique with very broad applications. Although it looks basic, it is one of the most robust techniques in the health services manager's repertoire.

GENERAL RULES

All techniques have specific rules and conventions. For example, mathematical forecasting relies on the rules of algebra to solve mathematical equations. Although not mathematical, general systems flow charting also has specific rules:

1. Charts flow from top to bottom and from left to right.
2. Decisions included in a chart must have either yes or no answers. If possible, the "routine" or "most common" answer flows downward; the nonroutine answer flows horizontally.
3. Lines on charts have arrowheads that indicate flow and sequence.
4. Specific symbols are used (Figure 4-1).

Using these rules, charts are constructed that describe the operation of a current work process. Managers create charts by identifying how current processes work and ensuring that all logical possibilities are included in the chart.

PREPARING THE CHART

Certain prerequisites must be satisfied before the actual general systems flow chart is constructed. The health services manager must know the goal of the system or work process being analyzed. The goal might be to prepare and mail a letter, to admit a patient into the hospital, or to render appropriate patient care to patients who arrive for service. Whatever the goal, the manager must know the goal and use it as the central and unifying theme of the general systems flow chart. Knowing the goal of the system or work process also provides the ability to use general systems flow charts to improve operations. Improvements can involve increased efficiency

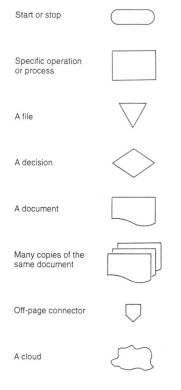

Start or stop	
Specific operation or process	
A file	
A decision	
A document	
Many copies of the same document	
Off-page connector	
A cloud	

(used to represent an aspect of the process that is unclear)

Figure 4-1.   Symbols used in general systems flow charting.

and/or increased quality of service. Rarely, if ever, will the manager be asked merely to analyze a system without an agenda for change, such as to fix a problem, increase efficiency, or enhance quality. Therefore, the agenda for change becomes an important aspect of the goal statement.

The general systems flow chart must describe how the current work operation is done. The creator of the chart must determine what is done, by whom, and in what sequence. Often this information is determined by interview and/or direct observation. Copies of documents created and used in the work process are collected and traced. This type of information is needed before the chart can be constructed. The description of the current system that emerges from these questions and documents is expressed in a general systems flow chart.

Creating general systems flow charts usually requires a few trials before the charts are completed and correct. The process of constructing and drawing the chart often identifies new questions or issues that lead to beginning again with a clean sheet of paper. The first time a chart is drawn is rarely the last. Novices usually produce many versions before the chart meets requirements. Experienced managers usually are more efficient—experience provides sharper senses to detect flow and sequence in a system. One must not underestimate the difficulty associated with using this simple technique. The only way to create a general systems flow chart is by trial and error, developing a version and then testing it to determine whether it actually reflects how the process is done. The manager must be prepared to do many drafts before the process is completed.

The first task, sometimes referred to as a *task list*, is to specify in order the individual *processes* in the overall process. Once the task list is established, the general systems flow chart can be created by adding decisions, files, documents, and other aspects of the process. Any chart must incorporate sufficient detail in order to be complete. Sometimes, for purposes of simplicity, charts are prepared in levels. Level I could be a simple summary chart that depicts the system at a macro level. This level is then backed up by numerous other charts (level II) that depict individual steps in the master process depicted on the level I chart.

A completed chart should be examined to verify the flow and sequence and determine whether the chart depicts the entire process. As can be seen in Figure 4-2, more detail could have been added by expanding the number of steps in this chart. This example could be considered a level I or macro chart, with other more detailed charts (level II) needed to cover each individual work process, such as "Collect data" and "Write first draft."

After the chart has been prepared and verified (verbally checked to ensure that all pathways and options lead to a logical stop point), the manager can use the chart to try some new ways to accomplish system goals. Perhaps, these new ways might involve simplifying procedures or the process. Often systems seem to "grow" needless steps that can be eliminated. In other instances, many steps can be repackaged into more efficient work packages. In still other instances, steps can be re-ordered and/or new steps added so that system outcomes better correspond with system goals. The primary point is that these new ideas for improvements must be developed as changes to the original system and field tested in the general system flow chart to ensure that desired outcomes are realized.

CONCLUSION

This chapter establishes general rules and conventions associated with general systems flow charting as a management method. Developing the skill to make a flow chart requires practice as well as patience. Although a basic method, it is very robust in identifying the operation of current work processes and options to enhance their efficiency and quality. Contemporary attempts to improve service quality, such as TQM and continuous quality improvement (CQI), rely on general systems flow charting as a basis for analysis.

Unlike other methods contained in the book, which rely on mathematics, general systems flow charting does not involve numbers and equations. In this sense it is not a quantitative method. It does, however, provide the manager with a form of symbolic logic to use to improve operations and design new systems. Therefore, general systems flow charting is a systematic method that should be incorporated into the repertoire of any health services manager.

EXERCISES

4-1. Develop a general systems flow chart that describes the process of filling a car with gasoline. After "Start," the first process should be "Arrive at gas station." Immediately before "Stop," the last process should be "Leave gas station."

4-2. Using a general systems flow chart, design a system for arrivals at the emergency room of a hospital.

GOAL: To complete an acceptable term paper

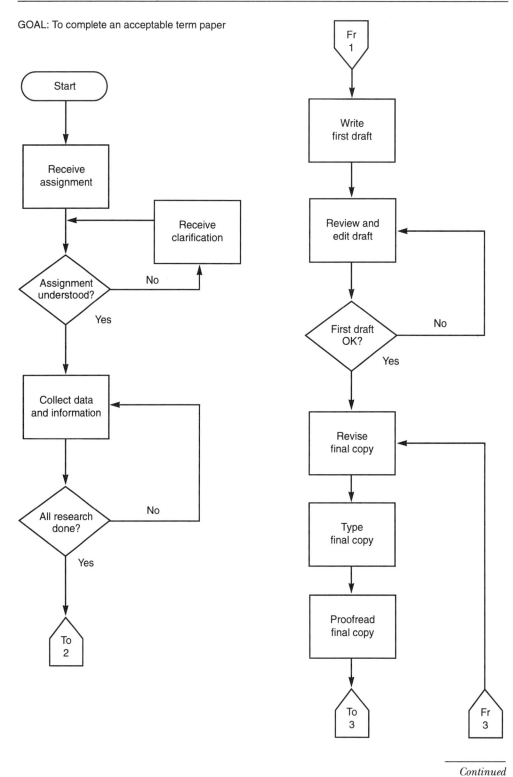

Figure 4-2. Example of a general systems flow chart.

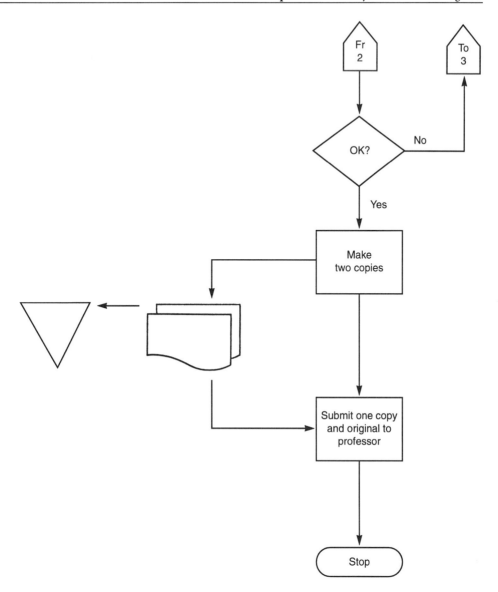

Figure 4-2. *continued*

4-3. Using the following narrative, create a general systems flow chart.

When a patient arrives at the clinic, the patient first sees the receptionist, who checks to see if the patient was seen before. If so, the receptionist pulls the medical record from the file. If the patient is new, the receptionist has the patient complete the necessary forms and then creates a medical record. Patients are seen by the physician in the order in which they arrive. If one of the two examination rooms is empty, the nurse escorts the patient to the examination room and records the complaint. The nurse performs routine tests. The nurse writes the complaint and findings on a Medical Examination Form, a form that will subsequently be filed with the patient's medical record. The physician examines the patient and orders medical tests, if necessary. A diagnosis and treatment plan is presented to the patient by the physician; a written copy of this plan and any other appropriate notes are written on the Medical Examination Form. When the patient is released by the physician, the patient returns to the receptionist, who prepares a bill. If the patient has health insurance, the bill is sent to the health insurance carrier. The patient leaves after either paying the bill (cash, check, or credit card) or signing the forms to authorize payment by his or her health insurance company. If the health insurance company refuses to pay the bill or only partially pays the bill, the receptionist bills the patient by mail. Any patient with an unpaid bill or bad credit history is refused subsequent treatment until the old bill is paid.

5

The Present and Future Value of Money

Chapter Objectives

1. To understand the concept of the time value of money
2. To be able to compute the future or present value of money (i.e., compounding and discounting)

Key Terms and Concepts

Compounding   Future value
Discount rate   Nominal or stated interest rate
Discounting   Opportunity cost
Effective annual interest rate   Present value

A manager is presented with an offer of $1,000 to purchase a new piece of laboratory equipment that her organization has begun developing. The prospective purchaser of this equipment has offered $1,000 for the rights to the equipment and has given the manager an option of receiving the money immediately or in 12 months. The rights to the equipment are going to be sold anyway, and there is no prospect of generating any revenue from the use of the equipment in the coming 12 months. Should the manager accept the money now or in 12 months? This is an easy choice: The manager elects to receive the $1,000 now, rather than waiting for 1 year. But what were the reasons behind her decision?

There are at least two factors that influenced the decision:

1. Assuming that some level of inflation will occur within the next 12 months, $1,000 can buy *more* today than in 12 months.
2. There is always an option of investing the $1,000 today or during the next year, an option that may result in greater financial return or gain in 12 months than accepting $1,000 in 12 months. At a minimum, the $1,000 could be put in a bank passbook savings account, where it would earn interest for the period of the investment.

This simple example illustrates one of the fundamental concepts of management: There is a time value associated with money. All other things being equal, money that you have today is worth more than the same amount of money received in the future. The concept of the time value of money comes from the field of finance.

Accountants and students of financial or managerial accounting typically are not concerned with the time value of money because they usually are working within relatively short time horizons (e.g., within the 12 months of an accounting cycle or a fiscal year). Over longer periods of time, however, and in many circumstances even over shorter periods of time, the relationship between time and the value of money is a critical management consideration. Given the fact that most investments or project opportunities have "lives" extending over time horizons greater than 12 months, the importance of the time value of money is magnified. Effective managers take a financial perspective of projects, not simply an accounting perspective.

Whereas the example above is simple, most financial decisions faced by managers are not as straightforward. For example, suppose the manager is offered the same $1,000 now for the equipment rights or $1,100 in 12 months. Should the manager sell the rights now, or sign an agreement to sell at the later time? Is it "better" financially to have the $1,000 in hand now, or is it more advantageous to wait for a year and receive a larger sum of money?

Responding to opportunities such as this requires competency in the management method of calculating what is known as the present value of money received at a later time. This competency enables managers to assess opportunities on an "apples and apples" perspective financially; in other words, it takes into account the time value of money. The overall objective of this chapter is to introduce the key management methods associated with the time value of money.

It must be added that, although financial factors should never be the only criteria used in making management decisions, particularly in health care, it is also true that such factors typically take precedence in decision making.

COMPOUNDING AND DISCOUNTING

The fundamental concepts underlying the idea that the value of money changes in relation to time are known as compounding and discounting. Compounding refers to the idea that, if money is invested (e.g., put in the bank or used to buy a bond with fixed return in the future), this amount of money grows or compounds in the future. Compounding refers to the process of going from today's value of money, known as the present value, to some future value of money.

It is useful to think of discounting as the inverse of compounding. Discounting is a way of looking at some future amount of money, known as the future value, and calculating its value today (i.e., calculating the present value). The following sections discuss the ideas of compounding and discounting and give several examples of how to compute future and present value. Additional examples of how to apply the ideas and tools introduced in this chapter are found later in the book.

Calculating the Future Value of Money: Compounding

The simplest example of the value of money growing over time (compounding) is a passbook savings account at a bank. Individuals choose to deposit money in the bank for a variety of reasons, including the knowledge that money invested in the bank grows because interest is earned on the money.

For example, if an initial deposit of $100 is made in a bank that promises to pay 4% interest annually, at the end of 12 months a total of $104 is available. The original deposit has grown or compounded from $100 to $104. The additional $4 is the interest earned on the deposit.

If the money is left in the bank for another year, assuming no change in the interest rate, at the end of year 2 a total of $108.16 is available in the account. The original $100 has grown or compounded by $8.16 as a result of interest earnings on the account. Thus, using conventional terminology, the future value of $100 invested for 2 years at an interest rate of 4% compounded annually is $108.16.

The increase in the account in the second year is $4.16 ($108.16 − $104.00), not $4.00, as was earned in year 1. This is because the amount in the account at the end of year 1 (i.e., the amount that is compounded for an additional [second] year) was $104 (the original $100 deposit + $4 of interest earned to that point in time). Thus, during year 2, 4% was earned on $104, not $100.

In situations involving compounding or discounting, it is helpful to create a "picture" or timeline of the investment scenario. A timeline is used to indicate the present and future value of money, the applicable interest rate, and the length of time involved. In fact, always beginning a time value of money analysis with a timeline may be a prerequisite for accurate calculations.

For example, Figure 5-1 depicts the situation just described. Note that time period "0" refers to the present time, and that the value refers to the size of the account at the end of the time period indicated. The compounding (interest) rate is shown on the timeline for the appropriate time periods. Creating a timeline is a simple, yet helpful tool to organize the "facts" of the investment opportunity and to help ensure that managers have all the information required for decision making.

In general terms, compounding is represented by the following equation:

$$\text{Future value} = \text{present value} + \text{interest earned (I)}$$

where

$$\text{Interest earned} = \text{present value} \times \text{interest rate}$$

Stated another way:

$$FV = PV \times i$$

or

$$FV = PV(1 + i) \qquad \qquad \text{(Eq. 5-1)}$$

where FV = future value
PV = present value
i = stated interest rate

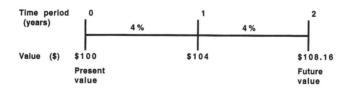

Figure 5-1.   Timeline showing present value (PV) and future value (FV) of $100 invested for 2 years at a 4% annual interest rate.

Using Equation 5-1 for the example described above, where the present value is the amount of the original deposit (i.e., $100) and the interest rate is 4%, the future value at the end of year 1 is calculated as:

$$FV_{yr\,1} = \$100(1 + 0.04)$$
$$= \$100(1.04)$$
$$= \$104$$

In the second year, another year's interest is earned. To reflect this second year of interest, Equation 5-1 becomes:

$$FV_{yr\,2} = PV(1 + i)(1 + i)$$
$$= PV(1 + i)^2$$

This is the same as:

$$FV_{yr\,2} = FV_{yr\,1} + FV_{yr\,1} \times i$$
$$= FV_{yr\,1}(1 + i)$$

because $FV_{yr\,1} = PV + PV(i)$. Each term $(1 + i)$, known as the compounding factor, indicates an additional period during which interest is being earned. In this example, it is said that interest is compounded for two periods. Substituting numbers in the equation, the future value at the end of year 2 is calculated to be:

$$FV_{yr\,2} = \$100(1 + 0.04)(1 + 0.04)$$
$$= \$100(1 + 0.04)^2$$
$$= \$100(1.04)^2$$
$$= \$100(1.0816)$$
$$= \$108.16$$

Equation 5-2 is a general equation for compounding that takes into account the number of compounding periods (n):

$$FV_n = PV(1 + i)^n \qquad \text{(Eq. 5-2)}$$

where FV_n = future value in time period n
PV = present value
i = stated interest rate
n = number of time periods

For example, if the original $100 remains in the bank and is compounded annually for a period of 7 years, the future value calculation is:

$$FV_{yr\,7} = \$100(1.04)(1.04)(1.04)(1.04)(1.04)(1.04)(1.04)$$
$$= \$100(1.04)^7$$
$$= \$100(1.3159)$$
$$= \$131.59$$

Equation 5-2 can be used without modification in any compounding problem, so long as there are no changes in the interest rate or the compounding period (examples in which these factors do change are considered later). Any standard calculator with an exponent key can be used to calculate future value easily.

Other options for computing the future value are available. Compounding factors may be obtained from published tables. Table 5-1 provides the compounding factors for various interest rates and periods of time. As reflected in Table 5-1, for the column corresponding to an interest rate of 4% and the row for 7 compounding periods, the compounding factor is 1.3159, the same number calculated above.

Business or financial calculators have a separate key for calculating the future value. The key requires that the present value, interest rate, and number of compounding periods be entered. In addition, spreadsheet software includes functions to calculate future value. It is recommended that either financial calculators or spreadsheet programs be used to compute the financial values described in this chapter.

The value of money grows more dramatically as the compounding rate increases. For example, the future value of $100 invested for 2 years at 8% is $116.64, compared with the value of $108.16 calculated at an interest rate of 4%.

Compounding More Frequently than Annually

In the simplest cases, described above, the value of money compounds once a year. In many cases, however, compounding occurs more frequently than annually. For example, interest on a passbook savings account may be compounded semiannually (i.e., twice a year). In this case, the number of compounding periods is doubled, but the interest rate is divided by 2 to account for the two periods.

The timeline in Figure 5-2 shows a situation in which the $100 in the earlier example is placed in an account that compounds interest semiannually. The $100 deposit will grow to $104.04 in 1 year when the 4% interest payment compounds semiannually. Using Equation 5-2, this calculation is:

$$FV_n = PV(1 + i)^n$$
$$FV_{yr\ 1} = \$100(1.02)^2$$
$$= \$100(1.0404)$$
$$= \$104.04$$

Note that the number of periods (n) has increased to 2, and the interest rate is now 2% for each compounding period. At the end of year 2, the account will be $108.24. Quarterly compounding results in a future value of $108.29 at the end of 2 years. Monthly compounding results in a future value of $108.31 at the end of 2 years. The account's value increases more rapidly with more frequent compounding.

Equation 5-3 is used to calculate future value when compounding takes place more frequently than annually:

$$FV_n = PV[1 + (i/m)]^{mn} \qquad \text{(Eq. 5-3)}$$

where m = number of compounding periods annually
n = number of years

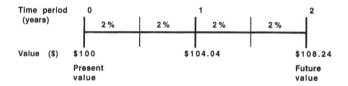

Figure 5-2.   Timeline showing present value (PV) and future value (FV) of $100 invested for 2 years at a 4% annual interest rate, compounded seminannually.

Table 5-1A. Table of compounding factors for interest rates of 1% through 11%

Period	1%	2%	3%	4%	5%	6%	7%	8%	9%	10%	11%
1	1.0100	1.0200	1.0300	1.0400	1.0500	1.0600	1.0700	1.0800	1.0900	1.1000	1.1100
2	1.0201	1.0404	1.0609	1.0816	1.1025	1.1236	1.1449	1.1664	1.1881	1.2100	1.2321
3	1.0303	1.0612	1.0927	1.1249	1.1576	1.1910	1.2250	1.2597	1.2950	1.3310	1.3676
4	1.0406	1.0824	1.1255	1.1699	1.2155	1.2625	1.3108	1.3605	1.4116	1.4641	1.5181
5	1.0510	1.1041	1.1593	1.2167	1.2763	1.3382	1.4026	1.4693	1.5386	1.6105	1.6851
6	1.0615	1.1262	1.1941	1.2653	1.3401	1.4185	1.5007	1.5869	1.6771	1.7716	1.8704
7	1.0721	1.1487	1.2299	1.3159	1.4071	1.5036	1.6058	1.7138	1.8280	1.9487	2.0762
8	1.0829	1.1717	1.2668	1.3686	1.4775	1.5938	1.7182	1.8509	1.9926	2.1436	2.3045
9	1.0937	1.1951	1.3048	1.4233	1.5513	1.6895	1.8385	1.9990	2.1719	2.3579	2.5580
10	1.1046	1.2190	1.3439	1.4802	1.6289	1.7908	1.9672	2.1589	2.3674	2.5937	2.8394
11	1.1157	1.2434	1.3842	1.5395	1.7103	1.8983	2.1049	2.3316	2.5804	2.8531	3.1518
12	1.1268	1.2682	1.4258	1.6010	1.7959	2.0122	2.2522	2.5182	2.8127	3.1384	3.4985
13	1.1381	1.2936	1.4685	1.6651	1.8856	2.1329	2.4098	2.7196	3.0658	3.4523	3.8833
14	1.1495	1.3195	1.5126	1.7317	1.9799	2.2609	2.5785	2.9372	3.3417	3.7975	4.3104
15	1.1610	1.3459	1.5580	1.8009	2.0789	2.3966	2.7590	3.1722	3.6425	4.1772	4.7846
16	1.1726	1.3728	1.6047	1.8730	2.1829	2.5404	2.9522	3.4259	3.9703	4.5950	5.3109
17	1.1843	1.4002	1.6528	1.9479	2.2920	2.6928	3.1588	3.7000	4.3276	5.0545	5.8951
18	1.1961	1.4282	1.7024	2.0258	2.4066	2.8543	3.3799	3.9960	4.7171	5.5599	6.5436
19	1.2081	1.4568	1.7535	2.1068	2.5270	3.0256	3.6165	4.3157	5.1417	6.1159	7.2633
20	1.2202	1.4859	1.8061	2.1911	2.6533	3.2071	3.8697	4.6610	5.6044	6.7275	8.0623

n											
21	1.2324	1.5157	1.8603	2.2788	2.7860	3.3996	4.1406	5.0338	6.1088	7.4002	8.9492
22	1.2447	1.5460	1.9161	2.3699	2.9253	3.6035	4.4304	5.4365	6.6586	8.1403	9.9336
23	1.2572	1.5769	1.9736	2.4647	3.0715	3.8197	4.7405	5.8715	7.2579	8.9543	11.0263
24	1.2697	1.6084	2.0328	2.5633	3.2251	4.0489	5.0724	6.3412	7.9111	9.8497	12.2392
25	1.2824	1.6406	2.0938	2.6658	3.3864	4.2919	5.4274	6.8485	8.6231	10.8347	13.5855
26	1.2953	1.6734	2.1566	2.7725	3.5557	4.5494	5.8074	7.3964	9.3992	11.9182	15.0799
27	1.3082	1.7069	2.2213	2.8834	3.7335	4.8223	6.2139	7.9881	10.2451	13.1100	16.7386
28	1.3213	1.7410	2.2879	2.9987	3.9201	5.1117	6.6488	8.6271	11.1671	14.4210	18.5799
29	1.3345	1.7758	2.3566	3.1187	4.1161	5.4184	7.1143	9.3173	12.1722	15.8631	20.6237
30	1.3478	1.8114	2.4273	3.2434	4.3219	5.7435	7.6123	10.0627	13.2677	17.4494	22.8923
35	1.4166	1.9999	2.8139	3.9461	5.5160	7.6861	10.6766	14.7853	20.4140	28.1024	38.5749
40	1.4889	2.2080	3.2620	4.8010	7.0400	10.2857	14.9745	21.7245	31.4094	45.2593	65.0009
45	1.5648	2.4379	3.7816	5.8412	8.9850	13.7646	21.0025	31.9204	48.3273	72.8905	109.5302
50	1.6446	2.6916	4.3839	7.1067	11.4674	18.4202	29.4570	46.9016	74.3575	117.3909	184.5648
60	1.8167	3.2810	5.8916	10.5196	18.6792	32.9877	57.9464	101.2571	176.0313	304.4816	524.0572

Note: Compounding factor for period n at interest rate $i = (1 + i)^n$.

Table 5-1B.   Table of compounding factors for interest rates of 12% through 20%, 25%, 30%, and 36%

Period	12%	13%	14%	15%	16%	17%	18%	19%	20%	25%	30%	36%
1	1.1200	1.1300	1.1400	1.1500	1.1600	1.1700	1.1800	1.1900	1.2000	1.2500	1.3000	1.3600
2	1.2544	1.2769	1.2996	1.3225	1.3456	1.3689	1.3924	1.4161	1.4400	1.5625	1.6900	1.8496
3	1.4049	1.4429	1.4815	1.5209	1.5609	1.6016	1.6430	1.6852	1.7280	1.9531	2.1970	2.5155
4	1.5735	1.6305	1.6890	1.7490	1.8106	1.8739	1.9388	2.0053	2.0736	2.4414	2.8561	3.4210
5	1.7623	1.8424	1.9254	2.0114	2.1003	2.1924	2.2878	2.3864	2.4883	3.0518	3.7129	4.6526
6	1.9738	2.0820	2.1950	2.3131	2.4364	2.5652	2.6996	2.8398	2.9860	3.8147	4.8268	6.3275
7	2.2107	2.3526	2.5023	2.6600	2.8262	3.0012	3.1855	3.3793	3.5832	4.7684	6.2749	8.6054
8	2.4760	2.6584	2.8526	3.0590	3.2784	3.5115	3.7589	4.0214	4.2998	5.9605	8.1573	11.7034
9	2.7731	3.0040	3.2519	3.5179	3.8030	4.1084	4.4355	4.7854	5.1598	7.4506	10.6045	15.9166
10	3.1058	3.3946	3.7072	4.0456	4.4114	4.8068	5.2338	5.6947	6.1917	9.3132	13.7858	21.6466
11	3.4785	3.8359	4.2262	4.6524	5.1173	5.6240	6.1759	6.7767	7.4301	11.6415	17.9216	29.4393
12	3.8960	4.3345	4.8179	5.3503	5.9360	6.5801	7.2876	8.0642	8.9161	14.5519	23.2981	40.0375
13	4.3635	4.8980	5.4924	6.1528	6.8858	7.6987	8.5994	9.5964	10.6993	18.1899	30.2875	54.4510
14	4.8871	5.5348	6.2613	7.0757	7.9875	9.0075	10.1472	11.4198	12.8392	22.7374	39.3738	74.0534
15	5.4736	6.2543	7.1379	8.1371	9.2655	10.5387	11.9737	13.5895	15.4070	28.4217	51.1859	100.7126
16	6.1304	7.0673	8.1372	9.3576	10.7480	12.3303	14.1290	16.1715	18.4884	35.5271	66.5417	136.9691
17	6.8660	7.9861	9.2765	10.7613	12.4677	14.4265	16.6722	19.2441	22.1861	44.4089	86.5042	186.2779
18	7.6900	9.0243	10.5752	12.3755	14.4625	16.8790	19.6733	22.9005	26.6233	55.5112	112.4554	253.3380
19	8.6128	10.1974	12.0557	14.2318	16.7765	19.7484	23.2144	27.2516	31.9480	69.3889	146.1920	344.5397
20	9.6463	11.5231	13.7435	16.3665	19.4608	23.1056	27.3930	32.4294	38.3376	86.7362	190.0496	468.5740

n												
21	10.8038	13.0211	15.6676	18.8215	22.5745	27.0336	32.3238	38.5910	46.0051	108.4202	247.0645	637.2606
22	12.1003	14.7138	17.8610	21.6447	26.1864	31.6293	38.1421	45.9233	55.2061	135.5253	321.1839	866.6744
23	13.5523	16.6266	20.3616	24.8915	30.3762	37.0062	45.0076	54.6487	66.2474	169.4066	417.5391	1178.6772
24	15.1786	18.7881	23.2122	28.6252	35.2364	43.2973	53.1090	65.0320	79.4968	211.7582	542.8008	1603.0010
25	17.0001	21.2305	26.4619	32.9190	40.8742	50.6578	62.6686	77.3881	95.3962	264.6978	705.6410	2180.0814
26	19.0401	23.9905	30.1666	37.8568	47.4141	59.2697	73.9490	92.0918	114.4755	330.8722	917.3333	2964.9107
27	21.3249	27.1093	34.3899	43.5353	55.0004	69.3455	87.2598	109.5893	137.3706	413.5903	1192.5333	4032.2786
28	23.8839	30.6335	39.2045	50.0656	63.8004	81.1342	102.9666	130.4112	164.8447	516.9879	1550.2933	5483.8988
29	26.7499	34.6158	44.6931	57.5755	74.0085	94.9271	121.5005	155.1893	197.8136	646.2349	2015.3813	7458.1024
30	29.9599	39.1159	50.9502	66.2118	85.8499	111.0647	143.3706	184.6753	237.3763	807.7936	2619.9956	*
35	52.7996	72.0685	98.1002	133.1755	180.3141	243.5035	327.9973	440.7006	590.6682	2465.1903	9727.8604	*
40	93.0510	132.7816	188.8835	267.8635	378.7212	533.8687	750.3783	1051.6675	1469.7716	7523.1638	*	*
45	163.9876	244.6414	363.6791	538.7693	795.4438	1170.4794	1716.6839	2509.6506	3657.2620	*	*	*
50	289.0022	450.7359	700.2330	1083.6574	1670.7038	2566.2153	3927.3569	5988.9139	9100.4382	*	*	*
60	897.5969	1530.0535	2595.9187	4383.9987	7370.2014	*	*	*	*	*	*	*

Note: Compounding factor for period n at interest rate $i = (1+i)^n$.

* Compounding factor greater than 9,999.

So, for this example with semiannual compounding, using Equation 5-3 to compute the future value at the end of year 1 yields:

$$FV_1 = \$100(1 + 4/2)^{2 \times 1}$$
$$= \$100(1.02)^2$$
$$= \$100(1.0404)$$
$$= \$104.04$$

Using Effective Annual Rates to Assess Opportunities

It is often important for a manager to compare different investment opportunities involving compounding, and these opportunities may not have the same compounding periods. In the examples described above, the annual interest rate is 4%, but, because the compounding frequencies differ, the future values of the investments differ. In order to facilitate a meaningful comparison among investment opportunities, it is important that adjustments be made to account for the differing compounding patterns (i.e., to compare apples with apples). This adjustment is made by calculating what is known as the effective annual rate.

The effective annual rate is the compounding rate that would have increased the initial investment to the higher future value (i.e., the amount calculated for the scenario with more frequent compounding), assuming annual compounding. In the example with semiannual compounding, the effective annual rate is the rate that would have increased the initial $100 deposit to $104.04 after 1 year ($108.24 after 2 years), assuming annual compounding. This effective annual interest rate can be calculated as follows:

$$\$100(1 + i) = \$104.04$$
$$(1 + i) = (\$104.04/\$100.00)$$
$$i = (\$104.04/\$100.00) - 1$$
$$= 0.0404$$
$$= 4.04\%$$

The effective annual rate of 4.04% is greater than the stated or nominal rate of 4%. Therefore, the opportunity with semiannual compounding is more attractive.

It should be clear that, when compounding occurs annually, the effective annual rate is equal to the stated or nominal rate. A manager evaluating the impact of different compounding periods should compare the effective annual rates and draw conclusions about the relative attractiveness of the opportunities. When assessing opportunities, assuming comparable risk levels, the same stated interest rates, and the same present value, those opportunities with more frequent compounding have higher future values.

Equation 5-4 is the general equation for the effective annual rate (EAR):

$$EAR = [1 + (i/m)]^m - 1.0 \qquad \text{(Eq. 5-4)}$$

where i = stated or nominal interest rate

m = number of compounding periods per year

If a bank changes its policy and compounds interest daily, what is the future value of $100 at the end of year 1 at 4% stated interest? What is the effective annual interest rate?

Using Equation 5-2, the future value may be calculated as:

$$FV = \$100[1 + (0.04/365)]^{365}$$
$$= \$100(1 + 0.0110)^{365}$$
$$= \$100(1.0408)$$
$$= \$104.08$$

Using Equation 5-4, the effective annual interest rate is:

$$EAR = [1 + (0.04/365)]^{365} - 1.0$$
$$= (1 + 0.01100)^{365} - 1.0$$
$$= 1.0408 - 1.0$$
$$= 0.0408$$
$$= 4.08\%$$

Daily compounding of interest enhances the attractiveness of the investment compared with less frequent compounding.

There may be instances when investments are made for periods of less than a full year. In such cases, the same equations presented above are used, but the value for n, the number of years of the investment, is adjusted to reflect the fractional period. For example, the $100 deposited at 4% compounded annually, may remain in the account for only 8 months. Eight months represents 8/12ths of a year, or 0.67 year. The timeline for this scenario is shown in Figure 5-3.

Using Equation 5-2, the future value of the account at the end of 8 months would be:

$$FV_{8\,mo} = \$100(1 + 0.04)^{8/12}$$
$$= \$100(1 + 0.04)^{2/3}$$

Algebraically, this is equivalent to:

$$FV_{8\,mo} = \$100(1.04)^{2/3}$$
$$= \$100\left(\sqrt[3]{1.04^2}\right)$$
$$= \$100\left(\sqrt[3]{1.0816}\right)$$

Rather than calculating a cube root, it is recommended that a calculator with an exponent key be used to solve this problem, and that the fractional exponent be translated to its decimal equivalent. The equation becomes:

$$FV_{8\,mo} = \$100(1 + 0.04)^{0.67}$$
$$= \$100(1.04)^{0.67}$$
$$= \$100(1.0266)$$
$$= \$102.66$$

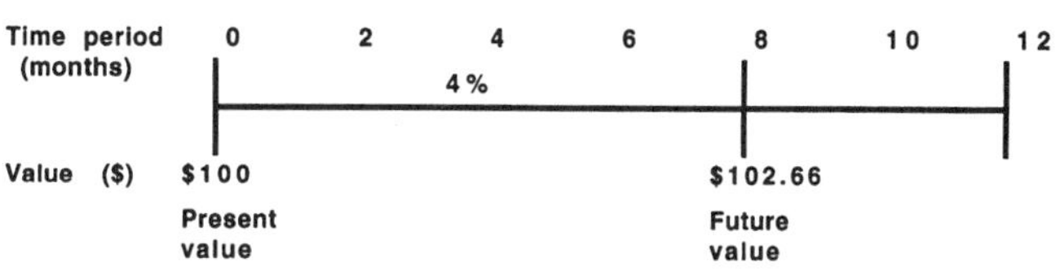

Figure 5-3. Timeline showing present value (PV) and future value (FV) of $100 invested for 8 months at a 4% annual interest rate, compounded annually.

It is not unusual for the compounding rate to change during a time period. For example, a $100 deposit may be made in a passbook account at a stated annual interest rate of 4%. After 6 months, however, the deposit may be transferred to a bank paying a stated annual rate of 4.5%. After 9 more months, the money may be transferred back to the original bank, which is now paying a stated annual rate of 5%. What is the total value of the account at the end of 2 years? The timeline for this situation is shown in Figure 5-4. This type of problem is essentially the same as those presented thus far. The future value for each compounding period is computed separately and each value then becomes the present value for the next compounding period.

At the end of 6 months the value of the account has grown to $101.98. This becomes the present value for the next 9 months, during which the account is compounding at a rate of 4.5%. The value of the account at the end of this period (i.e., 15 months after the initial deposit) is $105.40, which is considered the present value for the final 9 months, during which the account compounds at a rate of 5%. The final value of the account at the end of 2 years is $109.33. Assuming no fees or penalties associated with transferring funds, this alternative generates an amount greater than the future value of $108.16 computed earlier for a compounding rate of 4% over 2 years. Effective management of organizational finances often involves decisions related to finding the most attractive compounding opportunities.

Calculating the Present Value of Money: Discounting

Earlier in the chapter, a manager was presented with an opportunity to receive $1,000 now or $1,100 in 12 months. This is a typical financial management decision. The manager's choice is based on determining the present value of an amount of money to be received in the future, in this case $1,100. That is, how much is this sum of money worth today? This is essentially the reverse of the compounding question discussed in the first part of this chapter. Equation 5-2 states that:

$$FV_n = PV(1 + i)^n$$

where FV_n = future value
PV = present value
n = number of periods
i = interest rate (discount rate)

This new problem requires solving for the present value, so:

$$PV = FV_n / (1 + i)^n$$

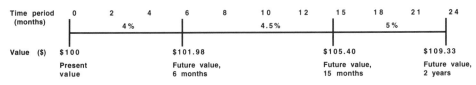

Figure 5-4. Timeline showing present value (PV) and future value (FV) of $100 invested for 2 years at a changing annual interest rate, compounded annually.

Restating this formula gives:

$$PV = FV_n[1/(1 + i)]^n \qquad \text{(Eq. 5-5)}$$

By looking at Equation 5-5, it should be apparent that, as it stands, there is not enough information to solve the problem; an interest rate (i) must be assumed. One technique typically used to identify an interest rate (also known as the discount rate or cost of capital) to be used in present value calculations is based on the idea of opportunity cost.

A manager typically has multiple options for investing money. For example, the manager may decide to deposit the $1,000 in a passbook savings account at 4%, compounded annually. The future value of this choice is $1,040 (using Equation 5-1 to calculate this number). In this case, the manager has an opportunity cost of 4%, or $40; this is the amount the organization would forego by accepting the 12-month offer from the prospective buyer. The concept of opportunity cost, as used here, assumes that the investment opportunities are of equal risk.

If 4% is the best alternative investment available, the manager would conclude that the offer to receive $1,100 in 12 months is more attractive than the bank deposit option and would accept the outside offer. In fact, the manager should be willing to accept any offer in excess of $1,040; at exactly $1,040, the manager should be indifferent between the opportunities; that is, there is no financial advantage to choosing one option over the other.

If a manager is offered an opportunity to invest in a project that will pay $1,000 after 5 years, how much should the organization be willing to invest now for this opportunity? Again, a key factor is the opportunity cost or discount rate to use. Because there is no standard rate, reasoned judgment must be used in selecting a rate. Use of a regular savings account rate is likely to be conservative; using a discount rate that is too conservative (low) may result in overpaying for investments.

If, through research, the manager discovers an investment of comparable risk that pays a 7% return, this is the discount rate that should be used. A timeline for this investment is shown in Figure 5-5; the present value is the unknown variable. Using Equation 5-5, the present value of this opportunity is calculated to be:

$$PV = FV_{5\,yr}\,[1/(1 + 0.07)]^5$$
$$= \$1,000(1/1.07)^5$$
$$= \$1,000(0.9346)^5$$
$$= \$1,000(0.7130)$$
$$= \$713.00$$

Given this analysis and based on the stated parameters, the organization should invest no more than $713 in this project—a project expected to return $1,000 to the organization in 5 years. If the organization can capitalize this project for less than

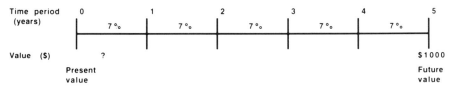

Figure 5-5.   Timeline showing the format for calculation of the present value (PV; unknown) and future value (FV) of $1,000 invested for 5 years at 7% interest, compounded annually.

$713, the project should yield a better financial return than the investment alternative. However, if the organization must capitalize this project for more than $713, then the investment alternative is a more financially attractive option. The manager should be willing to pay no more than $713 for this investment opportunity.

In Equation 5-5, the term $[1/(1 + i)]^n$ is known as the discounting factor. Table 5-2 provides discounting factors for various interest rates and periods of time. A review of the table indicates that the discounting factors decrease as the period of time lengthens and as the interest rate increases. Discounting factors can be used to compute present values. A more efficient way to complete the calculation, however, is to utilize a business or financial calculator or a spreadsheet program.

USING THE FUTURE VALUE AND PRESENT VALUE EQUATIONS

In the examples given thus far, the manager was asked to calculate the present or future value of money; these are the most frequent uses for the future and present value equations. They are not the only uses, however.

For example, a manager may be presented with an opportunity to purchase a certificate of deposit (CD) for $14,500 that will pay $20,000 after 5 years. In this scenario, the present value is $14,500 and the future value is $20,000. The period of time for the investment is 5 years; missing is the interest rate (i). This timeline is shown in Figure 5-6. This problem utilizes Equation 5-2 and solves for i:

$$FV_5 = PV(1 + i)^5$$
$$\$20,000 = \$14,500(1 + i)^5$$
$$\$20,000/\$14,500 = (1 + i)^5$$

This equation can be solved algebraically by taking the fifth root of both sides:

$$\sqrt[5]{20,000/14,500} = (1 + i)$$
$$i = \sqrt[5]{1.3793} - 1$$
$$= (1.3793)^{1/5} - 1$$
$$= (1.3793)^{0.20} - 1$$
$$= 1.06646 - 1$$
$$= 0.06646$$

This problem can be solved most easily, however, using a business or financial calculator. For most calculators, note that the present value must be entered as $-\$14,500$ to indicate that this amount of money must be invested to purchase the CD (i.e., it is a cash outflow). In this example, the interest rate (i) is calculated to be 6.64%.

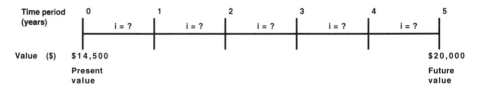

Figure 5-6. Timeline showing the format for calculating the annual interest rate (i) required to produce a future value (FV) of $20,000 for a 5-year investment of $14,500 (present value; PV).

Table 5-2A. Table of discounting factors for interest rates of 1% through 11%

Period	1%	2%	3%	4%	5%	6%	7%	8%	9%	10%	11%
1	0.9901	0.9804	0.9709	0.9615	0.9524	0.9434	0.9346	0.9259	0.9174	0.9091	0.9009
2	0.9803	0.9612	0.9426	0.9246	09070	0.8900	0.8734	0.8573	0.8417	0.8264	0.8116
3	0.9706	0.9423	0.9151	0.8890	0.8638	0.8396	0.8163	0.7938	0.7722	0.7513	0.7312
4	0.9610	0.9238	0.8885	0.8548	0.8227	0.7921	0.7629	0.7350	0.7084	0.6830	0.6587
5	0.9515	0.9057	0.8626	0.8219	0.7835	0.7473	0.7130	0.6806	0.6499	0.6209	0.5935
6	0.9420	0.8880	0.8375	0.7903	0.7462	0.7050	0.6663	0.6302	0.5963	0.5645	0.5346
7	0.9327	0.8706	0.8131	0.7599	0.7107	0.6651	0.6227	0.5835	0.5470	0.5132	0.4817
8	0.9235	0.8535	0.7894	0.7307	0.6768	0.6274	0.5820	0.5403	0.5019	0.4665	0.4339
9	0.9143	0.8368	0.7664	0.7026	0.6446	0.5919	0.5439	0.5002	0.4604	0.4241	0.3909
10	0.9053	0.8203	0.7441	0.6756	0.6139	0.5584	0.5083	0.4632	0.4224	0.3855	0.3522
11	0.8963	0.8043	0.7224	0.6496	0.5847	0.5268	0.4751	0.4289	0.3875	0.3505	0.3173
12	0.8874	0.7885	0.7014	0.6246	0.5568	0.4970	0.4440	0.3971	0.3555	0.3186	0.2858
13	0.8787	0.7730	0.6810	0.6006	0.5303	0.4688	0.4150	0.3677	0.3262	0.2897	0.2575
14	0.8700	0.7579	0.6611	0.5775	0.5051	0.4423	0.3878	0.3405	0.2992	0.2633	0.2320
15	0.8613	0.7430	0.6419	0.5553	0.4810	0.4173	0.3624	0.3152	0.2745	0.2394	0.2090
16	0.8528	0.7284	0.6232	0.5339	0.4581	0.3936	0.3387	0.2919	0.2519	0.2176	0.1883
17	0.8444	0.7142	0.6050	0.5134	0.4363	0.3714	0.3166	0.2703	0.2311	0.1978	0.1696
18	0.8360	0.7002	0.5874	0.4936	0.4155	0.3503	0.2959	0.2502	0.2120	0.1799	0.1528
19	0.8277	0.6864	0.5703	0.4746	0.3957	0.3305	0.2765	0.2317	0.1945	0.1635	0.1377
20	0.8195	0.6730	0.5537	0.4564	0.3769	0.3118	0.2584	0.2145	0.1784	0.1486	0.1240

(continued)

Table 5-2A. (continued)

Period	1%	2%	3%	4%	5%	6%	7%	8%	9%	10%	11%
21	0.8114	0.6598	0.5375	0.4388	0.3589	0.2942	0.2415	0.1987	0.1637	0.1351	0.1117
22	0.8034	0.6468	0.5219	0.4220	0.3418	0.2775	0.2257	0.1839	0.1502	0.1228	0.1007
23	0.7954	0.6342	0.5067	0.4057	0.3256	0.2618	0.2109	0.1703	0.1378	0.1117	0.0907
24	0.7876	0.6217	0.4919	0.3901	0.3101	0.2470	0.1971	0.1577	0.1264	0.1015	0.0817
25	0.7798	0.6095	0.4776	0.3751	0.2953	0.2330	0.1842	0.1460	0.1160	0.0923	0.0736
26	0.7720	0.5976	0.4637	0.3607	0.2812	0.2198	0.1722	0.1352	0.1064	0.0839	0.0663
27	0.7644	0.5859	0.4502	0.3468	0.2678	0.2074	0.1609	0.1252	0.0976	0.0763	0.0597
28	0.7568	0.5744	0.4371	0.3335	0.2551	0.1956	0.1504	0.1159	0.0895	0.0693	0.0538
29	0.7493	0.5631	0.4243	0.3207	0.2429	0.1846	0.1406	0.1073	0.0822	0.0630	0.0485
30	0.7419	0.5521	0.4120	0.3083	0.2314	0.1741	0.1314	0.0994	0.0754	0.0573	0.0437
35	0.7059	0.5000	0.3554	0.2534	0.1813	0.1301	0.0937	0.0676	0.0490	0.0356	0.0259
40	0.6717	0.4529	0.3066	0.2083	0.1420	0.0972	0.0668	0.0460	0.0318	0.0221	0.0154
45	0.6391	0.4102	0.2644	0.1712	0.1113	0.0727	0.0476	0.0313	0.0207	0.0137	0.0091
50	0.6080	0.3715	0.2281	0.1407	0.0872	0.0543	0.0339	0.0213	0.0134	0.0085	0.0054
60	0.5504	0.3048	0.1697	0.0951	0.0535	0.0303	0.0173	0.0099	0.0057	0.0033	0.0019

Note: Discounting factor for period n at interest rate $i = 1/(1 + n)^n$.

Table 5-2B.   Table of discounting factors for interest rates of 12% through 20%, 25%, 30%, and 36%

Period	12%	13%	14%	15%	16%	17%	18%	19%	20%	25%	30%	36%
1	0.8929	0.8850	0.8772	0.8696	0.8621	0.8547	0.8475	0.8403	0.8333	0.8000	0.7692	0.7353
2	0.7972	0.7831	0.7695	0.7561	0.7432	0.7305	0.7182	0.7062	0.6944	0.6400	0.5917	0.5407
3	0.7118	0.6931	0.6750	0.6575	0.6407	0.6244	0.6086	0.5934	0.5787	0.5120	0.4552	0.3975
4	0.6355	0.6133	0.5921	0.5718	0.5523	0.5337	0.5158	0.4987	0.4823	0.4096	0.3501	0.2923
5	0.5674	0.5428	0.5194	0.4972	0.4761	0.4561	0.4371	0.4190	0.4019	0.3277	0.2693	0.2149
6	0.5066	0.4803	0.4556	0.4323	0.4104	0.3898	0.3704	0.3521	0.3349	0.2621	0.2072	0.1580
7	0.4523	0.4251	0.3996	0.3759	0.3538	0.3332	0.3139	0.2959	0.2791	0.2097	0.1594	0.1162
8	0.4039	0.3762	0.3506	0.3269	0.3050	0.2848	0.2660	0.2487	0.2326	0.1678	0.1226	0.0854
9	0.3606	0.3329	0.3075	0.2843	0.2630	0.2434	0.2255	0.2090	0.1938	0.1342	0.0943	0.0628
10	0.3220	0.2946	0.2697	0.2472	0.2267	0.2080	0.1911	0.1756	0.1615	0.1074	0.0725	0.0462
11	0.2875	0.2607	0.2366	0.2149	0.1954	0.1778	0.1619	0.1476	0.1346	0.0859	0.0558	0.0340
12	0.2567	0.2307	0.2076	0.1869	0.1685	0.1520	0.1372	0.1240	0.1122	0.0687	0.0429	0.0250
13	0.2292	0.2042	0.1821	0.1625	0.1452	0.1299	0.1163	0.1042	0.0935	0.0550	0.0330	0.0184
14	0.2046	0.1807	0.1597	0.1413	0.1252	0.1110	0.0985	0.0876	0.0779	0.0440	0.0254	0.0135
15	0.1827	0.1599	0.1401	0.1229	0.1079	0.0949	0.0835	0.0736	0.0649	0.0352	0.0195	0.0099
16	0.1631	0.1415	0.1229	0.1069	0.0930	0.0811	0.0708	0.0618	0.0541	0.0281	0.0150	0.0073
17	0.1456	0.1252	0.1078	0.0929	0.0802	0.0693	0.0600	0.0520	0.0451	0.0225	0.0116	0.0054
18	0.1300	0.1108	0.0946	0.0808	0.0691	0.0592	0.0508	0.0437	0.0376	0.0180	0.0089	0.0039
19	0.1161	0.0981	0.0829	0.0703	0.0596	0.0506	0.0431	0.0367	0.0313	0.0144	0.0068	0.0029
20	0.1037	0.0868	0.0728	0.0611	0.0514	0.0433	0.0365	0.0308	0.0261	0.0115	0.0053	0.0021

(continued)

Table 5-2B. (continued)

Period	12%	13%	14%	15%	16%	17%	18%	19%	20%	25%	30%	36%
21	0.0926	0.0768	0.0638	0.0531	0.0443	0.0370	0.0309	0.0259	0.0217	0.0092	0.0040	0.0016
22	0.0826	0.0680	0.0560	0.0462	0.0382	0.0316	0.0262	0.0218	0.0181	0.0074	0.0031	0.0012
23	0.0738	0.0601	0.0491	0.0402	0.0329	0.0270	0.0222	0.0183	0.0151	0.0059	0.0024	0.0008
24	0.0659	0.0532	0.0431	0.0349	0.0284	0.0231	0.0188	0.0154	0.0126	0.0047	0.0018	0.0006
25	0.0588	0.0471	0.0378	0.0304	0.0245	0.0197	0.0160	0.0129	0.0105	0.0038	0.0014	0.0005
26	0.0525	0.0417	0.0331	0.0264	0.0211	0.0169	0.0135	0.0109	0.0087	0.0030	0.0011	0.0003
27	0.0469	0.0369	0.0291	0.0230	0.0182	0.0144	0.0115	0.0091	0.0073	0.0024	0.0008	0.0002
28	0.0419	0.0326	0.0255	0.0200	0.0157	0.0123	0.0097	0.0077	0.0061	0.0019	0.0006	0.0002
29	0.0374	0.0289	0.0224	0.0174	0.0135	0.0105	0.0082	0.0064	0.0051	0.0015	0.0005	0.0001
30	0.0334	0.0256	0.0196	0.0151	0.0116	0.0090	0.0070	0.0054	0.0042	0.0012	0.0004	0.0001
35	0.0189	0.0139	0.0102	0.0075	0.0055	0.0041	0.0030	0.0023	0.0017	0.0004	0.0001	0.0000
40	0.0107	0.0075	0.0053	0.0037	0.0026	0.0019	0.0013	0.0010	0.0007	0.0001	0.0000	0.0000
45	0.0061	0.0041	0.0027	0.0019	0.0013	0.0009	0.0006	0.0004	0.0003	0.0000	0.0000	0.0000
50	0.0035	0.0022	0.0014	0.0009	0.0006	0.0004	0.0003	0.0002	0.0001	0.0000	0.0000	0.0000
60	0.0011	0.0007	0.0004	0.0002	0.0001	0.0001	0.0000	0.0000	0.0000	0.0000	0.0000	0.0000

Note: Discounting factor for period n at interest rate $i = 1/(1 + i)^n$.

Another situation requires a manager to compute the number of periods required to generate a specified future value, given a known present value and interest rate. This is the same as solving for n in Equation 5-2:

$$FV_n = PV(1 + i)^n$$

Again, the easiest way to solve this problem is to use a business or financial calculator; alternatively, in many instances, Table 5-1 can be used. The compounding factor $(1 + i)$ for the identified interest rate can be computed as:

$$(1 + i)^n = FV_n/PV$$

Then, using this factor at the stated interest rate, the correct number of periods can be read directly from Table 5-1.

For example, if the present value is $250, the future value is $800, and the interest rate is 8%, what is the number of periods? Using Equation 5-2:

$$(1 + i)^n = \$800/\$250$$
$$= 3.20$$

Looking at Table 5-1 for an interest rate of 8% indicates that approximately 15 periods are required.

Time period problems also can be solved using Equation 5-5:

$$PV = FV_n[1/(1 + i)]^n$$

The discounting factor—$[1/(1 + i)]^n$—for the identified interest rate can be computed as:

$$[1/(1 + i)]^n = PV/FV_n$$

Table 5-2 is then used to identify the number of time periods corresponding to this computed discounting factor at the stated interest rate.

CONCLUSION

All management decisions involving the time value of money require the use of the tools of compounding and discounting. Competency in these two skills enables the manager to evaluate a wide variety of situations. In essence, managers must be able to compute the present value of money with compounding/discounting periods of various lengths and at different interest rates.

Often, the greatest challenges for managers involve: 1) identifying the unknown variable—that is, what is it that must be determined (e.g., present value, future value, interest rate, number of time periods), and 2) determining the appropriate discount rate. This subject will be addressed in greater depth later in the book. Regardless of the situation being analyzed, however, the simplest and most important tool at the disposal of the manager is a timeline, which indicates the information provided and assists in identifying what variable or factor is missing. The first step in assessing the time value of money should always be to draw such a timeline.

EXERCISES

5-1. The ambulance service of a rural community will need to purchase a used ambulance at the end of 3 years. An arrangement has been made to obtain the ambulance of a neighboring town for $13,500 at that time. The community has recently completed a fund drive that raised $11,250 to be used toward the purchase of the ambulance. What annual interest rate (stated or nominal interest rate) will the community need to obtain on its invested funds (the $11,250) in order to have the money needed to purchase the ambulance at the necessary time?

5-2. You are the new business manager of a medical group practice. You have been instructed to seek the highest available short-term interest rate in managing the group's investments. Following these guidelines, you deposit $950 of the group's net revenues in a bank savings account paying 5%, compounded quarterly. After 7 months, you transfer your funds to a different bank that pays 5.25%, compounded semiannually. Nine months later, with the approval of the board of directors of the group, you again withdraw your funds and loan the money to a local investor who has promised to pay back the loan plus 9% interest (per year) in 2 years. When the investor pays you back, as promised, how much money do you receive from the investor? (*Note:* There are no transfer or withdrawal fees charged by the banks.)

5-3. A business investment pays 6.5% interest, compounded monthly. What is the effective annual rate of this opportunity?

5-4. For the first time, the board of trustees of a community hospital has voted to purchase a medical practice. The negotiated purchase price is $450,000. Several meetings earlier, the board had designated funds in the amount of $300,000 to be used to acquire physician practices. While awaiting the identification of potential practices to purchase, the $300,000 was used to purchase a certificate of deposit (CD) at an interest rate of 8.5%. Selling the CD now will yield exactly the required amount of $450,000. How many years have you held the CD? (*Note:* Interest on the CD is compounded and paid annually.)

5-5. A health maintenance organization (HMO) is offered an opportunity to invest in a new outcomes indicator information system under development. The required investment is $300,000, and the HMO's return will be $450,000 in 5 years. An appropriate opportunity cost is 6%. Should the investment be made?

II

FORECASTING MODELS

Forecasting is a way of looking into the future in the hope of anticipating change. Forecasting is both an art and a science, and different managers use different techniques. Some managers look into the future and decide what will happen "by the seat of their pants." Others use the opinion of other persons they respect. Still others use mathematical techniques to make the best forecast they can, using past data from their organizations or data from outside sources. In the next three chapters, concepts and mathematical techniques of forecasting are presented.

The key to good forecasting is to make the forecast as close to reality as possible. Based on a forecast of patient days in a hospital, for example, the organization will order supplies and food and schedule staff. If the manager forecasts low, the organization will pay for expensive quick orders or overtime labor. If the manager forecasts high, the organization pays for unnecessary labor and materials.

Chapter 6, "The Art and Science of Forecasting," reviews the definitions of forecasting, the use of rates in forecasting, and how to use an equation to forecast. Chapter 7, "Trend Extrapolation Techniques," describes the use of moving averages and exponential smoothing techniques. These are used when past values of the data reflect a trend that is expected to continue. For example, past levels of patient days in a nursing home might show a trend that can be used to predict next year's level. Chapter 8, "The Regression Model," describes the use of explanatory variables for forecasting. This technique is used when independent variables, rather than past variables of the data being predicted, explain the variability of the data. For example, the number of students enrolled in a university might predict the number of visits to the university health center.

Forecasting is an important mathematical technique for a health services manager. The ability to forecast, however, presumes the ability to minimize the guaranteed error in the forecast. This message permeates this entire section.

6

The Art and Science
of Forecasting

Chapter Objectives

1. To describe the concept of forecasting
2. To describe the difference between analytical forecasting and genius forecasting
3. To describe the challenges forecasting presents to the health services manager

Key Terms and Concepts

Age-adjusted rates	Independent variable
Analytical forecasting	Method bias
Dependent variable	Random error
Genius forecasting	Sensitivity analysis
Health-related events	Systematic error

A forecast is intended to predict the future. No one is clairvoyant—able to see into the future or predict the future with absolute certainty. Nevertheless, managers must anticipate the future in order to prepare for it. Budgets are based on forecasts. The number and type of employees needed are based on present as well as future demands for service. Hirings and staff reductions are based on forecasts of the future.

Any forecast is, at best, an imprecise estimate of the future. Few forecasts will be absolutely accurate. Every forecast includes an error factor. The challenge faced by managers and analysts is to minimize the inherent *error* (*E*) included in any forecast—to minimize the difference between what is predicted and what actually happens.

For example, in a relationship in which F = the forecast made yesterday of today's temperature and *TEMP* = today's actual temperature, the only way F can equal *TEMP* is if:

1. The forecast was absolutely correct, *or*
2. The equation is revised to be $F = TEMP + E$, where E is the positive or negative error of the forecast.

If today's temperature was forecast to be 65° and the actual temperature is 65°, then the error in the forecast would be 0. However, if the forecast for today's temperature was 80°, given the equation:

$$F = TEMP + E \qquad \text{(Eq. 6-1)}$$

the error would be:

$$80° = 65° + E$$
$$E = 80° - 65°$$

or 15 degrees. In reality, the first forecast was a forecast where the error (E) was 0. This initial forecast absolutely minimized the error in the forecast.

Managers are interested in methods that can minimize the error that is included in all forecasts. The challenge with forecasting is to strive for accuracy and to minimize error. Error can be thought of as systematic error—that error that can be minimized by appropriate forecasting—and random error—that error that is inherent in every forecast and cannot be averted. The "best" forecast is the forecast with the least amount of systematic error.

ANALYTICAL AND GENIUS FORECASTING

Forecasting as a body of knowledge is composed of two main branches: genius forecasting and analytical forecasting.

Genius Forecasting

Genius forecasting involves either finding a clairvoyant or treating opinions rendered by people—usually experts—as the equivalent of the statements of clairvoyants. For example, the Delphi method is a systematic method to collect opinions (usually from experts) and use them in multiple round-robin cycles in an effort to arrive at a forecast that captures the essence of the individual opinions all the experts used in the forecasting exercise. Other examples of genius forecasting can be found in various forms: in newspapers on or around New Year's Day when notable geniuses(??) forecast what the new year will bring or in the multiple opinions or guesses of "experts" found in print or on television, usually involving some issue of contemporary importance.

Except for the Delphi method, all forms of genius forecasting are based on individual opinion. Obviously, sometimes the individual will be right and other times he or she will be wrong. It is important to remember that the inherent challenge in forecasting is to minimize the error inherent in all forecasts. Genius forecasting is usually used to forecast distant events that defy other approaches. Generally, the error inherent in genius forecasting is considered large but unavoidable.

For example, what if the assignment was to forecast the year when a cure would be available for AIDS? The only reasonable and logical approach would be to identify either an expert or multiple experts and ask their opinion(s) on this question. The thesis is that the error in their forecast will be less than the error in other forecasts because they are the experts and have greater knowledge of the area than others.

Before leaving the topic of genius forecasting, it is important to note that sometimes a forecasting problem requires the use of genius forecasting, such as in the example involving AIDS. Genius forecasting is still forecasting, even though it can be highly judgmental and is not based on mathematical models.

Analytical Forecasting

In contrast to genius forecasting, analytical forecasting attempts to be more systematic and is usually mathematical. Most forecasting problems faced by the health services manager will be solved using some form of analytical forecasting. Analytical forecasting methods are based on either one of the following assumptions.

Assumption A: The Past Can Predict the Future

The assumption that the past can predict the future means that what will occur in the future is (assumed to be) strongly related to what is occurring today and what has occurred in the past. Under this assumption, analytical approaches are used to examine past and present events and extend or extrapolate the values of these past events into the future. In using analytical approaches based on this assumption, managers count on the past being a valid and reliable predictor of the future.

This assumption must be thoroughly considered by health services managers who use analytical forecasting approaches. For example, if the assignment is to forecast the number of patient days a hospital would generate (or produce) next month, or even next year, basing the forecast on past patient day production or generation would seem appropriate because the past may be a reasonable predictor of the future. But, how far back in the past should a manager go in making the forecast?

Alternatively, what if the assignment is to forecast hospital patient days for the next 10 years? Ten years is a very long time in the future, and many things could happen to change the number of hospital patient days. Given the ambiguity associated with such a long time interval, most health services managers would be very reluctant to base a 10-year forecast solely on the past.

Methods explored in Chapter 7 that are based on this assumption include:

1. Extrapolations using average change
2. Moving averages as forecasts
3. Using exponential smoothing in forecasting

These methods are used best when the health services manager is confident that the past is an appropriate predictor of the future.

Assumption B: The Future Can Be Predicted Based on Cause and Effect

Many forecasting approaches are based on cause and effect and are known as causal models. The models used in this category of forecasting attempt to capture the primary factors that are believed to cause (hence the name causal) or influence the future. For example, consider a forecast of the number of patient days to be generated by a hospital: Patient days can be considered the "effect." Using the number of patient days forecast (PD_f), a conceptual as well as analytical cause-and-effect model or relationship can be constructed. Based on knowledge of patient day generation in a hospital, the following mathematical relationship or model can be examined:

$$PD_f = \text{ALOS} \times \text{admissions}$$

where ALOS = average length of stay for patients in the hospital (in days)
admissions = number of patients to be admitted into the hospital next year

Knowing that:

Admissions = Hospital admission rate per 1,000 people × Number of
people in the hospital's service area

provides the ability to express the cause-and-effect model as:

PD_f = ALOS × (Hospital admission rate per 1,000 people × Number of
people in the hospital's service area)

In this model, PD_f is the dependent variable (its value is dependent on the causal factors included in the model). It will take on a given value based on the mathematical interaction of the independent variables. It is the model's "effect." The ALOS, the hospital admission rate per 1,000 people, and the number of people in the hospital's service area are all independent variables or "causes." These are considered independent because their values are not affected by the value of the dependent variable. In other words, the forecast number of patient days will not affect the ALOS. (In contrast, however, the ALOS will affect the forecast number of patient days.) Usually the dependent variable is to the left of the equal sign in any equation and the independent variables are to the right of the equal sign. Independent variables are what you put into the model or equation to get the result—the result is the dependent variable because it is dependent on what is put into the model or equation (the independent variable[s]).

In this example, the hospital admission rate per 1,000 people can be estimated based on characteristics of the population. The number of people in the hospital's service area also can be estimated using census data and knowledge of patient origin. Average length of stay (ALOS) also can be estimated. Therefore, each independent variable in this model can be quantified and used to solve for the number of patient days. Chapter 8, "The Regression Model," covers one forecasting technique based on assumption B.

Sensitivity Analysis Sensitivity analysis provides the manager with the ability to examine the cause-and-effect relationship developed as the basis for forecasting. It involves determining the impact that change in one or more factors (independent variables) has on the final answer (the dependent variable).

Using the previous model involving hospital patient days, if:

Average length of stay (ALOS) is 5.0 days
Hospital admission rate per 100,000 per year is 118
Number of people in hospital's service area (in thousands) is 250

then:

PD_f = ALOS × (Hospital admission rate per 1,000 people × Number of
people in the hospital's service area)

= 5.0 (118 × 250)
= 5.0 (29,500)
= 147,500 patient days

However, if the population decreases by 10% to 225,000, ALOS decreases by 10% to 4.5 days, and the admission rate decreases 10% to 106.2 admissions per 100,000, then the new forecast (107,527.5 patient days) would be 27% [(107,527.5 − 147,500)/(147,500 × 100)] below the original forecast or answer.

Sensitivity analysis examines multiple "what if" questions to determine which variable in the model has the most power to change the overall answer or forecast. It also is used to determine the overall effect of changes in specific variables. In this last example, each variable was adjusted downward by 10%; the overall effect of these adjustments was a 27% decrease in the forecast number of patient days.

USING EPIDEMIOLOGY IN FORECASTING

Epidemiology is the science that describes and analyzes the need for health and medical care. It is usually defined as the distribution and determinants of health-related events in human populations. If managers or policy analysts know who has disease, injuries, pregnancies, and so forth and the risk factors associated with these, they can design service systems accurately either to treat the health-related event or to prevent it through risk reduction. Epidemiology produces many rates that can be incorporated into the use rate types of forecasting methods. Epidemiological information is critical whenever the manager or policy analyst is required to forecast the need for health and medical care.

Epidemiological rates include:

Natality (birth rate)
Fertility
Rates of mortality
    Crude death rate
    Cause-specific mortality rates
    Infant death rates and other age-specific rates
Rates of morbidity
    Incidence rates
    Prevalence rates

National use rates also include utilization rates of health and medical services. Examples include:

Hospital
    Discharges per 100 or 1,000 people
    Average length of stay
    Rate of occupancy
    Average daily census
Ambulatory care
    Average number of visits to a physician's office per year per person

Whenever epidemiological rates are used to forecast, care must be taken to adjust the rates so that approximate equality is achieved in demographic variables involving age, gender, race, income, and other factors thought to have a significant influence on death and disease. A national crude annual death rate of 8.7 deaths per 1,000 people, for example, could not be applied to a specific community or market area without adjusting or modifying the figure to reflect local demographic data. The demographic variables used to calculate the national rate must be matched with the demographic variables in the population being forecast. If the average age in the nation was 35 and the average age in a specific community was 28, using the national average of 8.7 deaths per 1,000 people would grossly overestimate the number of anticipated deaths because of the age discrepancy between the national rate and the rate for the demographic composition of the specific community. Rates must be age adjusted.

Forecasting with use rates appears simple but requires a high degree of caution because of changes in the population over time, especially with respect to age and socioeconomic status. In other words, use rates themselves change over time—they are not static. Also, whenever rates are used, the demographic characteristics represented in the national rate must be matched with the equivalent demographic characteristic in the population being forecast. Adjusting rates to match on demographic variables is a challenge when use rates are used in forecasting.

FORECASTING AS MANAGERIAL ART AND SCIENCE

Forecasting is approached systematically and thoughtfully. In this sense, forecasting is scientific—it is governed by rules and conventions. Being proficient at forecasting requires knowing these rules and conventions and being able to use them. Developing a forecast that minimizes systematic error requires a high level of proficiency, judgment, and common sense. In this sense, forecasting is an art form. Science is unable to provide health services managers with explicit rules to govern these judgmental aspects of forecasting. Experience and organizational convention, however, will help develop the ability of the manager to use forecasting as an art.

Merely performing accurate calculations does not make for a good forecast. Managers prepare forecasts. Computers and calculators can perform calculations, but it is the responsibility of the manager to minimize the error in forecasts. The primary test of any forecast is whether it minimizes the systematic error. Sometimes managers forecast the same thing using multiple techniques to determine which forecast provides the least error using historical data. In this sense, forecasting can be considered a heuristic, or learning, process.

Each and every forecast should teach the manager something. Expert forecasters use multiple methods and continue to ask themselves what each forecast has taught them about the forecast and the phenomena under study, such as hospital patient days. They search for new ways and new insights to minimize the excess error associated with their forecasts. They attempt to learn from every forecast they prepare. Comparing the forecast or prediction with the actual data enables the manager to determine how to perfect the craft of forecasting.

Analytical forecasting does involve mathematics. If forecasting were just math, however, mathematicians—not managers—would prepare forecasts. Forecasting also requires a knowledge of the phenomena being forecast, such as hospital patient days, as well as the ability to analyze the phenomena using mathematics for the purpose of forecasting. The manager needs to know what variables drive one another. Analytical forecasting is not just very complex mathematics. Any form of forecasting is a reasoned judgment made by a manager after considered study. Managers must know their data. Managers should be able to choose the appropriate variables to use in cause-and-effect models. In the final analysis, managers are responsible for their forecasts. The future, not the manipulation of equations, will indicate whether the forecast was responsible and logical.

Generally, four questions must be addressed in forecasting:

1. What (variable) is being forecast? What answers are needed from the forecast?
2. What variable(s) is/are associated with the variable being forecast? What information is available or will need to be made available on these variables?
3. How much time is there to do the forecast?
4. What is known about the relationships regarding the phenomena being forecast? To what degree are the variables associated (i.e., correlated)?

The number one rule of forecasting is *to always plot the data on a graph*. If the assignment is to forecast the number of inpatient admissions or clinic visits, any and all historical data should be plotted as well as the variables that might influence them. This will illustrate any association that might exist and can assist the manager in developing the appropriate forecast. For the most part, forecasts will be prepared based on both historical and current information, using a trend extrapolation technique. The availability of this information often will drive the decision as to which forecasting method or methods can be used.

The choice of a forecasting method or methods is the manager's alone. No table or textbook exists that tells exactly which method to use when. The textbooks only explain how to use the methods, not the exact conditions associated with when to use them. Experienced forecasters usually use multiple methods and compare the answers. Similar answers using different methods should add some confidence. Very different answers using different methods should suggest the existence of method bias—one or both methods are biasing the forecast based on some inherent assumption—and should force the manager to proceed with caution. When faced with the need for a forecast, the manager should use as many methods as possible and appropriate and compare the results. Often, the method(s) used will be dependent on the available information.

Managers are responsible for knowing their data. A classic example in which this is relevant to the health services manager involves the use of months in forecasting. Sometimes (not always), it is important to remember that months have a different number of days. For example, February usually has 28 days; March has 31 days. Sometimes the different number of days per month is significant. Also, different months have a different number of weekdays and weekend days. For example, July 1992 had 31 days, of which 23 were weekdays and 8 were weekend days. In contrast, August 1992 had 31 days, of which 21 were weekdays and 10 were weekend days. These types of minor changes in the number and type of days per month can create artificial variation in data that must be minimized. Managers are responsible for knowing their data and adjusting as needed.

When asked to prepare a forecast, managers are expected to use recognized methods and generate a forecast that is logical and reasonable given the state of existing knowledge and data. If, in the future, it is found that the forecast was highly inaccurate but reasonable, given the available information possessed at the time the forecast was prepared, most organizations will understand the high degree of inaccuracy. However, if, in the future, a forecast was found to be inaccurate because the manager failed to consider certain information or to use certain methods, then it may be appropriate to question the competence of the manager.

EXERCISES

6-1. Indicate the different ways an individual could forecast his or her weight 10 years from now. Do these methods change based on whether the individual is 5, 14, 24, or 45 years old? If so, why?

6-2. Using the concept of error, write an equation for the weight forecast in Exercise 6-1.

6-3. Provide examples from the field of health services management of phenomena that are probably best forecast using genius forecasting. Why?

6-4. When using any form of analytical forecasting, what is the number one rule? Why?

6-5. Determine the number of weekdays and weekend days in the current month. Compare this with the equivalent number for next year and last year. What phenomena forecast by the health services manager might be influenced by variation in the number and types of days in a month? Be specific and cite examples.

6-6. Calculate the expected number of infants needing neonatal intensive care in a hospital if the historic rate is 5 per every 1,000 births, and you expect 575 births this year.

6-7. If the annual death rate resulting from smoking is 154 deaths per 100,000 persons and the annual death rate resulting from firearms injuries is 13.5 deaths per 100,000 persons, how many deaths from these causes would you expect in a community of 1 million people?

7

Trend Extrapolation Techniques

Chapter Objectives

1. To be able to use appropriate mathematical models to forecast using historical data
2. To be able to select a specific mathematical forecasting model based on the calculated mean absolute deviation

Key Terms and Concepts

- Absolute deviation
- Exponential smoothing
- Extrapolation based on average change
- Extrapolation based on average percentage change
- Extrapolation based on a confidence interval

- Forecast error
- Naive models
- Mean absolute deviation
- Moving average
- Smoothing constant
- Standard error
- 95% confidence interval

The purpose of this chapter is to develop the ability to use each of the following time series forecasting techniques:

Extrapolation based on average change
Extrapolation based on a confidence interval
Extrapolation based on average percentage change
Moving averages
Exponential smoothing

Each of these methods is based on the assumption that the past (and present) can predict the future. These models and techniques are sometimes referred to as naive models in the sense that they recognize and incorporate only the past (and current) state into a forecast. They are naive as to the potential for change in the future and believe or assume that the past is the best and only predictor of the future.

Being naive does not make these models inappropriate for use in forecasting. Usually, naive models are used when detailed information on the near past is available, and the need is to forecast the near future.

THE IMPORTANCE OF TIME INTERVALS

Time intervals define forecasts. It is essential that forecasts be prepared in the same time interval as the historical data. For example, if the historical data are expressed in weeks, the forecast should also be expressed in weeks. If the historical data are expressed in years, the forecast should not be expressed in months, weeks, or days. In contrast, if the historical data are expressed in days, it is acceptable to express a forecast in a larger time interval, such as weeks, months, or years.

Equal time intervals are essential. The primary goal of any forecast is to minimize the systematic error associated with the forecast. Some of this systematic error can be minimized by examining the historical data critically and determining whether the time intervals are equal or approximately equal.

For example, if the task is to forecast the number of student visits to the Urgent Care Clinic at the University Health Service for the month of September, the forecaster must consider whether the number of visits that occurred in June, July, and August should be used to forecast the visits for September. Given that the student population in these summer months is very different from the student population in September, when all students are back from summer vacation, these months probably should not be used.

In this example, previous Septembers probably have more bearing on the forecast for a future September than would the preceding August. In other words, June, July, and August are not equal to September in the sense that the phenomenon being forecast (e.g., clinic visits) is fundamentally different in these summer months than in September, October, or November, when the campus is fully populated. Thus, the forecast is dependent on months.

Equal time intervals can also refer to the length of the time intervals. Some months have a different number of weekdays and weekend days and unequal total numbers of days. In some situations, failure to recognize this may artificially distort the forecast.

In addition, a day may not be a day. The number of clinic visits may (naturally) vary by day of the week. For example, an urgent care clinic may be closed Saturdays and Sundays or have shorter hours on weekend days than on weekdays. Utilization may be higher on certain days of the week, especially those days after a day the clinic was closed, such as a Monday. Although any forecast will have some degree of time interval difference, the challenge is to minimize the excess error in the forecast and do what can be done to achieve time intervals that are as equal as possible.

FORECASTING GUIDELINES

The first rule of forecasting is always to plot the data. Although many forecasting techniques use mathematical approaches, the essence of forecasting is the judgment of the manager preparing the forecast. Prior to performing any calculation on the data, it is essential that the data be plotted on a traditional x, y axis. The distribution of the plotted data points will describe the phenomenon under study. For example, it will indicate whether cycles or seasons exist in the data or whether a linear relationship with a positive or negative slope has characterized the past. Knowing such factors will assist in the selection of appropriate forecasting approaches. When plotting the data, the x axis is used to plot time and the y axis is used to plot the variable.

The length of the forecast generally should not exceed one third the length of the historical data. If 24 months of historical data exist, the forecast should be no longer than 8 months, or one third of 24. If 6 weeks of historical data exist, the forecast should be no longer than 2 weeks into the future. This convention is looked on as a guide, not as a rule. However, it is important that the length of the forecast be appropriate given the historical data. Forecasting the next 5–10 years based on 2 or 3 months of past data, regardless of the approach used, is an example of the inappropriate use of trend extrapolation techniques.

Another guiding principle of forecasting is to be conservative. Being conservative requires an understanding of circumstance. It is important to know whether it is worse to be 10% or 20% high or 10% or 20% low, given the circumstances of the forecast. For example, it is better to forecast high for a hospital's need for blood; a stock-out condition is medically unacceptable. It is better to forecast low for the number of hospital inpatient days because the forecast is used to establish budgets; it is usually easier to add temporary staff than to reduce core staff. Forecasts should be sensitive to the positive and negative implications associated with being high or low from the actual.

Some forecasting techniques permit the calculation of the standard deviation associated with the forecast. In these cases, 1.96 standard deviations above and below the forecast number (mean) provides a 95% confidence interval of where the actual value will fall. Setting the forecast at 1.96 standard deviations above the mean may be the conservative answer in some situations. In other cases, setting the forecast at 1.96 standard deviations below the forecast mean may be the conservative answer. Sometimes setting the forecast at the 50% level (forecast mean) also is the conservative approach. Judgment based on the implication of being high or low in the forecast is essential.

EXTRAPOLATION

As the name implies, time series techniques identify a historical trend and base the forecast on extending this trend into the future. At least three approaches can be used: 1) extrapolation based on average change, 2) extrapolation based on a confidence interval, and 3) extrapolation based on average percentage change. To illustrate the use of extrapolation, data on the number of live births in a hospital from January through June will be used to construct a forecast for the number of live births in July. The data in Table 7-1 are used for all examples in this section.

Table 7-1. Hospital live births for January through June

Month	Number of births
January	77
February	81
March	83
April	85
May	85
June	90
Total	501
Average	83.5

Prior to using any mathematical technique, the data must be plotted (e.g., Figure 7-1). Examination of the data plot suggests a linear relationship with a positive slope. One not very precise method to extend or extrapolate this historical trend to forecast the number of births for July would be to use a ruler to draw a straight line that "best" represented the historical data plot. Another method would be to calculate and use historical month-to-month change as a basis for extrapolation. The methods presented below, however, provide more systematic techniques.

If the data plot looks random—a circular cloud of data without any evident relationship—the first thing to do is to take the time series data apart, examine them in pieces, and then regroup the data and try again. For example, multiple years of Januarys, multiple years of Februarys, and so forth can be examined to see if this method of plotting the data presents a different image of the data. Also, the data can be regrouped by adding months together to create quarters (3-month periods) and years and examined again. Data can similarly be grouped by adding days into weeks, weeks into months, or months into years. If the data are regrouped, the forecast must be expressed in the new unit of time. It is the function of the manager to assemble the data in a manner that will lend itself to forecasting.

Extrapolation Based on Average Change

In order to extrapolate based on average change, the month-to-month change that occurred in the data must be calculated. Table 7-2 includes the month-to-month changes in the data as well as the average month-to-month change. With these additional calculations, a forecast of births for July using the average change method of extrapolation can be prepared. The basis for this forecast is the mean or average level of births (i.e., 83.5) experienced over the history of the available data. This

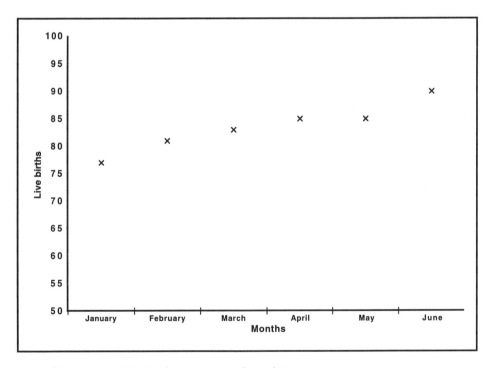

Figure 7-1. Hospital live births for January through June.

Table 7-2. Hospital live births for January through June and month-to-month change

Month	Number of births	Change from previous month
January	77	
February	81	4
March	83	2
April	85	2
May	85	0
June	90	5
Total	501	13
Average	83.5	2.6

approach ensures that no single value (e.g., June = 90) artificially distorts the forecast. Because the average or mean represents all available data, the use of the mean to extrapolate the data is appropriate.

For this example, the mean is 83.5. As the mean, it should be the number of births exactly in the middle of the historical data distribution. For this example, 6 month of historical data are available. The midpoint of this historical data sequence is between March, the third period, and April, the fourth period. Therefore, the midpoint of the data distribution is the number of historical data points [i.e., $(6 + 1)/2$, or 3.5]. If the example had 7 months of data, the midpoint would be $7 + 1/2$, or 4.

Extrapolation based on average change uses the following equation:

$$\text{Forecast month} = \text{Average} + (\text{Midpoint} \times \text{Average change}) \qquad \text{(Eq. 7-1)}$$

For this example, the average or mean = 83.5 births per month, the midpoint in the historical data distribution = 3.5, and the average change = 2.6 births per month. Therefore:

$$\begin{aligned} \text{July forecast} &= 83.5 + (3.5 \times 2.6) \\ &= 83.5 + 9.1 \\ &= 92.6 \end{aligned}$$

Note that it is merely coincidence that the forecast value for July, 92.6 births, is the same as the value for June (90 births) plus the average change (2.6).

Extrapolation Based on a Confidence Interval

As the name implies, this method uses a confidence interval to forecast. It is important to remember that 1.96 standard deviations above and below the mean represents a 95% confidence interval. Therefore, if a forecast is based on this method, the manager can be 95% confident that the actual number of births will be included in this interval. To use this approach, the standard deviation for the data must be calculated.

A standard deviation for a population, not a sample, is best calculated by:

1. Subtracting the mean from each month (e.g., January value − mean = 77 − 83.5, or −6.5).
2. Squaring each answer: for January, $(-6.5) \times (-6.5) = 42.25$.
3. Summing the squares from each individual month (i.e., 95.5) and then dividing by the number of data points (i.e., 6); 95.5 divided by 6 = 15.92.
4. Taking the square root of this number (15.92), which equals 3.99.

Table 7-3 shows the detailed calculation of the standard deviation. Note that 1.00 standard deviation = 3.99 births and that 1.96 (the 95% confidence interval) standard deviations = 1.96 * 3.99 = 7.82 births. For the example, the 95% confidence interval is the mean ± 1.96 standard deviations, or 83.5 ± 7.82 (i.e., 83.5 + 7.82 = 91.32 births, and 83.5 − 7.82 = 75.68 births). Using this method of extrapolation based on a confidence interval, the number of births for July is forecast to be between 91.32 and 75.68, or 92 and 76 births, with a 95% confidence level.

Extrapolation Based on Average Percentage Change

Extrapolating based on average percentage change requires revising the data in Table 7-1 to include the month-to-month change in the number of births and the percentage change from a previous month. Table 7-4 shows these revisions. Note that percentage change is calculated as, for example, (February − January) divided by January × 100%.

Having determined that the average percentage change per month is +3.19% (see Table 7-4), the forecast for July, using this method of extrapolation based on average percentage change, is calculated to be:

$$\text{July forecast} = \text{June actual} + 3.19\% \text{ of June actual}$$
$$= 90 \times 1.0319$$
$$= 93.51$$

A Note on Mathematics

When forecasting, the appropriate number of significant figures must be used throughout any mathematical calculations and the answers rounded at the end. A general rule of thumb is to work in one decimal place more than the original data and round at the end to no more than one additional decimal place than that represented by the original data. In the example, the historical data are furnished in whole numbers (no decimal points). Calculations are worked using one additional decimal place and then rounding back to a whole number. There can never be 93.5 births—93.5 means 94 births.

Table 7-3. Calculation of the standard deviation

Month	Number of births	Number of births minus mean	Number of births minus mean squared
January	77	−6.5	42.25
February	81	−2.5	6.25
March	83	−0.5	0.25
April	85	1.5	2.25
May	85	1.5	2.25
June	90	6.5	42.25
Mean	83.5		
Total			95.5
Number of data points	6		
Total divided by number of data points			15.92
Square root			3.99

Table 7-4. Calculation of percentage change

Month	Number of births	Change		% Change
January	77			
February	81	4	4/77 × 100	5.19
March	83	2	2/81 × 100	2.47
April	85	2	2/83 × 100	2.41
May	85	0	0/85 × 100	0.00
June	90	5	5/85 × 100	5.88
Total	501	13		15.95
Average	83.5	2.6		3.19

Comparison of Extrapolation Techniques

At this point, it is important to compare the different answers to the problem of forecasting the number of births for July using the different extrapolation methods:

Technique	July forecast
Extrapolation based on average change	92.6
Extrapolation based on a confidence interval (95%)	91.3–75.7
Extrapolation based on average percentage change	93.5

Although each technique yields a different answer, collectively the techniques provide sufficient information for the manager to venture a forecast. The issue is not which of the answers is the correct forecast for the number of births in July. Each technique or method provides a "right" answer. The issue is what number of births the manager will forecast given these findings. Forecasting requires judgment, not just the ability to solve mathematical equations.

In retrospect, each of these basic methods is based on different properties of the data used in the forecast. Each assumes a certain degree of linearity in the data and an inherent relationship between time (as the independent variable) and births (as the dependent variable) that has a positive slope. For example, the level of births forecast for July (e.g., 93.5) is higher than the actual number of births recorded for June (i.e., 90).

Although helpful in forecasting, these three techniques may be too simple for most applications. These techniques mask variability in the data. In the example used, some of this natural variability is based on a different number of days per month. These methods also distill the data using the average or average percentage change calculations. Except for the confidence interval approach, each method assumes that the forecast will be on the theoretical line that best represents the past data. Therefore, these methods are offered as a starting point for forecasting, not as definitive methods that can be relied on exclusively to provide a relevant forecast.

MOVING AVERAGES

In the preceding section, the possibility of variability in the historical data plot was mentioned. Moving averages, as a basis for forecasting, provide a method to examine variability in data and use this pattern of variability in constructing a forecast.

To demonstrate moving averages, the data in Table 7-1 have been revised by adding more historical data (July through December) and changing one of the original historical data points (March, from 83 to 63). The revised data are shown in Table 7-5. The initial step in any forecast is to plot the data. Figure 7-2 is the plot of the data included in Table 7-5. Note that the scale used in this historical data plot has been selected to magnify the variability of the historical data.

Using a moving (time period–to–time period) average to forecast is a method that first examines the variability in the historical data and then provides the ability to mathematically "smooth" or "soften" the historical variability in search of a master or underlying trend. The first operation is to calculate an n-period moving average for forecasting, where n = the number of time intervals that will be used in the moving average, such as a 2-month ($n = 2$), 3-month ($n = 3$), or 4-month ($n = 4$) moving average. To do this:

1. Select an n to try (n must be greater than 1). Twelve months of historical data are included in Table 7-5, so n could be 2, 3, 4, 5, or 6. To begin, $n = 2$ has been selected.
2. Calculate the n-period moving average, starting with the oldest data and working forward. For example, the forecast for September, using a 2-month moving average, is (July + August)/2. The forecast for October, using a 2-month moving average, is (August + September)/2.

In other words, to calculate the n-period moving average, take the n number of months preceding the month to be forecast, add their values, and then divide by n. Table 7-6 provides various n-period moving averages for the data included in Table 7-5. For example, the 2-month ($n = 2$) or two-period moving average for September is [68 (July) + 79 (August)]/2 = 73.5. The 3-month ($n = 3$) moving average for October is [68 (July) + 79 (August) + 81 (September)]/3 = 76. The 6-month moving average for May is calculated as follows:

$$\text{May moving average} = (\text{Nov.} + \text{Dec.} + \text{Jan.} + \text{Feb.} + \text{Mar.} + \text{Apr.})/6$$
$$= (71 + 60 + 77 + 81 + 63 + 85)/6$$
$$= 437/6$$
$$= 72.8$$

Table 7-5.   Revised hospital live births for 12 months

Month	Number of births
July	68
August	79
September	81
October	55
November	71
December	60
January	77
February	81
March	63
April	85
May	85
June	90
Total	895

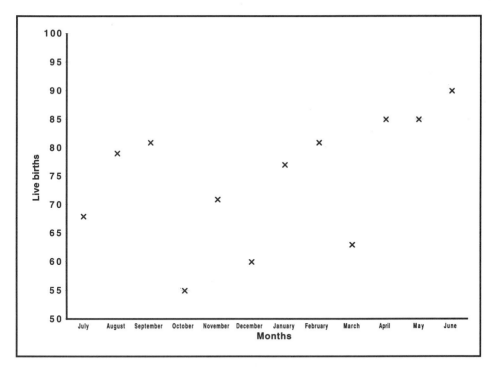

Figure 7-2.   Revised hospital live births for 12 months.

The next operation in moving averages forecasting involves selecting the "best" n to use in the moving average forecasting model. The concept used is forecast error *(FE)*. If F = forecast number of births for the month (using the moving average) and A = actual number of births for the month, then

$$FE = (A - F)$$ (Eq. 7-2)

Table 7-7 shows the calculated *FE* values for the n-periods used in Table 7-6. In addition, it includes the absolute deviation (AD) and the mean absolute deviation (MAD) calculations. The absolute deviation is calculated by adding the absolute

Table 7-6.   Birth data with moving average calculations for n = 2, 3, 4, 5, and 6

Month	Number of births	$n = 2$	$n = 3$	$n = 4$	$n = 5$	$n = 6$
July	68					
August	79					
September	81	73.50				
October	55	80.00	76.00			
November	71	68.00	71.67	70.75		
December	60	63.00	69.00	71.50	70.80	
January	77	65.50	62.00	66.75	69.20	69.00
February	81	68.50	69.33	65.75	68.80	70.50
March	63	79.00	72.67	72.25	68.80	70.83
April	85	72.00	73.67	70.25	70.40	67.83
May	85	74.00	76.33	76.50	73.20	72.83
June	90	85.00	77.67	78.50	78.20	75.17
Total	895					

Table 7-7. Forecast error (FE) with absolute deviation (AD) and mean absolute deviation (MAD)

Month	Number of births	n = 2		n = 3		n = 4		n = 5		n = 6	
		Moving average	FE	Moving average	FE	Moving average	FE	Moving average	FE	Moving average	FE
July	68										
August	79										
September	81	73.50	7.50								
October	55	80.00	-25.00	76.00	-21.00						
November	71	68.00	3.00	71.67	-0.67	70.75	0.25				
December	60	63.00	-3.00	69.00	-9.00	71.50	-11.50	70.80	-10.80		
January	77	65.50	11.50	62.00	15.00	66.75	10.25	69.20	7.80	69.00	8.00
February	81	68.50	12.50	69.33	11.67	65.75	15.25	68.80	12.20	70.50	10.50
March	63	79.00	-16.00	72.67	-9.67	72.25	-9.25	68.80	-5.80	70.83	-7.83
April	85	72.00	13.00	73.67	11.33	70.25	14.75	70.40	14.60	67.83	17.17
May	85	74.00	11.00	76.33	8.67	76.50	8.50	73.20	11.80	72.83	12.17
June	90	87.50	2.50	77.67	12.33	78.50	11.50	78.20	11.80	75.17	14.83
AD			105.00		99.34		81.25		74.80		70.50
MAD			10.50		11.04		10.16		10.69		11.75

96

values of the forecast errors (i.e., the value without regard to + or − signs). The mean absolute deviation is calculated by dividing the absolute deviation by the number of forecast errors. The "best" interval n is then selected based on the minimum MAD value.

In this example, $n = 4$ (4-month moving average) can be selected as the best n because, when $n = 4$, the mean absolute deviation is at the minimum level (Table 7-8). This indicates that the 4-month moving average, in contrast to the 2-, 3-, 5-, or 6-month moving average, best minimizes the variation in the historical data and is the recommended moving average to use to forecast. In Table 7-9, the 4-month moving average has been used to forecast births for the month immediately after the historical data.

A variation on this model enables the manager to use moving averages to forecast beyond 1 month (or period) into the future. Once a specific month is forecast (e.g., July = 80.75), it can be used for the "actual" value in the forecast error equation and the moving average calculation continued. Table 7-10 shows forecasts for the next 6 months using this method. Note, however, that the forecast becomes damped as it moves forward; that is, less variable as it moves into the future. This means the forecast is likely to be further from the actual (i.e., observed) value as it is extended further into the future.

Moving averages provide the ability to recognize the variability in time series data and use the pattern of variability to construct an appropriate forecast. Unlike

Table 7-8. Mean absolute deviation (MAD) summary

n	MAD
2	10.50
3	11.04
4	10.16[a]
5	10.69
6	11.75

[a]Lowest MAD.

Table 7-9. Four-month moving average and forecast for next month

Month	Number of births	Moving average
July	68	
August	79	
September	81	
October	55	
November	71	70.75
December	60	71.50
January	77	66.75
February	81	65.75
March	63	72.25
April	85	70.25
May	85	76.50
June	90	78.50
July		80.75[a]

[a]Forecast value.

Table 7-10. Four-month moving average and expanded forecast

Month	Number of births	Moving average
July	68	
August	79	
September	81	
October	55	
November	71	70.75
December	60	71.50
January	77	66.75
February	81	65.75
March	63	72.25
April	85	70.25
May	85	76.50
June	90	78.50
July	**80.75**	**80.75**
August	**85.19**	**85.19**
September	**85.23**	**85.23**
October	**85.29**	**85.29**
November	**84.12**	**84.12**
December	**84.96**	**84.96**

Note: Forecasts are indicated by bold type.

previous methods, moving averages also provide the ability to extend the forecast many time intervals into the future. However, this ability should be used with caution. Mean absolute deviation is used to select the best number of periods (n) to use in calculating the moving average.

It must be noted that moving averages possess a potential methodological flaw as a forecasting technique. Once the forecast is extended beyond the selected n, the entire forecast is based on calculated, not observed, values. A general convention is to use moving averages with at least one actual data point. Therefore, a forecast based on $n = 4$ should extend only three periods into the future.

A Note on Time Periods

Before covering additional techniques, it is appropriate to clarify some terms regarding time periods. As has been demonstrated in the examples, all extrapolation models rely on the past to forecast into the future. They are all naive models. In this type of calculation, the present is a point or moment in time (e.g., 12:00 P.M. on December 31, 1995), not a period of time such as a day, week, month, or year. In contrast, the future and the past are time periods. To describe the time intervals in forecasts, consider the following scale:

$$t_{-n} \cdots t_{-5}, t_{-4}, t_{-3}, t_{-2}, t_{-1}, t_0, t_1, t_2, t_3, t_4, t_5 \cdots t_n$$

where t_0 = the present as a point in time

t_{-n} = the oldest time period in the historical data

t_n = the furthest time period in the future (away from the present) in the forecast

Many forecasting models use this type of time interval notation. In such notation, for example, t_{-3} represents the third most recent historical period, and t_2 the second forecast period. (The actual time interval represented by t is determined by the data for the problem being solved.) Because time series data are used in forecasts, it is important to appreciate this time scale. It provides the ability to acknowledge the difference between the present—a point in time—and the past and future—intervals of time.

EXPONENTIAL SMOOTHING

Examination of the data in Table 7-5 reveals that it starts at 68 and ends at 90 births. As demonstrated in the data plot in Figure 7-2, the data suggest that the future more likely will involve numbers toward the higher values (i.e., 90) than numbers with the lower values (i.e., 68). In other words, it seems appropriate to base a forecast more on the most recent data than on the older data.

Exponential smoothing provides a technique to take these types of consideration into account. To smooth, and thereby minimize the effect of this fluctuation in the forecast, the initial step is to select a smoothing constant (*SC*). The smoothing constant must be between 0 and 1.00. In practice, the most common smoothing constants are between 0.10 and 0.50.

Exponential smoothing uses the following general equation:

$$F = (SC \times O) + [(1 - SC) \times F_{t-1}] \qquad \text{(Eq. 7-3)}$$

where *SC* = smoothing constant (a number between 1 and 0)
  F = forecast for next period in the future
  O = observed value for the last or most recent period
  F_{t-1} = forecast value for the last or most recent historical period

This equation indicates that the forecast for the next period (e.g., *F*) will equal the observed value for the most current time period (*O*) times the smoothing constant (*SC*) plus the forecast for the most recent historical period (F_{t-1}) times 1 minus the smoothing constant. For example, if a forecast for hospital patient days for the past month (F_{t-1}) was 550 and the observed (actual) number of patient days (*O*) was 525, the forecast for next month (*F*), arbitrarily using a smoothing constant of 0.3, can be calculated as follows:

$$
\begin{aligned}
F &= (SC \times O) + [(1 - SC) \times F_{t-1}] \\
&= (0.3 \times 525) + [(1 - 0.3) \times 550] \\
&= 157.5 + 0.7 \times 550 \\
&= 157.5 + 385 \\
&= 542.5 \text{ patient days}
\end{aligned}
$$

Note that this type of forecast is an expected value based on a weighted average of two variables: the most recent actual value and a forecast. The smoothing constant is a weighting factor that influences the degree to which the forecast value and the observed value for a past period influence one another in calculating the forecast for a future period. This last example "combined" 30% (0.30) of the observed value for a previous month with 70% (0.70) of the forecast value for that previous month to calculate the forecast for a future month.

This forecasting technique presents certain challenges. A smoothing constant must be determined using systematic methods. How should one select which is best for the forecast? Another challenge is to determine a forecast based on past data to use in predicting future data.

Dealing with the second challenge first, the need is to generate a preliminary forecast for the historical data from the historical data. Actual historical data values are referred to as observed values (*O*). The challenge is to generate forecast values (*F*) for those historical time periods and to compare these forecast values with the actual historical values observed.

The actual or observed value (*O*) for the oldest period in the data is used to begin the calculation of the forecast for the next period. Table 7-11 provides actual as well as forecast values for the live birth data in the earlier example, beginning with the actual value for July (*O* = 68) and using a smoothing constant of 0.3. The forecast for each month is calculated as follows:

$$F_{\text{Sept}} = (SC \times O \text{ for Aug}) + [(1 - SC) \times F_{t-1} \text{ for Aug}]$$
$$= (0.30 \times 79) + [(1 - 0.30) \times 68]$$
$$= 23.7 + 47.6$$
$$= 71.3$$

$$F_{\text{Oct}} = (SC \times O \text{ for Sept}) + [(1 - SC) \times F_{t-1} \text{ for Sept}]$$
$$= (0.3 \times 81) + 0.7 \times 71.3$$
$$= 74.21$$

and so on. This process meets the first challenge—to generate the forecast for past time periods (e.g., F_{t-1}).

The next challenge is to select, using an appropriate method, the most appropriate smoothing constant. The principle again used is mean absolute deviation (MAD). In order to determine which smoothing constant works best in an exponentially smoothed forecast, at least three different forecasts must be developed: one using a smoothing constant of 0.1, another using a smoothing constant of 0.3, and another using a smoothing constant of 0.5. By calculating the difference between the forecasts and the actual observation ($O - F_{t-1}$), the lowest MAD can be

Table 7-11. Exponential smoothing with smoothing constant = 0.30

Month	Observed value (*O*)	Forecast value (*FV*)	*O* − *FV*
July	68		
August	79	68.00	11.00
September	81	71.30	9.70
October	55	74.21	−19.21
November	71	68.45	2.55
December	60	69.21	−9.21
January	77	66.45	10.55
February	81	69.61	11.39
March	63	73.03	−10.03
April	85	70.02	14.98
May	85	74.51	10.49
June	90	77.66	12.34
Absolute sum			121.45
N			11
MAD			11.04

used to select which smoothing constant is best based on its ability to minimize MAD.

Table 7-11 presents the MAD calculations for a smoothing constant of 0.3, Table 7-12 for a smoothing constant of 0.1, and Table 7-13 for a smoothing constant of 0.5. According to these three tables, the forecast with a smoothing constant of 0.3 yields a MAD of 11.04, a smoothing constant of 0.1 yields a MAD of 11.33, and a smoothing constant of 0.5 yields a MAD of 11.12. Based on the minimum MAD value, a smoothing constant of 0.3 should be used with this example.

Table 7-12. Exponential smoothing with smoothing constant = 0.10

Month	Observed value (O)	Forecast value (FV)	O − FV
July	68		
August	79	68.00	11.00
September	81	69.10	11.90
October	55	70.29	−15.29
November	71	68.76	2.24
December	60	68.98	−8.98
January	77	68.09	8.91
February	81	68.98	12.02
March	63	70.18	−7.18
April	85	69.46	15.54
May	85	71.02	13.98
June	90	72.41	17.59
Absolute sum			124.64
N			11
MAD			11.33

Table 7-13. Exponential smoothing with smoothing constant = 0.50

Month	Observed value (O)	Forecast value (FV)	O − FV
July	68		
August	79	68.00	11.00
September	81	73.50	7.50
October	55	77.25	−22.25
November	71	66.12	4.88
December	60	68.56	−8.56
January	77	64.28	12.72
February	81	70.64	10.36
March	63	75.82	−12.82
April	85	69.41	15.59
May	85	77.21	7.79
June	90	81.10	8.90
Absolute sum			122.37
N			11
MAD			11.12

To forecast July (F_{t-1}), the exponential smoothing equation is applied to the actual observation and the forecast for June, using a smoothing constant of 0.3. That is:

$$F_{July} = (SC \times O) + [(1 - SC) \times F_{t-1}]$$
$$= (0.3 \times 90) + (0.7 \times 77.66)$$
$$= 81.36$$

To forecast beyond July while still in June, the same approach is continued but the forecast values are substituted for the actual values, remembering that a forecast generally should not exceed one third of the number of historical periods. Given that the example has 12 months, a 4-month forecast for July, August, September, and October, or one third of the 12 months of historical data, can be justified (see Table 7-14). Note that the forecast becomes damped as it moves forward. The variation in the forecast decreases, and eventually the string of numbers will become totally damped, with the forecasting formula yielding the same answer for each month. Again, this is another reason to use caution and not extend a forecast too far into the future.

Advanced users, instead of using three trial smoothing constants (e.g., 0.1, 0.3, 0.5), solve for the smoothing constant that yields the minimum value for the mean average deviation. When this approach is used, a smoothing constant above 0.5 can result. When simple exponential smoothing yields a best constant above 0.5, it should be disregarded as a forecast—too many variations are present in the data to be captured adequately with the use of a single smoothing constant. Advanced users are referred to Holt's method of exponential smoothing with trends and Winter's method of exponential smoothing with seasonality. Each of these more advanced approaches introduces multiple smoothing constants into the forecasting model to capture and use these trends in the forecast.

Table 7-14.   Four-month forecast using exponential smoothing

Month	Observed value	Forecast value
July	68	
August	79	68.00
September	81	71.30
October	55	74.21
November	71	68.45
December	60	69.21
January	77	66.45
February	81	69.61
March	63	73.03
April	85	70.02
May	85	74.51
June	90	77.66
July	77.66	**81.36**
August	81.36	**80.25**
September	80.25	**80.58**
October	80.58	**80.48**

Note: Forecasts are indicated by bold type.

THE RELATIONSHIP BETWEEN MEAN
ABSOLUTE DEVIATION AND STANDARD DEVIATION

Knowing the relationship between the mean absolute deviation and the standard deviation can prove useful to distinguish these concepts and relate the standard deviation to the basis of selecting a specific smoothing constant. Assuming that the error of a forecast is distributed normally, then:

$$\text{Standard deviation of the forecast} = 1.25 \times \text{MAD} \qquad \text{(Eq. 7-4)}$$

This equation provides an estimated standard deviation. In the example of live births and exponential smoothing, MAD (with a smoothing constant of 0.30) was calculated to be 11.04. Applying this to the forecast:

$$
\begin{aligned}
\text{Standard deviation of the forecast} &= 1.25 \times \text{MAD} \\
&= 1.25 \times 11.04 \\
&= 13.8
\end{aligned}
$$

Using 1.96 standard deviations, which equals a 95% confidence interval, it can be expected that, for about 0.95×4, or between 3 and 4 months of the 4-month forecast, the forecast would be off by 1.96×13.8, or 27.04, births per month.

SELECTING AN APPROPRIATE FORECASTING MODEL

Both moving averages and exponential smoothing approaches attempt to soften the variation in past data while searching for a master trend and using this master trend to forecast. Moving averages do this by calculating grouped, or pooled, averages. A two-period ($n = 2$) moving average groups the data in units of two. It calculates averages based on every consecutive 2-month period. A three-period moving average does the same in groups of three. Exponential smoothing does not group data together in different combinations (e.g., $n = 2, 3, 4,$ or 5). Instead, it bases a forecast on ascribing different powers to months and includes all months, with less weight given to periods the further in the past. For example, a smoothing constant of 0.3, used in the forecasting equation, bases 30% of the forecast on the actual level of the preceding time period or month and 70% on the forecast for the preceding time period. Changing the smoothing constant to 0.5 bases a forecast equally (i.e., 50% and 50%) on the actual and forecast values for the preceding time period. Both moving averages and exponential smoothing are mathematical approaches used to soften the time period–to–time period variability in time series data in order to determine a master trend.

The literature is silent on whether the MAD calculated as part of the moving average method can be compared with the MAD calculated as part of the exponential method. It seems logical and reasonable, however, to conclude that they are comparable. Therefore, the manager should be able to use the MAD calculated for each method to select the most appropriate approach to forecast a trend. In the example, comparing the previous calculations of MAD by both methods (Table 7-15) indicates that the moving average method with $n = 4$ is the most appropriate approach.

Methods other than MAD do exist as a basis for selecting specific forecasting models. For example, some methods use the standard error associated with many

Table 7-15. Comparison of calculated MAD values

Method	Period (n) or smoothing constant (SC)	MAD
Moving average	$n = 2$	10.50
	$n = 3$	11.04
	$n = 4$	10.15[a]
	$n = 5$	10.68
	$n = 6$	11.75
Exponential smoothing	SC = 0.1	11.33
	SC = 0.3	11.04
	SC = 0.5	11.33

[a]Lowest MAD.

forecasts and select the specific forecasting model with the lowest standard error. The formula for standard error (*SE*) is:

$$SE = \Sigma (x_1 - x_{f_1})^2 / n \qquad \text{(Eq. 7-5)}$$

where x_1 = observed value for a specific time period
x_{f_1} = forecast value for a specific time period
n = number of time periods

Using either MAD or the standard error provides a systematic basis to evaluate many forecasts and select the specific forecast that best represents past events. Obviously, the belief exists that a forecast best able to represent past events will be better able than other forecasts to represent and predict the future. Either approach is acceptable.

CONCLUSION

Moving averages and exponential smoothing approaches provide the health services manager with robust forecasting models to extrapolate trends. Both are naive forecasting models. Each depends on the wisdom of the health services manager to select and use these models when reasoned judgment indicates that the past may be a reasonable predictor of the future.

EXERCISES

7-1. Use the data in Table 7-16 to provide a forecast of the number of clinic visits for week 17 using the following approaches:

    a. Extrapolation based on average change.
    b. Extrapolation based on a confidence interval.
    c. Extrapolation based on average percentage change.
    d. Extrapolation based on moving averages.
    e. Extrapolation based on exponential smoothing.

7-2. Of all methods used, which is best and why?

Table 7-16. Clinic visits by week (data for Exercises 7-1 through 7-5)

Week	Visits
1	154
2	136
3	178
4	170
5	185
6	170
7	199
8	232
9	187
10	165
11	190
12	159
13	178
14	180
15	220
16	190

8

The Regression Model

Chapter Objectives

1. To be able to construct a linear regression model as a forecasting model
2. To be able to determine whether the constructed regression model is an appropriate forecasting model

Key Terms and Concepts

Dependent variable   Linear regression
Independent variable   Residuals

Unlike the linear correlation coefficient, which merely acknowledges a relationship or lack of relationship between two variables, the regression model is used to examine and, if appropriate, establish a predictive relationship between two (or more) variables. The regression model is sufficiently robust to be used in many management applications. It is the primary statistical model technique used to develop a predictive model or equation. This chapter explains how to apply the linear regression model as a forecasting method.

Accurate predictive models can assist the manager in understanding the relationships between factors under management control and those out of management control (e.g., models that predict service demands and service levels). In general, a model is a replication or simplification of reality. For example, a photograph can be considered a model because it describes reality. Whereas some models are merely descriptive, such as a photograph, others are also predictive. An algebraic equation is also a predictive model. It describes the relationship between the variables included in the equation and indicates or predicts the level of one variable given a change in the other variables. Like algebraic equations, models resulting from using regression analysis are quantitative expressions that describe as well as predict. Forecasting is one form of prediction, so managers can use regression models in forecasting.

Generally, models are not given; they must be constructed. For example, managers in hospitals may need to know the relationship between inpatient days and the number of staff hours. Managers in ambulatory care clinics may need to know the relationship between the number of clinic visits and number of laboratory tests ordered and performed. Managers in nursing homes may want to know the relationship between staff hours and measures of quality of care. Knowing these types of relationships provides managers with the ability to predict the number of staff hours given forecast hospital inpatient days for next year, the number of laboratory tests given anticipated clinic visits for next month, or levels of patient care quality in the nursing home given the number of staff hours anticipated for the next 3 months. Regression analysis provides the tools to construct models for these types of relationships in algebraic form.

Models should not be taken as fact, even when used historically in an organization, because many of the relationships that interest managers are situational and subject to change. For example, the relationship between the number of inpatient days in a hospital and the number of staff hours is different from hospital to hospital and can change over time as a result of technology or the population being served. Health services managers need to know both how to construct a model using regression analysis and how to update the model so that it remains a valid expression of reality.

A primary assumption associated with the regression model is that the past relationship between variables is a reasonable predictor of the future relationship. Regression models are constructed using past data. The resulting equation describes the relationships between the variables used in the equation. Once these relationships are developed as an equation, the equation can then be solved for a new answer (the y variable) by substituting the anticipated level of the input variable (the x variable). As long as the past relationship between x and y remains valid, the regression model will yield a valid prediction.

REGRESSION AS A QUANTITATIVE MODEL

The purpose of regression analysis is to construct an appropriate mathematical relationship among two or more variables. The regression model establishes the equation that best represents or fits available data. Once established, and within appropriate limits, the equation can be used to predict levels of the dependent, or y, variable given values of the x, or independent, variable.

The difference between these variables is important. In regression, y is used to represent the dependent variable; the value that y takes on depends on the value of x. The x variable is the independent variable; a change in x changes the value of y.

Using the regression model requires the ability to calculate appropriate coefficients for the regression equation, and to test the model to ensure that it satisfies certain conditions. Many spreadsheet programs can calculate models from data; however, most do not perform the statistical tests necessary to test the assumption of regression.

Although multiple forms of the regression model exist, this chapter restricts attention to the simple linear model. The linear regression model is usually expressed as:

$$y = b_0 + b_1 x \qquad \text{(Eq. 8-1)}$$

where b_0 = the y intercept
    b_1 = the slope

When the variables in the regression model or formula are reversed, the regression formula looks exactly like the formula for a straight line:

Regression model: $y = b_1 x + b_0$
Generic formula for a straight line: $y = mx + b$

where b and b_0 are the y intercept and b_1 and m are the slope.

The regression model establishes the best fit between a straight line equation and the available data that describe a relationship between x and y. The regression equation is often referred to as the line of best fit. Mathematically, regression analysis relies on the least squares method to determine the coefficients of the straight line that best (but not necessarily perfectly) establishes the equation representing the relationships between x as the independent variable and y as the dependent variable. The least squares method minimizes the mathematical distance between the line developed using the regression model and the actual x and y data points. Regression fits the best straight line to the available data.

Table 8-1 provides data on the number of laboratory tests per week (y) as the dependent variable and the number of clinic visits (x) as the independent variable. On average, during this 8-week period, 1.84 laboratory tests were performed for each clinic visit. In some weeks, however, this level ranged from a low of 1.56 tests per visit to a high of 2.08 tests per visit. Using just the average of 1.84 lab tests per visit might mask this variation and not produce as accurate a model as provided using regression analysis. The average is not necessarily the estimate that minimizes the forecast error.

In order to apply the regression model, two coefficients must be calculated from these data:

b_0 = the (predicted) y intercept
b_1 = the (predicted) slope

The y intercept is also the predicted level of y when x equals zero. These coefficients are calculated as follows:

$$b_1 = \frac{n\Sigma(xy) - (\Sigma x)(\Sigma y)}{n\Sigma x^2 - (\Sigma x)^2}$$

Table 8-1. Clinic visits and laboratory tests for an 8-week period

Week	Clinic visits (x)	Lab tests (y)	Lab tests per visit (y/x)
1	65	105	1.62
2	65	125	1.92
3	62	110	1.77
4	67	120	1.79
5	69	140	2.03
6	65	135	2.08
7	61	95	1.56
8	67	130	1.94
Total	521	960	1.84

$$b_0 = \frac{\Sigma y - b_1(\Sigma x)}{n}$$

where n = the number of paired observations.

Table 8-2 provides the additional calculations on the clinic data to determine the predicted y intercept and slope:

$$
\begin{aligned}
b_1 &= \frac{n\Sigma(xy) - (\Sigma x)(\Sigma y)}{n\Sigma x^2 - (\Sigma x)^2} \\
&= \frac{(8)(62,750) - (521)(960)}{(8)(33,979) - (521)(521)} \\
&= \frac{502,000 - 500,160}{271,832 - 271,441} \\
&= \frac{1840}{391} \\
&= 4.7
\end{aligned}
$$

$$
\begin{aligned}
b_0 &= \frac{\Sigma y - b_1(\Sigma x)}{n} \\
&= \frac{(960) - 4.7(521)}{8} \\
&= \frac{960 - 2448.7}{8} \\
&= \frac{-1488.7}{8} \\
&= -186.1
\end{aligned}
$$

Therefore, for the data contained in Tables 8-1 and 8-2, the regression model is:

$$y = -186.1 + 4.7x$$

If 65 clinic visits were forecast in the future (i.e., $x = 65$), the predicted number of laboratory tests (y) would be:

$$
\begin{aligned}
y &= -186.1 + (4.7 \times 65) \\
&= -186.1 + 305.5 \\
&= 119
\end{aligned}
$$

Table 8-2. Additional calculations for data on clinic visits and laboratory tests

Week	Clinic visits (x)	Lab tests (y)	x^2	xy	y^2
1	65	105	4,225	6,825	11,025
2	65	125	4,225	8,125	15,625
3	62	110	3,844	6,820	12,100
4	67	120	4,489	8,040	14,400
5	69	140	4,761	9,660	19,600
6	65	135	4,225	8,775	18,225
7	61	95	3,721	5,795	9,025
8	67	130	4,489	8,710	16,900
Σ	521	960	33,979	62,750	116,900

TESTING THE REGRESSION EQUATION

Before using the line of best fit (e.g., $y = -186.1 + 4.7x$) to describe the relationship between x and y, a statistical test must be performed to determined whether the predicted slope (i.e., 4.7) is not 0. By definition, slope is defined as:

$$\text{Slope} = \frac{\text{Change in } y}{\text{Change in } x} \qquad \text{(Eq. 8-2)}$$

A line with a slope of 0, when graphed, is perfectly horizontal because there is no change in y as x changes. A vertical line has an undefined slope because one cannot divide by zero.

When x changes, the change in y is 0. Zero divided by any number is zero.
When y changes, the change in x is 0. Any number divided by zero is undefined.

Having a regression equation with a slope of 0 would mean that y was a constant and did not change as the value of the x or independent variable changed. The value of x is irrelevant. For example, if $y = -186.1 + 0 \times x$, y would be a constant -186.1 regardless of whether x equaled 1 or 100, or any other number.

Many techniques exist to test a regression line. The technique used in this chapter tests whether (at 95% confidence) the slope of the regression line is other than 0. A three-step process is used:

1. Calculate the variance (s_e^2) of y about the regression line. The variance about the regression line—that is, the average squared deviation of the observed y from the predicted y, using the regression model—is defined as:

$$s_e^2 = \frac{(\Sigma y^2) - (b_0)(\Sigma y) - (b_1)(\Sigma xy)}{n - 2}$$

The denominator is $n - 2$ because two parameters are being estimated, b_0 and b_1.

For the clinic example,

$$s_e^2 = \frac{(116{,}900) - (-186.5)(960) - (4.7)(62{,}750)}{8 - 2}$$

$$= \frac{295{,}940 - 294{,}925}{6}$$

$$= 169.16$$

The square root of this variance is the standard deviation of y about the regression line. In this case, the standard deviation is $s_e = 13.01$.

2. Set up the statistical t test for the slope:

Hypothesis: $\qquad\qquad b_1 = 0$
Alternative hypothesis: $\quad b_1 \neq 0$

where b_1 is the slope.

A two-tailed t test will be used to test these hypotheses. The equation for a hypothesis test is:

$$\frac{\text{Actual parameter } - \text{ Estimated statistic}}{\text{Standard deviation of the statistic}} \qquad \text{(Eq. 8-3)}$$

The actual parameter is the value $= 0$. The estimated statistic is the estimate of the coefficient—in this case, 4.7. The standard deviation is calculated as:

$$s_{b_1}^2 = \frac{n(s_e^2)}{n(\Sigma x^2) - (\Sigma x)^2}$$

where s_e^2 = variance of y about the regression line
n = number of paired (x, y) observations

For the clinic example,

$$s_{b_1}^2 = \frac{8\ (169.16)}{8(33{,}979) - (521)(521)}$$

$$= \frac{1353.28}{271{,}832 - 271{,}441}$$

$$= 3.46$$

The standard deviation of the slope $(s_{b_1}) = 1.86$ (the square root of the variance).

3. Calculate the t test statistic.

$$t = \frac{0 - b_1}{s_{b_1}}$$

$$t = \frac{0 - 4.7}{1.86}$$

$$= 2.526$$

Recall that the t has the same mean as the z test statistic, but is used when the sample size is less than 30.

To determine the critical value of the t test statistic requires access to a table of critical values for the t test statistic, two-tailed (see Table 8-3). The most common level of significance used in this test is 95% or the 0.05 level of confidence. Note that degrees of freedom $(df) = n - 2$ for a simple linear regression equation. If the calculated t statistic equals or exceeds the critical value, reject the hypothesis that the slope equals 0 and accept the alternative hypothesis that the slope is not 0. If the calculated t statistic is less than the critical value, fail to reject the hypothesis; the slope appears to be 0 and thus the regression is worthless.

Using the example and the table of critical values, the t test statistic was calculated to be 2.526, which exceeds with $n = 8$, the critical value with 6 degrees of freedom for the t test statistic (from Table 8-3; critical value $= 2.45$). Because the calculated t test statistic (2.526) is greater than the critical value (95% confidence, two-tailed t test, $df = 6$) of 2.45, the appropriate decision is to reject the hypothesis that the slope of the line is 0 and accept the alternative hypothesis that the slope is other than 0. If the calculated t test statistic was less than 2.45, the appropriate decision would be to accept the hypothesis that the slope equals 0 and discard the previously calculated regression equation as useless.

Following this process provides the manager with the ability to conclude whether the calculated regression equation (e.g., $y = -186.5 + 4.7x$) is a valid expression of the relationship portrayed in the data. Whether the regression equation is usable can be determined only by following this process.

Table 8-3.   Critical values of the *t* test statistic (two tailed) at 95% level of confidence (0.05 level of significance) and degrees of freedom $(df) = n - 2$

Degrees of freedom	Critical value
1	12.70
3	3.18
4	2.78
5	2.57
6	2.45
7	2.36
8	2.31
9	2.26
10	2.23
15	2.13
20	2.09
25	2.06
29	2.05

TIME AS AN INDEPENDENT VARIABLE

When regression is used to forecast, time is often used as the independent variable. Time can be expressed in any appropriate unit, such as days, weeks, months, or years. To simplify calculations and provide equal units, it is important to express time intervals in small numbers. For example, instead of using 1988, 1989, and so forth as the *x* variable, time intervals of one integer are used. In that way, the coefficient is more easily interpreted as 1, 2, and so forth.

The data in Table 8-4 describe the number of hospital births during a 6-year period. Using the additional calculations presented in Table 8-5, we can determine that the regression model is $y = 18.87 + 7.8x$. The critical value of the *t* test statistic for 4 degrees of freedom at 95% confidence is 2.78. Given that the calculated *t* statistic is 28.59, the slope of the regression line is other than 0. Therefore, this regression model appears useful to forecast births (*y*), as in Table 8-6.

Any calculated regression equation must be tested to ensure, within acceptable limits of probability, that its slope is not 0. The *t* test provides the ability to conclude that the model may have some degree of utility in describing the relationship between *x* and *y*. Until this test is performed, the calculated regression equation is merely an algebraic equation that may or may not be useful.

Table 8-4.   Hospital births for 6 years beginning 1989

Time period	Time interval (x)	Births (y)
1989	1	25
1990	2	36
1991	3	43
1992	4	50
1993	5	58
1994	6	65
Σ	21	277

Table 8-5. Additional calculations for data on hospital births for 6 years beginning 1989

Time period	Time interval (x)	Births (y)	x^2	xy	y^2
1989	1	25	1	25	625
1990	2	36	4	72	1,296
1991	3	43	9	129	1,849
1992	4	50	16	200	2,500
1993	5	58	25	290	3,364
1994	6	65	36	390	4,225
Σ	21	277	91	1,106	13,859
n	6				
b_0	18.87				
b_1	7.80				
s_2	1.302				
$s^2_{b_1}$	0.074				
t	28.59				

Table 8-6. Forecasted number of births

Year	x	y
1995	7	73.47
1996	8	81.27
1997	9	89.07
1998	10	96.87

Testing the slope should be the first and primary test of the regression model. Additional information can be obtained from the size of the standard error of the regression—that is, the standard deviation of the "distance" between the observed (actual) data point and its mean, given the value of the independent variables (given the value represented by the regression line). The standard error (SE) should be small relative to the size of the predicted y. Also, an F test for significance of the overall regression line can be used. The value of F should be relatively larger than 1.0. Still another piece of information is R^2, which is the proportion of total variance of y explained by the regression model. The value of R^2 should be close to 1.0 because the regression model uses x to predict y more accurately than using the mean of y.

A data plot used to test a regression model plots the residuals. A residual is defined as the difference between an observed Y and the predicted Y, at a specific value of x, written as $(y - \hat{y})$ against x. The plot should look somewhat constant around the zero value of the residuals; that is, most residual values should be close to zero.

Mathematically, one should examine all available tests. In managerial practice, however, determining that the slope is greater than 0 at 95% confidence may provide sufficient justification to use the calculated regression model.

CONFIDENCE INTERVALS AND REGRESSION MODELS

Regardless of the type of independent variable in a regression equation, it is important that the resulting prediction be presented with a 95% confidence interval.

This is because a forecast is never totally accurate. As previously stated, the regression model establishes the line of best fit from the available data. However, the regression model is limited by the domain of these data. In the previous example (hospital births), x ranged from 1 to 6 and y ranged from 25 to 65. The calculated regression equation (i.e., $y = 18.87 + 7.8x$) is the line of best fit based on the available data. Extending the line beyond the domain of the original data (i.e., $x = 7$), while appropriate, has inherent risk.

The confidence interval is not a constant width for all values of x. This is because of the way in which least squares works and the fact that the equation for regression is rooted in the values for the mean of x and the mean of y. Thus, for predictions based on values of the independent (x) variable close to the mean, the confidence interval is the narrowest (most precise). The farther away from the mean, the less precise or wider the confidence interval becomes.

Thus, the confidence interval for a predicted value of y depends on the value of x that predicts it (using the regression formula). The following method can be used to calculate the confidence interval for the mean value (expected value) of y. The confidence interval is even larger if the confidence intervals for individual values of y are used.

To calculate the 95% confidence interval:

1. Calculate the mean value of x. Using data from Table 8-7, the mean for $x = 3.5$.
2. Select the y to be forecast. In this case, the example is based on wanting to predict y for the next time interval.
3. Select the value of x to be used as the basis for the 95% confidence interval. Using the data in Tables 8-5 and 8-6, $x = 7$ (1995) has been selected as the point for which the 95% confidence interval will be calculated. Using the regression equation to solve for y:

$$\begin{aligned} y &= 18.87 + 7.8x \\ &= 18.87 + (7.8)(7) \\ &= 18.87 + 54.6 \\ &= 73.47 \end{aligned}$$

According to Table 8-5, $s_e^2 = 1.303$ and $s_e = 1.141$. The critical value of t with $df = 4$ (from Table 8-3) is 2.78 (.05 level, two-tailed).

Table 8-7.   Calculating the mean value of x

Time period	x
1989	1
1990	2
1991	3
1992	4
1993	5
1994	6
Σ	21
n	6
Mean	3.5

4. Solve for the 95% confidence interval (CI) using the following formula:

$$CI(y) = \text{prediction} \pm (t)(s_e)\sqrt{\frac{1}{n} + \frac{(x_0 - \bar{x})^2}{n(\Sigma x^2) - (\Sigma x)^2}} \qquad \text{(Eq. 8-4)}$$

Using data and calculations from Table 8-5, when $x_0 = 7$, and $\bar{x} = 3.5$ with $df = 4$:

$$CI(y) = 73.47 \pm (2.78)(1.141)\sqrt{\frac{1}{6} + \frac{(7 - 3.5)^2}{6(91) - (21)^2}}$$

$$= 73.47 \pm 3.172 \times \text{SQRT}(0.1667 + 0.1167)$$
$$= 73.47 \pm 3.172 \times (0.5323)$$
$$= 73.47 \pm 1.688$$
$$= 75.12 \text{ and } 71.78$$
$$= 71.78 \text{ and } 75.16 \text{ when } x = 7$$

Using the 95% confidence interval provides the ability to extend the line of best fit beyond the domain of the original data, such as in the case of using the data on Table 8-4 to forecast 1994 using regression. A 95% confidence interval can be calculated for any level of X, including an X value included in the domain of the original data. Based upon the results of these calculations, the regression model indicates a 95% probability that births in 1994 ($x = 7$) will not exceed 76 and be no less than 71.

In any situation where the calculated regression model is used outside of the domain of the original data, a 95% confidence interval should be calculated. As such, this covers all situations when the independent variable (i.e., x) is time. Any time regression is used to forecast, the 95% confidence interval should be calculated for the forecast.

USING RESIDUALS AND MAD

A residual is defined as $Y - \hat{Y}$, where Y is the observed value and y is the predicted value for a specific value of x. Using the example (Table 8-5), residuals can be calculated and are included in Table 8-8. Values of predicted Y have been calculated using the regression formula:

$$y = 18.87 + 7.8x$$

The total of the residuals is 65.08. It is interesting to note what the value of the residuals would be if the mean was used as a basis for prediction. ($Y_{\text{mean}} = Y_{\text{predicted}}$) Consider Table 8-9. Since the regression model (total residual = 65.08) is less than

Table 8-8. Calculation of residual values

Time period	Time interval (x)	Births (y)	Predicted y	Residual (y − predicted y)
1989	1	25	23.57	1.43
1990	2	36	28.27	7.73
1991	3	43	32.97	10.03
1992	4	50	37.67	12.33
1993	5	58	42.37	15.63
1994	6	65	47.07	17.93
Total				65.08
Mean		46.17		10.85

the absolute residual created by using the mean (i.e., 69.00), the regression model better fits the historical data than does the mean.

The mean value of the regression residuals (e.g., 10.85) can be comparable with the MAD calculation used in trend extrapolation. In developing a forecasting model, assuming a valid regression model, select the approach that minimizes the value, either mean average deviation or mean residual. That approach best explains the historical data and should provide the more accurate forecast.

Although the calculations necessary to develop and use the regression model, especially in a forecasting situation, can be cumbersome, regression remains the premier statistical model to construct an algebraic equation of the relationship among two or more variables. Even though this chapter has been restricted to the linear regression model and one x value, it demonstrates the power and utility of this model.

OTHER REGRESSION MODELS

Other regression models should be used when the data do not present a linear relationship. For example, multiple regression covers situations with two independent variables. Polynomial or curvilinear models also exist. To decide which type of model to use, the manager should always plot the data and examine the resulting image to determine whether the data plot looks linear, with either a positive or negative slope.

If the data plot looks like a straight line, then the regression model can be used. If the data plot looks more like a random cloud or has a clear curvature, then the linear model may not be the best model. If the data look like they have cycles, the forecasting models that smooth the data may be more appropriate than the linear regression model.

After calculating the regression model, additional data plots must be examined to see if a linear relationship holds. To do this, the predicted y for various values of x is calculated, and the values of the predicted y are plotted against the values for x. The plot should look linear, with a positive slope or a slope around 1. Other types of plots exist to examine the appropriateness of a linear regression model. For example, plotting the difference between y and predicted y (called the residuals) as a histogram should produce a data display that resembles the shape of the standard normal data distribution (i.e., bell shaped).

Testing the calculated slope of the regression equation also provides the ability to evaluate the appropriateness of the linear regression model. Only linear regression equations that have a slope other than 0, at 95% confidence, should be used.

Table 8-9.   Comparison of y and predicted y values using mean y for predicted y

Time period	Time interval (x)	Births (y)	Predicted y	Residual (y − predicted y)
1989	1	25	46.17	−21.17
1990	2	36	46.17	−10.17
1991	3	43	46.17	−3.17
1992	4	50	46.17	3.83
1993	5	58	46.17	11.83
1994	6	65	46.17	18.83
Absolute total				69.00
Mean		46.17		11.50

If the slope of the calculated regression equation is not tested, then the user is potentially using a spurious model, one of many that could best fit the data, and will most likely make a forecast with large error.

CONCLUSION

Regression analysis is the primary statistical model used to produce a predictive equation. When used appropriately, it produces the line of best fit given the available data. Being able to apply the regression model to management situations and concerns is an essential competency associated with being a manager.

EXERCISES

8-1. For the data in Table 8-10, calculate and test the regression equation. Also indicate a 95% confidence interval for $x = 7$ (i.e., week 7).

8-2. For the data in Table 8-11, present a regression model. Calculate the mean residual.

8-3. For the data in Table 8-12, calculate the regression equation to predict the number of x-rays given different levels of clinic service (i.e., $x = $ visits). Test the regression equation.

Table 8-10. Data for Exercise 8-1

	Time interval (x)	Visits (y)	x^2	xy	y^2
Week 1	1	40	1	40	1,600
Week 2	2	46	4	92	2,116
Week 3	3	50	9	150	2,500
Week 4	4	59	16	236	3,481
Week 5	5	63	25	315	3,969
Week 6	6	68	36	408	4,624
Σ	21	326	91	1,241	18,290
n	6				

Table 8-11. Data for Exercise 8-2

Month	Births
July	68
August	79
September	81
October	55
November	71
December	60
January	77
February	81
March	63
April	85
May	85
June	90

Table 8-12.   Data for Exercise 8-3

	Visits (x)	X-rays (y)	x^2	xy	y^2
Week 1	24	17	576	408	289
Week 2	34	21	1,156	714	441
Week 3	50	35	2,500	1,750	1,225
Week 4	43	32	1,849	1,376	1,024
Week 5	48	37	2,304	1,776	1,369
Week 6	30	21	900	630	441
Σ	229	163	9,285	6,654	4,789

III

PROJECT ANALYSIS

Health care organizations change. New services are added. Existing services are modified or eliminated. New approaches are designed to enhance the efficiency and effectiveness of services. Change within the health care organization is not accidental. It is the product of managers working to design system modifications.

Project analysis is integral to organizational change. A manager must define project alternatives and decide among projects, determine their cost to and effect on the organization, schedule the tasks and activities that make up a project, and evaluate the financial impact of the project. Overall, managers are expected to provide the organization project proposals that improve the organization's ability to meet its mission.

In Chapter 9, "Decision Analysis," topics include the difference between decision alternatives, the effect of predicted states of the world on the decision consequences, and the effect of the likelihood of these states on the consequences. This is a formalized decision-making technique used by managers to list the alternatives, consequences, and probabilities associated with projects. It requires the use of the concept of expected value from statistics because *expected* consequences are what are compared in order to decide among alternatives.

Chapter 10, "Economic Analysis," uses the concept of decision analysis and expected consequences to evaluate the cost and cost-effectiveness of projects. Project inputs and methods to assign costs to inputs are covered. Also included is a discussion of the health consequences of decisions, a unique and important concern for health care managers.

Chapter 11, "Program Evaluation Review Technique (PERT)," provides a way to micro-plan for the implementation of a project. All activities associated with the project are identified, and the durations of each activity are estimated. From this, the total time for the project can then be calculated. When a project is implemented, PERT becomes a management scheduling and control system.

Chapter 12, "Financial Evaluation of Projects," presents methods based on the time value of money, used by managers to assess the financial implications associated with specific projects. Many of the concepts included in this chapter are drawn from finance. This chapter provides the manager with the ability to evaluate project proposals as well as the parameters to use when designing projects to facilitate the organization's mission.

The techniques in this section are day-to-day decision-making and project planning skills that all managers need in their repertoire. Each represents a critical understanding as well as a critical skill.

9

Decision Analysis

Chapter Objectives

1. To be able to construct and use decision trees as a method to examine decision alternatives
2. To be able to calculate expected payoff and select decision alternatives based on maximum payoff

Key Terms and Concepts

Decision alternative
Decision tree
Expected payoff

Payoff
States of the world
Probability of states

Managerial life is full of decisions. Managers must decide, given available resources, how best to meet the organization's mission. Managers adjust organizational goals and objectives based on internal capabilities and environmental changes. Managers search for ways to enhance the efficiency and effectiveness of their organization, which often requires making decisions that involve the reallocation of resources and tasks within the organization. As resources diminish, systems within the organization change. Each of these is a broad example of the types of decisions faced by the health services manager.

Management decision making is a systematic process. Although it is a process influenced by many factors, such as organizational culture, precedents, and the values of the managers, it is characterized by the reasoned consideration of these factors. Equally important, management decisions are usually made under conditions of uncertainty. It is almost always the case that the manager does not know for certain the full consequences of a decision. The outcomes associated with decision alternatives are governed by unknown probabilities. This means that there are two parts to any decision, only one of which is under the control of the decision maker. These are:

1. The *alternatives* among which the choice is made by the manager—what are the alternatives and, given appropriate considerations, which is "best."
2. The *state of the world* that will occur after the decision is made.

The interaction between these two parts creates a payoff or outcome with which the decision maker must deal.

DECISION MAKING UNDER UNCERTAINTY

Managers are expected to consider alternatives before making a decision. Some alternatives are different strategies intended to realize the same outcome or payoff. In other instances, the alternatives will result in very different payoffs or outcomes, and managers must select among the alternatives given their assessment of the payoffs and outcomes associated with each. For example, should a college student or professor carry an umbrella to class in the spring? Intuitively, each of us makes this decision using reasoned judgment. We listen to the weather reports. Then we think about how far we have to go to cross campus. Then we might think about what we are wearing that day. The alternatives are to carry the umbrella or not. The states of the world will be either that it will rain or it will not. Intuitively, we list each alternative with each state of the world, and then include the payoff for each interaction of alternative and state of the world. There are always as many possible payoffs as the product of the number of alternatives times the number of states of the world. In this case, for example, there are two alternatives and two states of the world, for a total of four payoffs:

Alternative	Outcome/Payoffs
1. Carry umbrella and it rains	1 in 10 chance of losing umbrella; outcome is $-$1$
2. Carry umbrella and it does not rain	1 in 10 chance of losing umbrella; outcome is $-$1$
3. Do not carry umbrella and it does not rain	No consequences; outcome is $0
4. Do not carry umbrella and it rains	Ruined clothing; outcome is $-$50$

This example demonstrates the basic decision-analytic approach covered in this chapter—the explicit identification of decision alternatives and states of the world and the comparison of outcomes and payoffs. It is a formal process very similar to the intuitive processes we use every time we hear of the chance of showers. The difference, however, is that the explicit approach has the power to assist health services managers to identify alternatives and select among the alternatives.

Payoffs are not always in monetary units. It is easier, however, to compare alternatives with some common unit. In health care and public health, outcomes are sometimes healthy life years gained or cases of disease or injury averted or medical procedures avoided by the decision made. Managers must choose some outcome measure that provides a good comparison measure in order to use these decision-analytic techniques.

One way of looking at the chronology and payoffs of a decision is to construct a decision tree. A decision tree has branches for each decision alternative and each state of the world. A square is used for a choice node; a circle is used for the states of the world nodes. The decision tree for the previous example is shown in Figure 9-1. Note that this tree shows the decision being made first and the weather condition occurring second. If it is raining when we leave the house, we are choosing under conditions of certainty; the payoff is known for certain, so we choose correctly every time. On any day when it is not raining when we leave the house, the state of the world later that day is not known *for certain*, so we cannot *be certain* of choosing correctly. Therefore, a dilemma exists. How should an individual choose what to do?

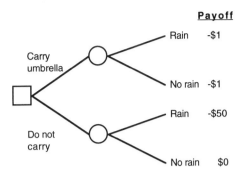

Figure 9-1. Decision tree for carrying or not carrying an umbrella.

Expected Payoff as the Decision-Making Criterion

Statistically, the expected value is expressed mathematically as:

$$E(x) = \Sigma \text{ probability of } (x) \times \text{ payoff if } (x) \qquad \text{(Eq. 9-1)}$$

where x is the possible outcome. This is the same as the equation for the mean when several of the data points are the same. For example, the mean of the five points $x = 2, 4, 2, 3,$ and 2 is the sum of $(3/5 \times 2)$ plus $(1/5 \times 3)$ plus $(1/5 \times 4)$. This is algebraically the same as $(3^{*}2/5) + (3/5) + (4/5)$, or

$$\frac{2 + 2 + 2 + 3 + 4}{5}$$

In decision analysis, the expected value is called the *expected payoff,* and the equation for calculating this is:

$$\Sigma \text{ probability of the payoff } \textit{multiplied by} \text{ the payoff}$$

Each decision alternative has an expected payoff. The rule is: *choose the alternative whose expected payoff is best.* In the example of carrying the umbrella, on any given day, what is the expected payoff for the decision to carry the umbrella compared to the decision not to carry one? That is, on average, over many days, what is the "damage" to our finances for each alternative?

The answer depends on the probabilities assigned to the states of the world. Meteorologists always give probabilities in their weather forecasts. They say that there is an 80% chance of rain. This means that given the meteorological conditions at the time of the forecast, 8 out of 10 days it rains and 2 out of 10 days it does not. The probabilities of states of the world must add up to 1. In this example, $.8 + .2 = 1.0$.

If there is an 80% chance of rain, the expected payoffs for our example, in the order illustrated by the decision tree, are:

Expected payoff [carry] $= (.8 \times -\$1)$ $+ (.2 \times -\$1) = -\$1$
Expected payoff [not carry] $= (.8 \times -\$50) + (.2 \times \$0)$ $= -\$40$

This is illustrated in the decision tree in Figure 9-2. Note that the expected payoffs are written inside the state of the world nodes. If we carry an umbrella, there is a chance of leaving it somewhere, but that cost is low (loss of $1) compared to not

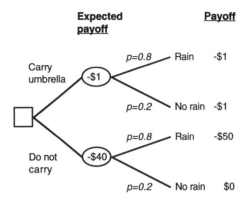

Figure 9-2. Decision tree for carrying or not carrying an umbrella, with associated probabilities of rain.

carrying the umbrella and ruining our clothes (loss of $40). We should choose, under these probabilities of rain, to carry an umbrella.

Break-Even Analysis

An important tool for evaluating alternatives is break-even analysis. The example can be expressed as a break-even question: How low does the probability of rain have to be before we leave our umbrella at home? In other words, with the payoffs we have estimated, what probability value will give an expected payoff if we do not carry an umbrella that is equal to the expected payoff if we do?

In this case, the expected payoff associated with not carrying an umbrella must be equal to $-$1$, the value of the expected payoff of carrying an umbrella. That is, algebraically, the break-even point occurs when:

$$-1 = (p \times -\$50) + [(1-p) \times 0]$$

where p represents the probability of rain and, because probabilities add up to 1, $1 - p$ represents the remaining probability of no rain. Solving this equation, we find that:

$$-1 = p \times -\$50$$

and thus

$$p = 1/50$$
$$= .02, \text{ or } 2\%$$

Given the parameters used in this example, the chance of rain must be 2% or less for us *not* to carry our umbrella.

Of course, maybe our clothes are not so valuable. If the loss associated with being rained on were equal to $20 rather than $50, then the break-even probability for carrying an umbrella would be:

$$-1 = p \times - \$20$$

and thus

$$p = 1/20$$
$$= .05, \text{ or } 5\%$$

Changing the value of loss from ruined clothes from $50 to $20 changes the break-even point associated with decision alternatives—the chance of rain must be 5% or less for us not to carry an umbrella.

EXAMPLES FROM HEALTH CARE

Health services managers make decisions under conditions of uncertainty all the time. In some instances, uncertainty may be relatively low. For example, purchasing a new imaging device in order to meet an existing and continuing need more efficiently is a choice with a low level of uncertainty. Conversely, purchasing a new imaging device to meet a potential demand might represent a situation characterized by a high level of uncertainty. Consider the following examples.

Clinic Renovation

An ambulatory care clinic administrator is trying to decide whether to renovate in order to accommodate possible increased demand. The manager could plan a major renovation costing $100,000 that would allow 50 patients per day to be served or a minor renovation costing $70,000 that would allow 35 patients per day to be served. A final alternative is the status quo—no renovation, and thus no ability to accommodate demand greater than the current 20 patients per day. Currently, the clinic earns $20 per patient served. Assume that the clinic is open 300 days per year and that the clinic management wants to cover the costs of the renovation from first-year earnings. What does the manager know?

There are three alternatives and three possible states of the world. This means that there are *nine* possible outcomes, as shown in Table 9-1. What are the payoffs for each of these nine alternatives?

Earnings are based on patients served; therefore, part of the payoff involves earnings. Thus, for the various demand levels, earnings are:

20 patients/day $\times$ $20/patient $\times$ 300 days = $120,000
35 patients/day $\times$ $20/patient $\times$ 300 days = $210,000
50 patients/day $\times$ $20/patient $\times$ 300 days = $300,000

The clinic renovation costs money; however, that must be charged against these earnings. The payoffs for each alternative are shown in Table 9-2. A minor renovation can accommodate 35 patients per day and a major renovation accommodates 50 patients per day.

Table 9-1.   Expected outcomes for clinic renovation alternatives

Alternative	State of the world	Outcome
1. No renovation	Demand remains at 20 patients per day	Demand is met
2. No renovation	Demand increases to 35 patients per day	Demand is not met
3. No renovation	Demand increases to 50 patients per day	Demand is not met
4. Minor renovation	Demand remains at 20 patients per day	Demand is met
5. Minor renovation	Demand increases to 35 patients per day	Demand is met
6. Minor renovation	Demand increases to 50 patients per day	Demand is not met
7. Major renovation	Demand remains at 20 patients per day	Demand is met
8. Major renovation	Demand increases to 35 patients per day	Demand is met
9. Major renovation	Demand increases to 50 patients per day	Demand is met

Table 9-2. Payoffs for each alternative for clinic renovation example

Alternative	Patients/day	Earnings ($)	Renovation ($)	Payoff ($)
1	20	120,000	0	120,000
2	20	120,000	0	120,000
3	20	120,000	0	120,000
4	20	120,000	70,000	50,000
5	35	210,000	70,000	140,000
6	35	210,000	70,000	140,000
7	20	120,000	100,000	20,000
8	35	210,000	100,000	110,000
9	50	300,000	100,000	200,000

It is important to remember that potential demand is uncertain. The clinic does not know for certain whether the demand will continue to be 20 patients per day or will increase to 35 or 50 patients per day. This is management decision making under uncertainty. The decision tree for this problem is shown in Figure 9-3.

At this point in this example, one management approach would be to use expert opinion or mathematical forecasting to predict the future demand and base the subsequent analysis on the "certainty" associated with the forecast. That is, knowledge of the future level of demand would enable management to choose the best alternative for that level of demand. This approach, however, requires management to risk financial loss on a probabilistic estimate of the future.

Another approach is to assume that all states of the world are equally likely to happen. With three states, this means that the probability of current demand is .33, moderate demand is .33, and high demand is .33. Using these probabilities, we can calculate the expected payoff [EP] for each decision alternative:

$$\text{EP [no renovation]} = \$120,000$$
(because all payoffs are the same, regardless of state)

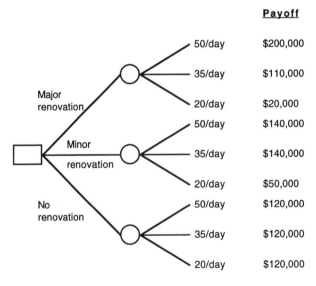

Figure 9-3. Decision tree for clinic renovation example.

$$\text{EP [minor renovation]} = (.33) \times \$50,000 + (.67) \times \$140,000$$
$$= \$110,000$$

$$\text{EP [major renovation]} = (.33) \times \$20,000 + (.33) \times \$110,000 + (.34) \times \$200,000$$
$$= \$110,000$$

Expected payoffs are calculated *for each alternative* because the states of the world have probabilities associated with them and we must decide *among alternatives*. In this case, the clinic management is *indifferent* between the major and minor renovations because the expected payoff is the same in both cases. They would have to use other information to make the choice between the two, such as other anticipated expenditures or expected income.

Perhaps the clinic management will be doing some marketing in the community concurrent with construction in order to increase demand. They think that there is a 1-in-10 chance that demand will remain at 20 patients per day and that there is a 50% chance that demand will increase to 35 patients per day. This means that management is implicitly assigning the probabilities of .1 to low demand and .5 to a moderate increase. By definition of probabilities for states of the world, the remaining probability must be $1 - (.1) - (.5) = (.4)$.

Recalculating the expected payoffs (EPs), we obtain:

$$\text{EP [no renovation]} = \$120,000$$
(because all payoffs are the same, regardless of state)

$$\text{EP [minor renovation]} = (.1) \times \$50,000 + (.9) \times \$140,000$$
$$= \$131,000$$

$$\text{EP [major renovation]} = (.1) \times \$20,000 + (.5) \times \$110,000 + (.4) \times \$200,000$$
$$= \$137,000$$

In this case, the clinic management should choose the major renovation strategy because the expected payoff is the greatest, *even though* the probability of high demand is less than that of moderate demand. Thus, all conditions before the decision being equal, decision analysis tells the manager to choose the alternative of major renovation.

Bid for Services

You are part of a consulting firm that is considering bidding on a project to set up a pricing plan for cardiovascular treatment procedures. You determine the cost for each procedure—based on provider time, materials and supplies, lab work, anesthesia, and other factors—that will become the standard price that a specialty practice group bills for these procedures. If you get the bid, it will cost you $300,000 to complete the pricing project. Merely preparing the proposal, however, will cost you $100,000. You want to make a profit on this project, of course, so how much should you bid?

You have competitors who also want this project. The project will go to the lowest bidder, so bidding too high will mean losing the bid. However, the lower you bid, the lower your profit will be. You know something about your competitors and decide that you have four alternatives:

1. Bid $800,000.
2. Bid $575,000.

3. Bid $500,000.
4. Do not bid at all.

The states of the world are that:

1. There is no other bid less than $800,000.
2. There is no other bid less than $575,000.
3. There is no other bid less than $500,000.
4. At least one bid is less than $500,000.

(Because states of nature or the world must be mutually exclusive and exhaustive, the entire universe of possibilities must be represented by the states you choose.)

Because this is a complicated situation, the information is presented in another form in Table 9-3. Remember that it will cost $400,000 to complete the project if you get the bid ($100,000 for the proposal and $300,000 to perform the actual work of the project), and it will cost the consulting firm $100,000 to bid on the project even if it does not win the bid.

The next step is to assign probabilities to each state of the world. If you have no reason to think that any one state is more likely than another, you would assign equal probabilities to each state. There are four states, so each has a 1-in-4 (.25) probability of occurring.

In this case, where each probability is .25, the expected payoffs (EPs) will be:

$$EP \text{ [bid \$800,000]} = (.25) \times \$400,000 + (.75) \times - \$100,000$$
$$= \$25,000$$

$$EP \text{ [bid \$575,000]} = (.5) \times \$175,000 + (.5) \times - \$100,000$$
$$= \$37,500$$

$$EP \text{ [bid \$500,000]} = (.75) \times \$100,000 + (.25) \times - \$100,000$$
$$= \$50,000$$

$$EP \text{ [no bid]} = \$0$$

Under these conditions, you should bid $500,000 because that alternative has the highest expected payoff.

Medical Treatment versus Prevention

Mammography does not prevent breast cancer but can avert a more advanced stage of cancer through earlier diagnosis, thus preventing premature mortality from breast cancer. The average mammogram—including the technician, the equip-

Table 9-3. Alternatives in bid for services example (in dollars)

Other bids (states of the world)	Payoffs for various alternatives			
	Bid 800,000 (−400,000)[a]	Bid 575,000 (−400,000)[a]	Bid 500,000 (−400,000)[a]	Do not bid (−0)
None <800,000	400,000	175,000	100,000	0
None <575,000	−100,000[b]	175,000	100,000	0
None <500,000	−100,000[b]	−100,000[c]	100,000	0
At least one <500,000	−100,000	−100,000	−100,000	0

[a]Represents cost of proposal ($100,000) and cost of project ($300,000).
[b]Assumes at least one bid was less than $800,000.
[c]Assumes at least one bid was less than $575,000.

ment, and the radiological assessment—costs a hospital $50 to perform. Additional costs associated with false-positive screening, such as biopsies, add an expected cost to each mammographic screening of $5.

The medical treatments for advanced breast cancer are assumed to be $35,000. Mammography can reduce the chance of advanced breast cancer by 40% with proper screening. Given these parameters, should we screen for breast cancer? The decision tree for this example is shown in Figure 9-4.

The incidence of breast cancer is approximately 4 per 1,000 white women over age 50 per year in the United States. For the purpose of argument, let us assume that the 4 per 1,000 incidence rate is based on no screening for breast cancer and that introduction of screening would reduce this rate by 40%, to 2.4 per 1,000. If we assume that, without screening, this is the incidence rate of advanced breast cancer, a 40% reduction with screening means that the incidence rate would be 2.4 per 1,000. That is, 1.6 cases of breast cancer per 1,000 women would be averted.

In this simplified model, what are the expected payoffs for screening women over 50 years old? For every 1,000 women screened, the expected payoffs (EP) are:

$$
\begin{aligned}
\text{EP [screen]} &= \$55 \times 1{,}000 \text{ women} + \$35{,}000 \times 2.4 \text{ cases} \\
&= \$139{,}000 \\
\text{EP [no screen]} &= \$35{,}000 \times 4 \text{ cases} \\
&= \$140{,}000
\end{aligned}
$$

Although the difference is small, the expected payoff rule says that we would choose to screen women over 50. The savings from advanced cases averted would more than compensate for the costs associated with screening.

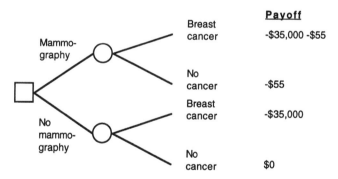

Figure 9-4.   Decision tree for breast cancer screening example.

CONCLUSION

Decision analysis provides the manager with a technique for specifying decision alternatives and estimating the payoffs and outcomes associated with each alternative. It also provides the manager with the opportunity to examine the impact that different probabilities of the states of the world can have on payoffs. It is a systematic approach that can be used in virtually any decision situation and moves management decision making further into the realm of reasoned judgment.

In health care management decision making, expected payoff should not be the only criterion. It is important to consider quality of life and other values important to the community at risk. It is also important to recognize that a decision is made up of two parts: 1) the alternatives and 2) the anticipated or forecast state of the world that will occur after the decision is made. It is not just the decision, but the consequences of the decision, that are important.

EXERCISES

9-1. Draw a decision tree for the consulting example.

9-2. In the clinic renovation example, suppose management thinks that the likelihood of demand remaining at the current level is 30%, the likelihood of a moderate increase is 25%, and the likelihood of a large increase is 45%. What should they do, according to the expected payoff rule?

9-3. In the clinic renovation example, suppose management thinks that a moderate increase is twice as likely as either demand remaining at the current level or high demand occurring. What does the rule tell them to do?

9-4. The Centers for Disease Control and Prevention (CDC) is predicting that a new influenza strain will strike the United States. It is not known for certain how infectious this strain is. Depending on its strength, the United States could have a major epidemic (1 in 100 persons affected), a minor epidemic (1 in 1,000 persons affected), or a trace epidemic (1 in 100,000 persons affected). It costs $5,000 to treat a severe case of the flu; minor cases will be assumed to be taken care of within a patient's health care provider group under their fixed cost contract with no additional costs. If a new vaccine must be provided, a dose costs $5, including drug and administrative costs.

There may be vaccine side effects; these are very rare (1 in 1,000,000 doses) but are estimated to cost $15,000 to treat.

a. Construct a decision tree for this problem.

b. The probabilities are estimated to be .01 and .03 for the major and minor epidemic cases. What should the President recommend? Assume that the vaccine will be given to all people (250 million) with a major epidemic predicted and to older adults and children (100 million) with a minor epidemic predicted and that no extra vaccine will be given if a trace epidemic is predicted.

c. If the probabilities are estimated as .10 and .30 with the same assumptions as in (b), does your decision change? Why or why not?

10

Economic Analysis

Chapter Objectives

1. To understand the basic elements of a cost-effectiveness analysis
2. To be able to calculate the cost-effectiveness of a specific project or intervention

Key Terms and Concepts

Cost–benefit analysis (CBA)

Cost-effectiveness analysis (CEA)

Cost of health-related event averted

Cost–utility analysis (CUA)

Direct medical care costs

Net costs

Based on the goals of the organization, a health services manager must make decisions and recommendations regarding what services to provide. Changing needs, demands, and desires, along with changing organizational goals and objectives, require the manager to revise existing services, add new services, and eliminate existing services. New technology constantly redefines the medical care frontier. The health services manager approaches these issues with two potentially conflicting perspectives and one stark realization.

The realization is that community and organizational resources are scarce and must be used wisely. Value or benefit is expected from every resource used in a service. Patients expect value. Health care organizations expect value. Communities expect value. Health care organizations and financing sources also continue to stress exactly how scarce resources are and that resources used for health care cannot be used for other purposes, such as economic development, transportation, education, amusement, and defense. Being scarce, resources must be allocated to meet prioritized goals and objectives. Personnel, organizational, and governmental budgets reflect how resources are allocated between and among competing needs, demands, and desires. Markets allocate resources based on the interplay of supply and demand. The need to allocate resources is a given; the question becomes, on what basis will they be allocated?

The health services manager, as an employee of a health care organization, feels the potentially competing perspectives of the "community" and the "organization." From an organizational perspective, any decision or recommendation must be evaluated based on its impact on the organization. Organizational profits and losses are real and are a dominant criterion used to evaluate a manager and his or her actions. From a community perspective, however, the health services manager is challenged to use organizational resources to improve the health status of the community served by the health care organization. From this perspective, the health status of the community is the dominant criterion used to evaluate the manager and the health care organization. Although these criteria can be compatible, they can also be mutually exclusive. Organizational benefit and community benefit can range from being the same to being opposite. Each is a dominant, real, and important perspective that every health services manager must consider when making a decision or recommendation involving new or revised projects.

The purpose of this chapter is to equip health services managers with the ability to formulate project recommendations that include community benefit. This does not imply that the manager should be insensitive to organizational profit and loss. It merely implies that the health services manager must examine *both* the organizational and community benefits associated with any project recommendation.

Health services managers are retained to exercise reasoned judgment. Their actions are expected to benefit their organization *and* the community served by their organization. Reasoned judgment requires that the health services manager be able to evaluate project alternatives from many perspectives, including an economic perspective that values community benefits as well as organizational costs and benefits. Sometimes, however, considerations other than economic will be the dominant influence on the health services manager (i.e., a political perspective based on stakeholder interests). To exercise reasoned judgment, the health services manager must be conversant in these many perspectives. This chapter expands the ability of the health services manager to consider the community implications associated with project recommendations. It is a continuation of the previous chapter and parallels the last chapter in this section (Chapter 12, "Financial Evaluation of Projects"), a chapter that provides methods to analyze organizational costs.

USING ECONOMIC ANALYSIS

Management decisions and recommendations can be made by comparing anticipated costs and anticipated benefits. To evaluate project alternatives, analyses must evaluate the costs and benefits associated with each project alternative, including the alternative of doing nothing. Analysis can be used to determine whether a proposed project is better in terms of the relationship of benefits to costs and the benefits to individuals than any of the alternatives. This concept is critical in managerial decision making in the health care field because it incorporates into the analysis the impact the project alternatives should have on clientele served by the health care organization.

Every health care organization intends to improve the health status of the populations it serves. This distinguishes health care organizations and their managers from other types of organizations and managers in the service sector. Community health status is important to health care organizations.

A community can be defined as a group of individuals with common attributes. These attributes can be demographic, behavioral, geographic, or disease specific. Health status is influenced by prevention programs and medical treatments available to the community as well as by factors involving behavior, genetics, and environment. For example, an immunization program should decrease the number of cases of infectious diseases, thus increasing health status. An anticholesterol drug, which lowers blood cholesterol associated with cardiovascular disease, can decrease the number of heart attacks in a community of "users" compared with "nonusers," thus increasing health status. A neonatal intensive care unit in the community hospital can enhance the likelihood of survival for low birth weight babies. All these programs use health care resources.

As health status in a community improves as a result of the prevention of adverse health outcomes, fewer health care resources should need to be spent in this community on treatment of the same health outcomes. When health status decreases, it is likely that more health care resources will be expended on treating avoidable adverse health events. The major question in health care economic analysis is how do *increased* expenditures on projects to improve health status compare to the *decreased* expenditures on health care resources resulting from health-related events (HREs) averted? This question is particularly relevant today. It is, for example, a fundamental question used in decisions regarding health insurance coverage, especially in managed care plans. It is also a basic question used to evaluate the actions and community benefit of health care organizations. In addition, it is a classical question from the field of public health—would society be better served by preventing a disease or by treating a disease?

Given these perspectives and these questions, a management decision regarding the initiation of a new project or service or the evaluation of existing services must include three parts:

1. *What is the total cost—per unit—of providing a particular service?* What is the cost per person screened or cost per magnetic resonance imaging performed or cost per immunization? Costs include fixed and variable costs associated with all resources consumed in the provision of this service. Analysis based on true resource costs must be used to determine the total or full cost associated with providing the particular unit of service associated with the existing program or project alternative. Service units also must be specified.

2. *What are the benefits (payoffs)—per unit—of this service?* Analysis must also determine the benefits associated with each unit of service. In some cases, the benefits associated with a service can be measured in economic terms. Examples include estimating the medical care costs *averted* by treating one case of a disease, injury, pregnancy, or other HRE, or the value of decreased job absenteeism as a result of averting a particular disease. In other cases, estimating the economic value associated with a particular service is more difficult. Examples include estimating the value of averted deaths and disabilities or increased quality of life.

3. *What proportion of individuals receiving this service will actually benefit?* This proportion represents the probability of an individual payoff, and determining it usually requires knowledge of the effect of the service on reducing the risk of an adverse HRE. For example, 100% of cervical cancer can be averted through early detection using Pap screening. Another example is that 50% of women's heart disease could be averted if all women took estrogen during and after menopause. The scientific literature can provide a reasoned basis to make these types of estimates.

Once these three pieces of information are collected and analyzed, one can proceed to the determination of the value of the service to the organization and community. Using the technique of decision analysis, which allows the comparison of alternative strategies—using costs, payoffs, and probabilities—one can choose the project alternative that is best. One alternative is always "do nothing"—that is, do not provide the service.

There are three evaluation techniques for projects:

cost–benefit analysis (CBA)
cost-effectiveness analysis (CEA)
cost–utility analysis (CUA)

This chapter focuses on CEA. For completeness, however, a brief discussion of CBA and CUA is provided.

Cost–benefit analysis evaluates all project inputs (i.e., costs) and outcomes (i.e., benefits) of a service in *monetary terms.* This means that not only are service costs calculated but all benefits are also calculated in terms of costs, even including the cost of a life saved. This is very difficult, especially because our society cannot come to any agreement on the value of a human life. For example, is life of any quality of the same value? In many cases, the benefit of a life saved is calculated as the present value of the individual's future income stream. This approach, however, values the lives of a young productive population and discounts the value of those either retired from productive labor or unable to be productive. Until we can address this issue as a society, CBA in its complete form generally cannot be used across all services and health interventions.

Cost–utility analysis also compares project costs and benefits. Benefits, however, are expressed in terms of consumer preferences. This is an economic and operations research concept that recognizes that individuals prefer certain goods to others and thus are assumed to *prefer* certain health states to others. Investigators spend time interviewing people, then calculating and refining these measures, called "relative weights." For example, a year of life after a heart attack has been said to be worth 80% of a healthy year of life. Thus, years after adverse HREs are valued less than years prior to these events. The application of CUA is limited and fraught with highly value-laden assumptions.

COST-EFFECTIVENESS ANALYSIS

In cost-effectiveness analysis, project and service costs are calculated in monetary terms. Benefits, however, are calculated in their *natural units,* such as the number of cases of heart disease or cancer averted. CEA compares alternative interventions (i.e., project A vs. project B) whose outcomes (benefits) are measured in identical *units.* This chapter uses examples of interventions and projects whose purpose is to prevent some specific disease, injury, or other HRE that consumes health care resources.

Basic Elements

To use CEA, a manager must be able to determine such factors as the cost of the intervention or project, the cost of any adverse side effects of the intervention or project, the cost of adverse health conditions (i.e., HREs) *averted* or other benefits, and the estimated proportion of current HREs averted by the intervention or project.

Project Costs

Every project intervention requires resources to implement and maintain itself. These include labor for services rendered, facilities and utilities, equipment and supplies, and administrative support. Direct and indirect project costs must be estimated.

Intervention Side Effects

All interventions have an effect, or one would not implement them. Some interventions have adverse side effects as well as beneficial results. As for all interventions, the benefits must exceed the risks in order for the intervention to be implemented ethically. Costs associated with these risks must be included in a CEA. Thus, the extremely small risk of severe vaccine reactions must be included in a mass vaccination program because, in a million doses, the cost associated with an adverse side effect may occur. Diagnostic procedures to rule out false positives in a screening intervention also must be included in a CEA.

Direct Medical Costs of HREs Averted

A prevention program is undertaken to avert adverse HREs. For every adverse HRE averted, the direct medical costs associated with that event do not occur. When sufficient numbers of HREs are averted, the cost savings may exceed the cost of the prevention intervention.

Personal Costs of a Specific HRE Averted

Personal costs are the economic impacts associated with an adverse HRE. Examples include earnings (productivity) losses to society as a whole as a result of the premature morbidity and mortality of persons who become ill with an adverse HRE. Thus, if one can avert adverse health outcomes, one averts the morbidity and mortality that occur with that health outcome and saves the productivity of that individual potentially afflicted.

Two methods of costing this morbidity and mortality are the *human capital* and the *willingness-to-pay* approaches. The human capital approach values personal loss as the income not earned by the individual who experienced the HRE. The willingness-to-pay approach values this loss as what someone might spend to avert this particular event—for example, how much an individual was willing to pay to install automobile seat belts or air bags in a car to avert death or injury. Although many CEAs include these personal costs, sometimes referred to as indirect cost factors, the approach used in this chapter concentrates on the resources used and direct benefits associated with averting a specific HRE.

Determining Resource Costs

Resources are those project inputs to an intervention without which the intervention would not exist. To determine the resource costs, the manager must:

1. Choose a time period for the intervention analysis.
2. Choose the service unit of the intervention.
3. List the resources required for all activities comprising the intervention.
4. Measure or count the units of each resource used in the time period.
5. Determine the cost per unit of each resource.
6. Multiply the cost per unit by the number of units (= the total cost of each resource).

7. Determine the cost of resources not measured per unit of services.
8. Add up all total resource costs to determine the total cost for the intervention for a specific period and based on an anticipated level of service.
9. Divide the total cost by the number of service units to determine the *expected* cost per service.

Following these steps will yield an estimate of the cost per unit of service and the total cost of the project.

Time Period

The time period for the CEA is important. It is recommended that at least 1 year of resource data be used to determine the cost of the intervention itself unless that year includes start-up time. In that case, a 3-month period for start-up should be omitted from data collection; the 1 year of data collection should begin after that.

Service Unit

The choice of the appropriate service unit(s) in advance of data collection is critical because it may drive the way in which data are collected. The cost-effectiveness calculation is predicated on a denominator of effectiveness; thus, the unit of this denominator must be chosen in advance.

Resource Inputs

The list of resources to be compiled may include the following:

Direct provider time for each type of service or activity, by provider type, and the salary and fringe benefit expenses
Supplies and materials for each type of service provided and their costs
The type of laboratory or other tests for each service provided and their costs
Lab controls and the like
Additional facilities, including rent and utilities, required for this intervention
Additional equipment
Maintenance of facilities and equipment
Additional support staff
Additional administrative staff
Other direct costs of providing services, such as courier services, cars and vans, uniforms or badges, additional insurance or permits, travel reimbursement, and computer database construction/maintenance

Not all interventions will require all of these resources. A table of unit costs should be constructed based on the final resource list.

In addition, information on the participants may need to be collected. Participation in prevention activities may be influenced by the time it takes and the extra expenses it entails. This is a form of personal or indirect costs, costs associated not with direct use of medical or health resources but with participation. Participant costs include:

Participant time—travel, wait, actual service
Participant expenses for travel, child care, and so forth

These costs can be determined by a survey of the participants as they enter the facility and by collecting information about arrival and service times.

Measuring Resources Consumed: Estimating Provider Time

There are five methods of estimating provider time: 1) direct observation, 2) random observation, 3) time diaries, 4) patient records, and 5) provider surveys. Because of the variable nature of service times, a large number of observations may have to be collected.

Regardless of the technique chosen, a histogram of service times should be produced. If service times are clustered about one number and look symmetrical, a sample of 30 may be sufficient as a basis for estimating mean service time. However, if the times are variable and asymmetrical, a larger sample (e.g., 100) will be needed. The Poisson distribution has a mean equal to the variance. This is the most conservative case and yields a sample size calculation of $n = 96$ for a 95% confidence level.

Direct Observation   Direct observation of services requires a trained observer who can determine how much time is spent providing a particular service. Data are collected on each component of the service. For example, to determine the time spent per breast cancer screening, the observer would measure the time spent on counseling, the mammogram, the radiologist's determination, and the clinical breast examination. If direct observation of the service were not possible, the time a woman enters and then leaves the examination or consultation room could be measured, and an estimate of the time spent on the various components could be made.

Random Observation   Random observation is a technique based on the proposition that the proportion of time spent on an activity is equal to the proportion of observations made of that activity during the workday. Each provider is assigned a code number. Before the beginning of the observation period, a schedule of observations is drawn up. A random number table is used to determine which provider is to be observed every t minutes. Time interval t is based on how far apart these providers are—that is, how long it will take to go from one to another. When a particular provider's code number comes up on the schedule, the observer goes to find him or her and notes what the provider is doing at that instant. This technique requires at least 5 observations of *each* type of service to obtain a confident proportion of time spent on each service.

To determine the time for each activity, the frequency of each activity is noted. Each activity frequency is a proportion of the total observations taken during the workday—that is, the proportion of time spent in that activity during the workday.

Time Diaries   Time diaries are a provider-based technique. Each provider is given a sheet to fill out during the workday that requires the notation of the time each activity begins. Because this is an intrusive method for the provider, it is important to study the types of activities the provider is usually engaged in and to construct a check-off list on the form for the provider. Personal time should always be included on the form. If the time diary option is used, the providers must be assured of the confidentiality of the diaries. The diaries should be collected in sealed envelopes and analyzed off site.

Patient Record   The patient record method requires that each patient be tracked through the intervention. The exact time the patient enters a new service and leaves an old service must be noted. This type of recording can yield information about patient flow and patient waiting time. Each patient carries a form on which each provider can note the time the patient begins and ends the service by that provider.

Survey of Providers A survey of providers is the least accurate method of data collection. Individuals do not generally remember how long they spend on a particular activity. Contemporaneous collection—that is, collection each day—may work, but asking a provider how much time he or she spent immunizing a child during a routine visit will not elicit an accurate response.

Determining Resource Costs per Unit

Calculation of Provider Time Costs The following equation is used to estimate the cost of service providers:

$$\text{Cost} = \text{each provider type} \times [\text{salary} + \text{fringe}] \times \text{duration of service}$$
$$\times \text{ number of services provided in time period} \qquad (\text{Eq. 10-1})$$

For example, suppose we wish to determine the cost per week for nutritionist services for a cholesterol screening program. The following calculations are needed:

$$\text{Nutritionist service cost per hour} = \frac{\text{salary/year} + \text{fringe}}{\text{number of weeks} \times \text{number of hours/week}}$$

$$= \frac{\$35,000/\text{year} + 15\% \text{ fringe}}{(52 \text{ weeks}) \times (37.5 \text{ hr/week})}$$

$$= \frac{\$49,250/\text{year}}{1,950 \text{ hr/year}}$$

$$= \$20.64/\text{hr}$$

Thus, the nutritionist service cost in a time period of 1 week is ($20.64 per hour) $\times$ (0.42 hours per service) $\times$ (118 services during the week of data collection) = $1,022.92 per week.

Calculation of Other Resource Costs per Unit of Service Materials, supplies, tests, and other resources are associated with particular services. Using expert opinion, a list of these is constructed. Costs should reflect those actually paid by the intervention program. This avoids confusion for other users of the data.

The following equation is used to calculate costs in a time period:

$$\text{Cost} = \text{materials and supplies per unit of service} \times \text{number of units} \quad (\text{Eq. 10-2})$$

To determine the cost per week for per-unit resources to provide a cholesterol screening service, the total cost per client must be calculated:

Materials handed out to clients:	$1.27
Finger-prick supplies:	$0.75
Laboratory test:	$3.50
Total cost per client for per-unit items:	$5.52

The total cost during a week of data collection is ($5.52 per client) $\times$ (118 service units) = $651.36.

Calculation of Resource Costs Not Expressed per Unit of Service

Resources such as facilities, equipment, administrative support, and other overhead costs may not be expressed per unit of service within a particular range of service volume. For example, an x-ray machine sits idle some proportion of every workday. The same equipment cost accrues whether 100 or 200 patients are screened per day. (Note that the x-ray film is a per-person expense.) Thus, the following calculations are suggested.

For facilities, it must be determined whether additional facilities will be acquired for the project. If so, the cost of this space plus utilities must be used. If not, it must be determined whether additional facility time is required. If so, the additional facility time for this intervention is calculated as a proportion of the total time the facility is in use. This proportion is multiplied times the total cost of space plus utilities. If neither additional facilities nor additional time is used, then the facility cost may be ignored.

For equipment, the total cost of the equipment plus maintenance, the useful lifetime of the equipment in years, and the proportion of that lifetime the equipment will be used by the project must be determined. The proportion of equipment lifetime should include the proportion of the useful life in years multiplied by the proportion of time in any year that the equipment is in use. The total cost is divided by the estimated lifetime of the equipment and then multiplied by the estimated proportion of that lifetime that the equipment is used in the intervention.

Administrative and staff support costs are calculated as a proportion of their time spent on this particular project. The salary plus fringe benefits for each person providing support is multiplied by the proportion of their time spent in support.

Other direct costs are collected through expert opinion. Only resources directly used by the project should be included. In an incremental (marginal) cost analysis, the fixed costs may be irrelevant because facilities and equipment are already in place, and no additional costs are associated with the intervention.

Thus, the fixed cost in a given time period includes:

Additional facility space × (cost of rent + utilities) for that space, or additional facility time × (cost of rent + utilities) for that proportion of time spent on the intervention
(Total cost of equipment and maintenance ÷ estimated lifetime of equipment) × proportion of that lifetime for this intervention
Proportion of administrators' time spent on intervention × (salary + fringe)
Proportion of support staff time spent on intervention × (salary + fringe)
Other direct costs of providing the intervention (e.g., travel, courier, outside agency charges)

Determining Facility Costs The facility costs (i.e., costs per year for rent and utilities) associated with the cholesterol screening project are $22,500 per year. Therefore, the cost per week is ($22,500 ÷ 52), or $432.69. The project will be associated with 36% of the time the organization spends on all programs. Therefore, the fixed facilities costs are ($432.69 × .36) = $155.77 per week for this project.

Determining Equipment Costs The computer costs associated with this cholesterol screening intervention are:

Cost of computer and software: $1,900
Lifetime of computer: 3 years
Salvage value of computer: $250

Thus, the computer cost is ($1,900 − $250) ÷ 3 years = $550 per year. A maintenance contract for the computer costs $45 per month.

The proportion of time the computer will be used for the project = 25%. Therefore, if:

$$\text{Computer costs per week} = (\$550/\text{year} \div 52 \text{ weeks/year})$$
$$+ (\$45/\text{month} \div 4.3 \text{ weeks/month})$$
$$= \$10.58/\text{week} + \$10.47/\text{week}$$
$$= \$21.05$$

the fixed computer costs are ($21.05 × 0.25) = $5.26 per week for this project.

Determining Travel Costs   The travel costs associated with this project are reimbursed at $0.28 per mile. Therefore, the cost of travel is (217 miles per week × $0.28 per mile) = $60.76 per week.

Determining Administrative and Support Costs   The annual administrative salary plus fringe benefits associated with this project is $52,375 + 23%; that for support staff is $12,500 + 15%. The proportion of time that administration and support staff are involved in this intervention is 5% and 13%, respectively. Therefore, if:

$$\text{Administration and support staff costs} = [(\$52,375 + 23\% \text{ fringe}) \times .05]$$
$$+ [(\$12,500 + 15\% \text{ fringe}) \times .13]$$
$$= \$3,221.06 + \$1,868.75$$
$$= \$5,089.81/\text{year}$$

the fixed administrative and support costs are $97.88 costs per week for this project.

Determining Participant Costs   To calculate participant costs, a participant survey should be conducted. Data collected should include how far participants travel and how much they spend to reach the facility (e.g., bus fare, tools, mileage, child care). The cost of participant time is based on average wages. Regional wage rates may be obtained from Bureau of Labor Statistics publications.

Participant time for travel, waiting, and service: 115 minutes (= 1.92 hours)
Average participant expenses: $2.59 per client

Therefore, if:

$$\text{Participant costs} = (1.92 \text{ hr}) \times \$10/\text{hr median wage}$$
$$= \$19.17 \text{ time cost/hr} + \$2.59 \text{ for expenses}$$
$$= \$21.76 \text{ per participant}$$

the total costs associated with participation are ($21.76 × 118 participants per week) = $2,567.29 per week for this project.

Determining Costs of Intervention Side Effects   Intervention side effects costs also must be determined or estimated. These can be adverse vaccine reactions, diagnostic workups on positive screening results, psychological support for persons told they are HIV positive, or presumed injuries associated with seat belt use. The scientific literature can be consulted for the costs associated with these events, or expert opinion can be used to determine the costs of dealing with these eventualities. Then, the probability of the occurrence of side effects must be determined. For example, if a vaccine reaction occurs in 1 out of every 10,000 persons vaccinated and the project vaccinates 5,000 children, the project can expect to incur one half (5,000 ÷ 10,000) of the cost of the vaccine reaction. These costs are added to the total costs of the intervention.

For example, suppose that for every 500 persons provided a cholesterol screening service, 1 person needs immediate medical attention. The time it takes the nutritionist to refer the patient is approximately 35 minutes, and the phone call costs are approximately $1.24. Therefore, the total cost of one referral is ($20.64 per hour × 0.58 hours) + $1.24, or $13.28. In 118 services per week, one would expect less than one side effect. If the expected number of persons with side effects is (118/500) = 0.236, the expected cost per week is ($13.28 × 0.236) = $3.13. This cost is a legitimate part of the cost of the project.

Total Costs for the Time Period

To calculate or estimate total costs, the manager must:

1. Sum the resource costs for the time period.
2. Sum the participant costs for the time period.
3. Sum any costs for side effects associated with the intervention.
4. Calculate the number of service units provided in the time period.
5. Calculate the total costs associated with the intervention [= (1) + (2) + (3)].
6. Divide total costs (5) by number of service units provided (4) to determine the cost per unit of intervention.

The total costs for the cholesterol screening project described above for 1 week can be calculated as follows:

Resources and costs per week

Provider time:	$1,022.92
Materials, supplies, lab:	$651.36
Facilities:	$155.77
Computer:	$5.26
Travel:	$60.76
Administration and support staff:	$97.88
Total project:	$1,993.95
Side effects:	$3.13
Participation:	$2,567.29
Total cost per week:	$4,564.37
Total cost per service:	($4,564.37 ÷ 118) = $38.68
Total cost of program per participant:	($1,997.08 ÷ 118) = $16.92

Direct Medical Costs of HREs Averted

To calculate or estimate the direct medical costs of HREs averted, the manager must:

1. List the HREs to be averted.
2. Determine the rate of occurrence per year in a "treated" compared to an "untreated" community. For example, the rate of severe injury may be 2.3 per 1,000 with the intervention but 4.2 per 1,000 without. Thus, the difference is 1.9 per 1,000—these are the expected number of HREs averted in 1,000 people participating in the intervention (i.e., the rate of HREs averted).

3. Multiply the rate of HREs averted by the number of persons participating in the project or intervention. That is, if 1,500 individuals participated, then one would expect $[(1.9 \div 1,000) \times 1,500] = 2.85$ HREs averted.
4. Consult the scientific literature or obtain expert opinion on the health care costs associated with treating each HRE.
5. Multiply the expected number of HREs averted by the costs associated with each HRE to obtain the direct medical costs averted through the project.

For example, the medical care costs associated with cholesterol-related diseases that could be averted through intervention can be calculated as follows:

Hypothetical costs per case:	$55,000
Rate of cholesterol-related disease:	1 in 1,000
Rate of disease among participants:	0.75 in 1,000
HREs averted in 10,000 persons screened:	$(1 - 0.75) = 0.25$ in 1,000, or 2.5 in 10,000
Medical costs of HREs averted:	($55,000 \times 2.5) = $137,500

Cost-Effectiveness Ratio of an Intervention

The cost-effectiveness (CE) ratio of an intervention is defined as

$$CE = \text{net costs} \div \text{benefits} \qquad \text{(Eq. 10-3)}$$

where

Net costs = (intervention costs + side effects costs) − direct medical care costs saved

and benefits are the effectiveness measure chosen, such as the specific HRE averted. Some managers present the net costs calculation as the measure of cost-effectiveness. Most analyses, however, go one step further and calculate the net costs per *unit* of effect. For example, the cholesterol screening intervention described above calculated a cost of $38.68 per screen. For 10,000 participants, the net cost is:

$$\text{Net cost} = \$386,800 - \$137,500$$

$$= \$137,113$$

If participant costs are *not* considered in this analysis:

$$\text{Net cost} = \$169,200 - \$137,500$$

$$= \$31,700$$

The CE ratio is ($137,113/2.5 cases averted) = $54,845 per case.

Timing of Costs and Benefits

This entire discussion presumes that the costs of the intervention and the benefits from the intervention occur in the same year. If this is not the case, discounting must be used to compare dollars spent in one period with dollars saved in future periods. For example, a dollar cost this year is of different value than a dollar saved in 20 years from now. (See Chapter 5 for a review.)

EXERCISES

Use the following information to do a cost-effectiveness analysis of a work site screening program:

Serum cholesterol is a major predictor of coronary heart disease. As the level of serum cholesterol increases, the risk of heart disease increases, particularly for those individuals with values over 200 mg of cholesterol per deciliter of blood.

Coronary heart disease (CHD) treatment is expensive. For example, assume that a CHD death costs $19,321 and a nonfatal case of CHD costs $58,025. For purposes of this analysis, assume that the expected lifetime benefits from coronary heart disease averted for persons less than 60 years old who lower their serum cholesterol by 5% are as follows:

Initial cholesterol level (mg/dl)	Present value of dollars saved
260	72–93
300	90–120
340	118–161

These figures represent the *present value* of health care dollars saved as a result of cases of CHD averted in the population lowering their cholesterol by 5%. Most individuals do not suffer from CHD, so the average cost saved over many people is quite low. These lifetime costs can be compared to the costs of a cholesterol-lowering intervention.

One way of reducing the costs of prevention interventions is to provide an intervention at the work site. This consists of two parts: 1) an initial screening for all participants and 2) a special intervention for those whose cholesterol is found to be 200 mg/dl or greater. The data in Table 10.1 represent the costs for an initial

Table 10-1.   Cholesterol intervention program: initial screening costs

	Time (in hours)	Numbers	Expense (in dollars)
Preparation time for screening	12.4		
Contact work site	7.3		
Collect equipment and supplies	1.8		
Arrange staff	2.1		
Train staff	1.2		
Travel time to site	1.3		
Time at site for screening	6.4		
Follow-up time of screening	7.8		
Mailings	2.3		
Telephone	1.5		
Checking forms	4.0		
Average number of screenees, per site		51	
Average number of hospital providers, per site		9.3	
Average provider salary plus fringe			25,000
Miles to site, from hospital		23	
Supplies, per participant			$3.70
Mail and phone charges, per participant			$0.19

screening. Costs for the special intervention were calculated to be an additional $27.55 per participant. This includes both fixed and variable costs at the site.

Effects on serum cholesterol, obtained from the baseline and 12-month re-screening of all participants whose initial values were 200 mg/dl or greater, were:

Initial intervention only	1.9% reduction
Initial plus special intervention	5.3% reduction

Use the worksheet shown in Table 10-2 to answer the following questions.

10-1. How much did it cost, per person screened, for the initial cholesterol testing? Remember that each provider on site incurs costs to travel from the health department to the site and back.

10-2. How much did it cost per person who participated in the special intervention as well as the initial screening?

10-3. What is the cost per percentage reduction in cholesterol for the initial screening only and for the initial plus special screening?

10-4. What is the marginal cost per percentage additional reduction in cholesterol attributable to the special intervention?

10-5. How does this compare to the lifetime coronary heart disease cost savings from reducing serum cholesterol?

Table 10-2. Worksheet for cost of activities per service

	Staff person	Cost per unit (in dollars)	Number of units	Cost (in dollars)
Site preparation time				
Contact work site	Clerk	_____	7.3 hr	_____
Collect equipment and supplies	Nutritionist	_____	1.8 hr	_____
Arrange staff	Nutritionist	_____	2.1 hr	_____
Train staff	Nurse	_____	1.2 hr	_____
Travel time to/from site	Nutritionist	_____	8 × 1.3 hr	_____
Time at site for screening	Nutritionist	_____	8 × 6.4 hr	_____
Follow-up time				
Mailing	Clerk	_____	2.3 hr	_____
Phone	Nutritionist	_____	1.5 hr	_____
Check forms	Nurse	_____	4 hr	_____
Materials and supplies				
Preparation		_____	_____	_____
At site		_____	51	_____
Follow-up		_____	51	_____
Travel reimbursement		_____	_____	_____
Postage		_____	_____	_____
Phone		_____	_____	_____

11

Program Evaluation Review Technique (PERT)

Chapter Objectives

1. To be able to use PERT to plan and manage project activities
2. To be able to construct a PERT network diagram

Key Terms and Concepts

Crash time
Critical path
Gantt charts
PERT COST
Project versus program
Slack

Time–cost relationship
Total system performance
   responsibility
Variance analysis
Work breakdown structure

This chapter presents program evaluation and review technique (PERT) as a methodology and demonstrates its application as a planning, scheduling, and control system to use with large-scale projects. PERT was developed to support complex research and development projects. It was used to plan and guide the development of NASA activities to develop, build, and test the systems used to begin travel into space. Designed as a management support system, PERT provides the manager with a protocol to identify and sequence the many activities that make up a complex project. It enables the manager to change the sequence of required activities as needed, either to finish the project by a specific date or to adjust to changing circumstances once the project has begun. It is a micro project management activity in that it focuses attention on the myriad of micro activities that make up a project.

    Many variations of this method exist. An almost identical approach is called the critical path method (CPM). This presentation is restricted to single-time-estimate PERT. Using PERT terminology, the single time estimate is the project manager's "most probable time." It is the time the project manager believes is highly likely to be needed to complete the activity. Other versions of PERT use multiple time estimates by adding estimates for the optimistic or ideal time and the pessimistic or worst-case time. By using an equation that weights the optimistic, pessimistic, and most probable time estimates, multiple-time-estimate PERT also yields a pooled time estimate.

PROJECT MANAGEMENT

A project is an activity done once. Building a new nursing home or modernizing a part of an existing hospital are examples of projects. Installing a new machine in a laboratory is a project. Developing a new capability, such as installing labor and delivery rooms in a hospital, also is a project. Installing a new computer system or new computer capability to process patient accounts is a project. A project is a one-time activity intended to change the capability of the organization.

The antonym of a project is a program. A program is a repetitive activity. Developing and installing a system for mothers to birth in the same hospital room that they will use for the duration of their maternity stay is a project. Using this capability over and over again for many mothers, however, is a program. Issuing patient bills using the new capability in the revised computer system is a program. Doing surgery in the newly renovated same-day surgical suite is a program.

A project has defining attributes. It seeks to achieve a desired capability or capacity (e.g., using a computer system to process a patient account). When that capability is achieved, by definition the project is completed. Therefore, a project has a formal start and end. Projects do not continue past when the desired capability has been achieved.

Projects evolve through many phases. Any project must move through at least three phases of development. During the initial or concept phase, different ways to achieve the desired capabilities are considered and evaluated. Broadly defined project options are identified. Usually one or two of these conceptual options are taken into the next project phase. The concept stage is characterized by the gathering of information and examining different ways to achieve the capability. Some projects spend minutes in this phase, whereas others spend years.

During the second or definition phase, managers define exactly what resources are needed in order to achieve the desired capabilities associated with the specific project option. During this phase, the project is defined in as much detail as possible. Usually a business plan or similar type of report is developed. At the completion of this phase, some type of organizational approval is sought to continue the project into its next phase. This approval may be based on a detailed economic and financial analysis. In health care, some projects also must secure regulatory approval, such as approval granted in the form of a Certificate of Need. If approvals are not received to move the project into the next phase, managers are expected to repeat the definition phase using different parameters or to return to the concept phase, or they are told that the organization no longer desires the capability.

During the third or implementation phase of project management (the last phase of any project), resources and capabilities are installed in the organization in keeping with the intent of the overall project. It is during this phase that a project may involve new construction, buying new equipment, training staff, hiring new staff, revising job descriptions, and the host of other activities needed to implement or install the desired capability. PERT is used in all phases of a project.

Projects typically involve altering existing capabilities as well as installing or implementing new capabilities. For example, expanding the capacity of a nursing home by 20% will require more rooms, beds, and staff to administer to the needs of additional residents. Such a project, however, also may require altering the nursing home's existing capacity to park cars (e.g., more visitors and staff), to process laundry (e.g., increased amount), to feed patients and staff (e.g., more meals), and to store heating oil.

Project managers have total system (or subsystem) performance responsibility (TSPR). TSPR characterizes all project management activities. Project managers are expected to install the "total package" of capabilities necessary to complete the project. Installing a new computer system that exceeds the capability of existing electrical circuits violates TSPR. Installing the equipment to do laser surgery without training the operating room staff to use the equipment violates TSPR. Installing new labor and delivery capabilities without informing the public violates TSPR. Having total system performance responsibility means defining the project to include all the capabilities needed to complete it.

Some projects are complex, involving many actions and steps, significant resources, and many people. However, the definition of "complex" is situational: What may be complex to one organization may not be to another. Complex can also refer to the duration of a project. A project that will require 2 years to complete may be complex; a project that takes 1 day may not be considered complex.

Formal project management methods, such as PERT, are reserved for complex projects. Typically, complex projects have significant financial implications created by the expenses associated with installing the new capability as well as the expense (e.g., lost revenue) associated with any delay in achieving the capability. Using PERT to plan a news conference or meet the deadline to submit a Certificate of Need application may be justified by the financial implications associated with being late or unprepared.

Complex projects also involve many actions and steps that must be accomplished by many people in a coordinated and efficient fashion. PERT assists managers to identify and sequence all the activities that must be completed in order to finish the project.

Generally, projects involve many activities performed in a predetermined sequence. Some activities must occur before other activities can or should occur. For example, new electrical service may need to be installed in a surgical suite before the actual laser surgery equipment is installed so that the technicians can connect the laser equipment to an appropriate power source. Existing equipment in a laboratory may need to be moved before the new equipment can be added. In any project, the order or sequence of activities is important. Similarly, some sequences are more efficient than others.

The sequencing of activities is also very important in other ways. For a project that requires a significant amount of time to complete, it may be inappropriate to train staff as an initial step. Training needs may change over the course of the project. Some trained staff may leave before the project comes on line. Staff may forget their training given the long gap between training and when they can use the newly acquired skill. Similarly, it would be inappropriate to hire new staff for an expanded nursing home months before the staff were actually needed.

When most managers think of a project, they think of the many steps or activities that will need to be completed in order to finish the project. For a project to expand a nursing home by 20%, an initial list of some of the needed activities or steps could include:

1. Get Certificate of Need (CON) approval.
2. Get zoning approval.
3. Hire an architect and approve plans.
4. Get the necessary construction financing.
5. Hire a construction company.
6. Build the expansion.
7. Advertise for staff.
8. Interview staff.
9. Select and train staff.
10. Revise existing insurance policies.
11. Change the operating budget to reflect the project.
12. Determine the necessary new equipment, issues bids, and select the equipment.
13. Get the equipment delivered, unpack it, and set it up. Test it. Secure replacements for any defective equipment.

When managers first define the activities or steps necessary to implement the required project capabilities, their lists imply a sequential order. Project activities are usually listed in an implied order. For example, the CON is obtained before the construction financing is arranged. Although some activities must be accomplished in a sequential order, other activities can be accomplished in parallel order. Accomplishing activities in parallel can shorten the total time between when a project is begun and when it is completed. By authorizing and managing activities to proceed in parallel, the manager can make projects more efficient as well as more difficult to manage and coordinate. PERT facilitates managing parallel activities in a project, especially when the sequence or order of activities influences the overall time a project will take.

WORK BREAKDOWN STRUCTURE

Before using PERT, any complex project must first be broken down into its component parts. Each piece of the project must be identified. A work breakdown structure (WBS) is used to divide the project into appropriate and logical components and then subdivide each component of the project into even more specific parts.

The WBS is a comprehensive listing of the components of the project. Some managers use a numbering system to ensure that macro as well as micro components of the project are identified and ordered. For example, the project to increase the capacity of a nursing home by 20% could be broken down into the following pieces:

    1.0 Regulatory approvals
        1.1 Certificate of Need
        1.2 Zoning
        1.3 Fire department
        1.4 Highway department
        1.5 Building inspection
        1.6 Certificate of Occupancy

2.0 Physical addition
   2.1 Design
      2.1.1 Building design—new space
         2.1.1.1 Resident rooms and baths
         2.1.1.2 Hallways and storage
         2.1.1.3 Work stations
         2.1.1.4 Common areas
         2.1.1.5 Other new space
      2.1.2 Changes to existing mechanical systems
         2.1.2.1 Heat
         2.1.2.2 Fire alarm
         2.1.2.3 Electrical
         2.1.2.4 Telephone
         2.1.2.5 Water
         2.1.2.6 Air
         2.1.2.7 Other mechanical systems
   2.2 Build
3.0 Staff
   3.1 Professional staff
      3.1.1 Registered nurses
      3.1.2 Licensed practical nurses
      3.1.3 Social workers
      3.1.4 Therapists
   3.2 Nonprofessional staff
   3.3 Consultants

This example merely illustrates the concept of a WBS; it is not a comprehensive WBS for this specific project.

Project managers, with input from many sources, create a WBS to define the project in terms of its scope and detail. A comprehensive WBS ensures a comprehensive project. To create a comprehensive WBS, project managers ask what is necessary to achieve the desired project capability, categorize their answers into logical big packages (e.g., regulatory approvals, building design, staff, financing), and then continue to define subcomponents of each large package until they think that the project has been adequately defined from the perspective of scope as well as detail.

How much detail to include in the WBS is a product of managerial judgment. The WBS must be sufficiently comprehensive to include all necessary components and must contain sufficient detail to guide the continued definition, implementation, and management of the project. A WBS lists *all* the pieces of the project.

Prior to the advent of PERT and similar methods in the 1960s, project managers used such a list of project activities to schedule activities. Gantt charts, for example, list all the activities associated with a project (i.e., WBS) on the vertical axis of a chart and use lines across a horizontal time axis to indicate when a specific activity is to begin and end. Figure 11-1 is one simplified form of a Gantt chart.

Gantt charts provide the manager with a list of project activities and the estimated duration of each activity. These charts also provide the estimated start date as well as the estimated completion date for each activity. From a project management perspective, however, these charts have one serious flaw—they do not repre-

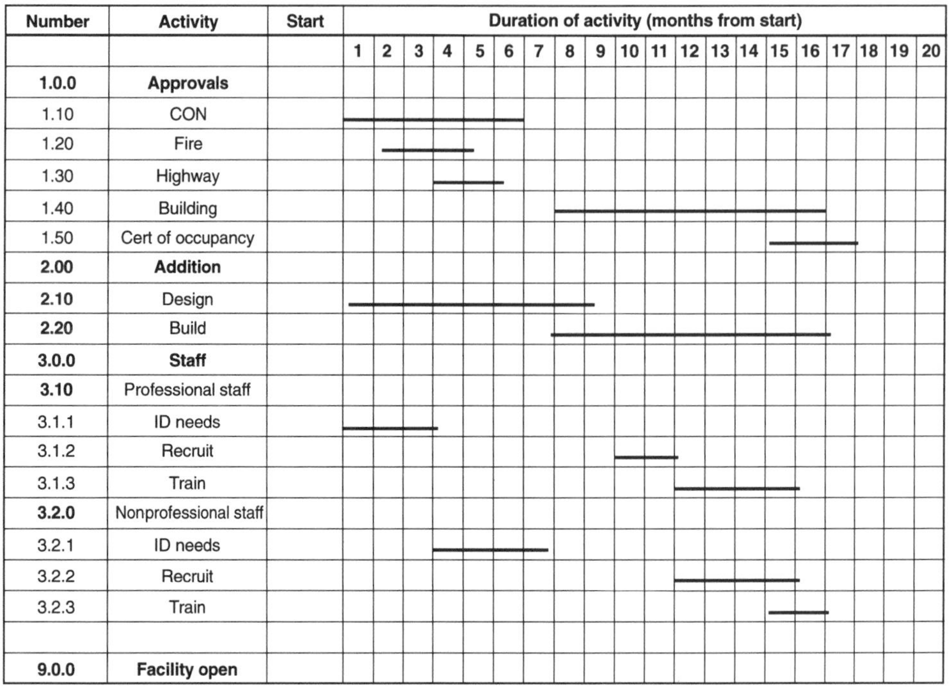

Number	Activity	Start	Duration of activity (months from start)																			
			1	2	3	4	5	6	7	8	9	10	11	12	13	14	15	16	17	18	19	20
1.0.0	**Approvals**																						
1.10	CON		▬	▬	▬																		
1.20	Fire			▬	▬	▬																	
1.30	Highway				▬	▬																	
1.40	Building										▬	▬	▬	▬	▬	▬	▬	▬					
1.50	Cert of occupancy																		▬	▬			
2.00	**Addition**																						
2.10	Design			▬	▬	▬	▬	▬	▬														
2.20	Build									▬	▬	▬	▬	▬	▬	▬	▬	▬					
3.0.0	**Staff**																						
3.10	Professional staff																						
3.1.1	ID needs		▬	▬																			
3.1.2	Recruit										▬	▬											
3.1.3	Train													▬	▬	▬							
3.2.0	Nonprofessional staff																						
3.2.1	ID needs					▬	▬	▬															
3.2.2	Recruit													▬	▬	▬							
3.2.3	Train																▬	▬					
9.0.0	**Facility open**																						

Figure 11-1.   Example of a Gantt chart.

sent the relationships between and among activities. Although Gantt charts do indicate which activities *can* precede other activities, they fail to indicate—although they do imply—which activities *must* proceed other activities. PERT was invented to overcome this significant flaw.

However, Gantt charts remain an effective project planning and control approach for simple, in contrast to complex, projects. These charts provide the manager with appropriate scheduling information and a yardstick to use to compare actual experience with planned actions.

PROGRAM EVALUATION REVIEW TECHNIQUE

Although misnamed "program" evaluation review technique, PERT is a formal method to define projects and support project management. Specifically, it helps project managers determine:

1. When the project will be completed
2. What the scheduled start and completion dates for each specific activity included in the project will be
3. What activities are "critical" and must be completed exactly as scheduled in order to keep the project on schedule (This feature of PERT makes PERT a much more robust project planning and control system than Gantt charts.)
4. How long "noncritical activities" can be postponed before they cause a delay in the total project

Based on timing and the specific activity, PERT segregates all activities into critical activities and noncritical activities. By definition, if the completion date of a critical activity is delayed, the date for the completion of the overall project will be delayed. If the completion date of a critical activity is earlier than estimated, the date for the completion of the overall project may be earlier than originally planned. Noncritical activities, also by definition, do not have an impact on the scheduled completion date of the overall project. As projects evolve and circumstances change, noncritical activities can become critical activities and vice versa.

Developing the Network

When completed, PERT will be a graphical network that shows the relationships between project activities and the time estimated for individual activities as well as for the total project.

Step 1: Using the WBS, all project activities are listed.

Each activity should be expressed using an action verb, such as "*secure* a Certificate of Need," "*build* the new addition," and "*train* new staff." The list must be comprehensive and indicate all the activities needed to complete the project. In Table 11-1, each area of project activity has been modified by the addition of an action verb. Using this approach, the WBS becomes an activity list—a "to do" list—that indicates all the activities that must be completed in order to complete the project.

Step 2: The immediate predecessor of each activity is indicated.

This step begins to identify the essential sequence of activities included in the project. Each activity must be considered separately to determine which individual activity or activities *must* occur immediately before it. The immediate predecessors of each activity are then listed (see Table 11-2). The list of immediate predecessor activities must be based on the essential sequence of activities in the project. For example, it is *essential* that the organization hire staff (E) before it trains staff (F).

Table 11-1. Activity list for project of opening a new clinic

Office
Identify site and lease
Make modifications
Install equipment
Acquire supplies
Staff
Hire staff
Train staff

Table 11-2. Activity list with predecessors

Activity list	Immediate predecessor
A. Identify site and lease	—
B. Make modifications	A
C. Install equipment	B
D. Acquire supplies	A, C
E. Hire staff	A
F. Train staff	E, D

Step 3: The time it will take to complete each activity is estimated.

Estimates of the time each activity will take (see Table 11-3) use a common unit of time, such as days, weeks, or years. The estimate should be a reasonable estimate, not based on ideal or pessimistic conditions or events.

Step 4: A network diagram, including the time estimate, is drawn.

PERT requires the use of specific symbols. A circle indicates the completion of a predecessor activity and the beginning of the next activity. A circle is referred to as an "event," which is a specific moment in time. The first event (Start) starts the project, and the last event (End) finishes the project.

Networks start at the left and end at the right of the diagram. Lines are used to indicate relationships among activities. Figure 11-2 illustrates the basic components of a network diagram. Figure 11-3 is the completed network diagram for the activity list shown in Table 11-3.

Step 5: The critical path determined.

The total time from start to end for each pathway through the network is calculated. The critical path is the path through the network that requires the most time. For our example, the critical path is the path represented by activities A, B, C, D, and F. On this path, the total minimum time is 11 weeks. Two other paths exist. For the path represented by activities A, E, and F, the total minimum time is 7 weeks. For the path represented by actiities A, D, and F, the total minimum time is 6 weeks.

As can be seen in Figure 11–3, this project can be completed in a minimum of 11 weeks. According to the information presented, the project cannot be done in less than 11 weeks. If any of the activities on the critical path takes longer than the time estimates as presented, the overall date for the completion of the project will be later than 11 weeks.

Given the sequence of activities included in a PERT network, each activity has an earliest start date—the earliest the activity can start after the project has begun. For example, activity B has an earliest start of 3 weeks; it can only start after activity A, estimated to take 3 weeks, has been completed. The latest start date is the latest time the activity can be begun without jeopardizing the total time estimated for the project. For example, activity E could begin as late as the seventh week without jeopardizing the 11 weeks estimated for the entire project. If activity E started in the seventh week, and took 3 weeks to be completed, it would still leave the 1 week necessary to complete activity F and complete the overall project in 11 weeks.

Slack is the amount an activity can increase in duration without changing the estimated completion date of the overall project. Along the critical path in the net-

Table 11-3. Activity list with predecessor activities and time estimates

Activity	Immediate predecessor	Time estimate (weeks)
A. Identify site and lease	—	3
B. Make modifications	A	3
C. Install equipment	B	2
D. Acquire supplies	A, C	2
E. Hire staff	A	3
F. Train staff	E, D	1

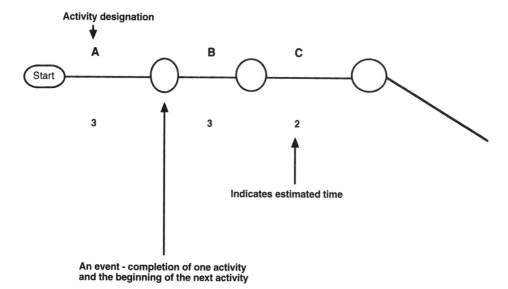

Figure 11-2. Basic components of a PERT network diagram.

work, by definition, slack equals zero. Therefore, slack is the amount of time an activity can increase in duration or be delayed without influencing the critical path.

Slack is calculated by subtracting the earliest start date from the latest start date for each activity. This calculation must equal zero or be a positive number. When slack equals zero, the activity is on the critical path. When slack is greater than zero, the activity is not on the critical path. Table 11-4 reports the slack calculations for our example.

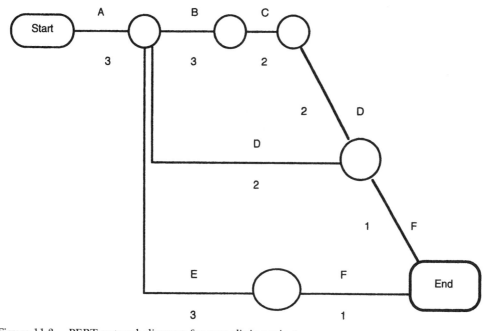

Figure 11-3. PERT network diagram for new clinic project.

Table 11-4.   Calculation of slack (weeks)

Activity	Earliest start date (E)	Latest start date (L)	Slack (L − E)	Critial path?
A	0	0	0	Yes
B	3	3	0	Yes
C	6	6	0	Yes
D	8	8	0	Yes
E	3	7	4	No
F	10	10	0	Yes

PERT establishes the sequential schedule of activities that comprise the overall project. By sequencing the activities in an appropriate order and adding time estimates, the overall time necessary to complete the project can be estimated. Equally important is the identification of those specific activities that must be monitored so as to be completed on time in order to complete the overall project on schedule—activities on the critical path.

Managing with a PERT Network

Once developed as a project planning technique, PERT provides the manager with the ability to evaluate and control the project. In projects with many activities and paths, PERT focuses the attention of the manager on those activities on the critical path. While all activities are important and essential for the completion of the project, PERT indicates those special or critical activities that the manager must monitor in order to complete the project within the original time estimate. If the manager can shorten the time associated with these critical activities, the completion date of the project can be shortened.

Once a project is begun, managers monitor all activities by comparing the estimated time for each activity with the actual time taken to complete an activity. The difference between the time estimated and the actual time is a variance. When the actual time is less than the original time estimate, a positive variance is recorded. When the actual time is more than the original time estimate, a negative variance is recorded.

Negative variances on the critical path will, by definition, delay the overall project. A delay is referred to as a slip or slippage. Managers must evaluate any negative variance to determine if it is associated with a critical path or noncritical path activity. If so, the overall completion date of the project will be affected, as will the date subsequent activities will begin. If the negative variance is not a slippage on the critical path, then the manager must determine the impact of the activity slippage. It is important to remember that extreme slippage of an activity that is not on the critical path can shift the critical path in the network.

Some managers use "rolling wave" PERT once a complex project has been begun. Rolling wave PERT is most frequently used with projects that involve long time durations. Under this approach, managers continue to update and change the original network based on project experience and new information. They add more detail in the near future than originally included in the network. To ensure appropriate project management, they break macro activities in the near future into many micro activities and monitor adherence to the revised detailed schedule of activities. They do this as a "rolling wave" throughout the project and within the

PERT network, keeping micro plans to use in the near future, until the project is completed.

PERT networks and charts, however, can be cumbersome. For large projects, the charts can fill walls. Therefore, some managers prepare PERT networks in levels, using a master network to show large activities and individual charts to plan and control smaller or subactivities. Some managers organize their charts based on the categories used in the WBS. Often activities are organized by scope. "Higher level" activities are those activities expressed in larger time durations. "Lower level" activities show the detail associated with one or a few higher level activities.

As an evaluation and control system, PERT provides the manager with the ability to monitor project activity and assess the impact of project accomplishments. It facilitates timely replanning of subsequent activities and provides the manager with the dual ability to monitor the micro as well as macro aspects of the project.

Time and Cost Trade-Off

Typically, but not always, a project can be shortened by adding more resources. Embedded in every time estimate is an implicit resource statement. For example, if modifying a clinic (i.e., activity B) is estimated to take 3 weeks, this could imply that the modification will take 3 weeks with a crew of four working 8 hours per weekday.

$$4 \text{ workers} \times 8 \text{ hours/day} = 32 \text{ worker hours/day}$$
$$32 \text{ worker hours/day} \times 15 \text{ workdays} = 480 \text{ worker hours}$$

At $14.00 per hour, this would equal $6,720 for worker time.

Of course, there are alternative ways to schedule 480 worker hours:

If two workers were scheduled to work the 480 hours, the activity could be completed in 30 workdays or 6 weeks (480 hours per 2 workers $\times$ 8 hours per day = 30 days).

If six workers were scheduled to work the 480 hours, the activity could be completed in 10 days or 2 weeks (480 hours per 6 workers $\times$ 8 hours per day = 10 days).

If four workers were used and required to work 12, in contrast to 8, hours per day, the activity also could be completed in 10 days or 2 weeks.

Requiring workers to work 12 hours per day, in contrast to 8 hours per day, however, would change the expenses related to this activity. Mandatory overtime would need to be paid, usually at a pay rate 50% higher than the base hourly rate. In this case, the trade-off between time and cost is very evident. As originally scheduled, using four workers, 8 hours per day for 480 hours, the worker cost was estimated to be $6,720. Using four workers 12 hours per day for 480 hours, given time-and-one-half overtime pay, this cost increases by $3,360 to a total of $10,080.

The project manager understands the trade-off between project time and project cost and knows that there are many strategies available to complete specific project activities. Some of these options take more or less time than the time chosen for project planning, and some options involve higher costs. The project manager also knows the limits of this type of thinking. For example, if 480 worker hours are needed to complete the activity, could this activity be completed in 1 hour if 480 individual workers worked side by side for 1 hour each? Given the sequential nature of tasks required to complete most activities, as well as the physical space needed to accommodate 480 workers, the answer is undoubtedly no.

Compressing time estimates by adding resources, such as more workers or more expensive workers, or both, or more work hours, has a boundary. If cost concerns are not a factor, a project can be rescheduled using crash time, the quickest time that an activity can be completed. Crash time activities and projects are usually very expensive.

Conversely, to lower project and activity costs, activities and projects can sometimes be lengthened. This will delay the project completion. Even though such an action may have a system cost impact (e.g., the cost impact of a delayed opening of a new clinic on patients), it may lower the cost of the project. Delay may be caused by using fewer workers or less skilled workers who are paid less but require more time to complete the project. Delay may mean using manual labor to accomplish a task even though the task could be done quicker, although more expensively, if the project used a specific piece of equipment.

The central point is to acknowledge the fundamental relationship between time and cost in project management. Within boundaries, the project manager is able to trade off one for another. Costs can usually be lowered by slowing the project. Increasing the speed of the project usually requires added costs.

OTHER PERT METHODS

Multiple-Time-Estimate PERT

Multiple-time-estimate PERT provides the project manager with a probabilistic range of estimates of the time required to complete individual project activities and the overall project. Using multiple-time-estimate PERT, the manager can trade off different levels of probability (i.e., the probability of completing an activity in a specified amount of time), which is sometimes referred to as a time-probability trade-off. Because multiple-time-estimate PERT utilizes optimistic, pessimistic, and most probable time estimates, it emphasizes the implicit probabilities associated with using single time estimates. Interestingly, given the probabilistic nature of the time estimates used in PERT, other versions of PERT incorporate formal methods for the project manager to assess and trade off time, cost, and the probability of completion or risk of success or failure. Although some managers continue to use multiple-time-estimate PERT, the complexity associated with it seems beyond the needs of most projects.

PERT COST

PERT COST was developed as a companion to PERT. It adds the ability to assess and trade-off time and cost at the activity level. It requires each activity to have three costs estimates, an estimate associated with the optimistic time, pessimistic time, and most probable time. Other versions use boundary limits (e.g., crash time cost estimates) as a basis for these multiple cost estimates. PERT COST is a complex system best used in very specific settings. Project managers of major construction and research and development projects use PERT COST to plan, evaluate, and control project activity. By comparing the planned value of work scheduled with the planned value of work accomplished, the project manager is able to extend his or her ability to use variance analysis to manage project costs as well as project times. Computer programs exist to develop PERT networks and support a project manager's use of multiple-time-estimate PERT and PERT COST. The application of these more advanced versions of PERT usually is restricted to large-scale, highly complex projects.

CONCLUSION

Overall, PERT remains the premier method to define, plan, schedule, and control a project. It provides the manager with the ability to consider alternative plans and to change plans once the project has begun. As a formal method, PERT has a proven history of providing the project manager with project status information and alternatives.

Groups of managers and experts are typically used to construct the WBS and do PERT. The PERT network is the outcome of the combined insight of many. PERT also provides the ability to do "What if. . . .?" analysis—for example, what if the project had to be completed in 8 weeks instead of 12; how could this be done? "What ifs" are common questions that project managers consider.

Initially, PERT forces comprehensive project planning. As circumstances change or develop, the project may need to be replanned to accomplish it differently. During the concept and definition phase of a project, project managers construct and consider many different project approaches using PERT as a basis for project planning. Once begun, PERT forces project managers to replan specific activities as needed within the context of the entire project and provides a basis to use variance analysis. In essence, PERT provides project managers with many capabilities and forces them to address many questions and issues.

The health services manager can use single-time-estimate PERT in many situations. The version described in this chapter can be used to determine the micro plan for a project, and then provide a system to manage (e.g., evaluate and control) the project once the project has been begun. PERT stresses the interrelationship between project activities and the impact activities on the critical path have on the overall project.

EXERCISES

11-1.   Using the information in Table 11-5, construct a PERT network and answer each of the following questions:

a.   What is the expected project completion date?
b.   What is the scheduled start and completion date for each activity?
c.   Which activities are on the critical path?
d.   How long can noncritical path activities be delayed without jeopardizing the overall completion date for this project?

Table 11-5. Information for Exercise 11-1

Project: To convert a 20-bed unit in a nursing home to accommodate patients with infectious disease.

Activity	Immediate predecessor	Time estimate (weeks)
A. Secure state approval	—	4
B. Identify 20-bed unit to be used	A	1
C. Move residents to other part of nursing home	B	1
D. Clean existing space	C	2
E. Develop architectural plans	A	9
F. Install new heating and ventilation system	E	4
G. Install security systems	E	2
H. Move walls; renovate as necessary	F	4
I. Identify new equipment	A	1
J. Order new equipment	I	1
K. Unpack and inspect new equipment	J	1
L. Install new equipment	K, H	3
M. Reassign staff to new unit	A	1
N. Identify need for new staff	M	1
O. Advertise for new staff	N	3
P. Interview for new staff	O	2
Q. Select new staff	P	3
T. Train staff	S, M, P	1
S. Develop clinical care protocols	M	1
U. Modify Quality Assurance Plan	S	2
V. Coordinate with hospital discharge planners	U	4

11-2. Assess the impact of the following changes (in bold type) to the information provided in Exercise 11–1. Individually, what is the impact if:

Activity	Predecessor	Time estimate		
a.	O	Advertise for new staff	N	**4**
b.	P	Interview for new staff	O	**6**
c.	Q	Select new staff	P	**1**
d.	T	Train staff	S, M, **Q**	1

Collectively, what is the impact of these changes?

11-3. As project manager for the example included in Exercise 11-1 what would you recommend doing to preserve the original project completion date even though activity A will take 8 weeks, not the 4 weeks originally estimated? Provide a detailed plan.

11-4. Develop a WBS and PERT network with no more than 20 activities for each of the following projects.

  a. To acquire a car.

  b. To screen 1,000 school-age children for high blood pressure and report results to the children's physicians.

12

Financial Evaluation of Projects

Chapter Objectives

1. To develop skills in evaluating the financial consequences of alternative projects
2. To understand what comprises a cash flow
3. To be able to compute discounted cash flow and to use three tools to evaluate the financial impact of projects (i.e., net present value, internal rate of return, and adjusted rate of return)

Key Terms and Concepts

Annuity

Cash flow

Cost of capital

Discounted cash flow

Internal rate of return

Net present value

Risk

The concept of the time value of money, including the tools of compounding and discounting, was introduced in Chapter 5. For a health services manager, the most important use of these tools is in evaluating potential organizational projects. This chapter provides examples of how to apply these tools in organizational decision making.

Any project must compete for organizational approval and the capital or funding associated with approval. Capital is limited and must be allocated to meet the many goals and objectives faced by the contemporary health care organization. New projects must be designed to be competitive within this context of organizational priorities and realities.

Every project must compete for capital with existing projects, other new projects, and alternative uses of capital, such as capital investment opportunities (e.g., certificates of deposit [CDs], passbook accounts). If an existing project must be stopped in order to furnish the capital needed for a new project, the termination expenses associated with stopping the first project must be added as an expense associated with the new project. Generally, however, new projects compete against other new projects and alternative capital uses, not existing projects.

In well-managed health care organizations, a project never competes only against itself for organizational approval. When organizations consider a new project, it is not enough to know how much a project will cost and how much it can be expected to earn. The manager must also compare a given project with other project alternatives and alternative uses of capital. Well-managed health care organizations evaluate projects based on the implications and alternatives associated with each project and the capital needed to support it.

Most situations requiring managers to evaluate the attractiveness of a potential project or investment opportunity involve understanding and building on the concept of the time value of money. An investment almost always requires an immediate outflow of cash, known as the initial investment, or present value. In future years, a series of cash flows will be required to support the project, and revenues will accrue as a result of the investment. By convention, all cash flows—both negative and positive—are determined at the end of a defined time period, such as 1 month or 1 year. The sum of these cash flows is known as the future value. Cash flows may involve either uneven amounts or equal amounts of money. Cash flows of equal size are known as annuities or payments.

In the discussion of compounding and discounting in Chapter 5, it was noted that the rate at which the value of money grows (going forward in time, known as compounding) or declines (going backwards in time, known as discounting) is known as the discount rate, cost of capital, or opportunity cost; the number of time periods involved in the project or investment is the final factor.

The key variables addressed so far—present value; cash flow in time period n; future value in time period n; annuity (cash flows of equal size separated by equal time periods); discount rate/cost of capital/opportunity cost; and number of time periods, or particular time period n—are critical for evaluating a project. Using the formulas and techniques presented in the discussion of the time value of money in Chapter 5, it is possible to compute any unknown key variable, given sufficient information regarding other variables. For example, the present value can be computed if the future value in time period n, the number of time periods, and an appropriate discount rate are known.

In this chapter, tools for analyzing and comparing the attractiveness of a potential project or investment are described. These tools, the net present value and the internal rate of return, build on the concept of the time value of money.

So fundamental are these concepts to management decision making that financial and business calculators have keys for each of the important variables to facilitate computation. Readers are encouraged to use such calculators to solve problems of the type presented in this chapter. Multiple spreadsheet programs are also available to assist in financial analysis of projects.

CASH FLOWS

Managers of health care organizations must consider many elements when evaluating potential projects. For example, market and competitive factors may influence the effect of the project on market share, the likely impact on the organization's image, and the organization's ability to establish and maintain a competitive distinction. Epidemiology also may influence the effect of the project. Health services managers should assess the likely impact of a project on the health status of the community. Managers must always be sensitive to the impact of new projects on existing personnel and the organization's ability to attract and retain well-qualified staff. The well-educated and highly trained nature of large portions of the typical health services organization's staff make these factors especially important.

Among all relevant factors, however, financial issues are usually weighted most heavily by managers. In particular, managers assess a project's impact on the organization's ability to generate cash. This is not surprising because it is the availability and flow of cash that, in a very real sense, "fuel" the organization and its activities. Without an acceptable cash flow, the organization's survival is in question. For this reason, it is critical to consider cash flow.

As the words suggest, cash flow reflects the actual movement of funds into or out of an organization. Revenues generated by a project are cash inflows. Expenses, such as payroll or supply purchases, are cash outflows. The difference between cash inflows and cash outflows is known as the net cash flow. For example, if cash inflows for a new patient care service are $100,000, and cash outflows associated with the project are $95,000, then the net cash flow for the service is $5,000. Net cash flows for any period of time may be either positive or negative.

Most projects involve a series of events that entail either the outflow or inflow of cash. For example, a multispecialty group practice might decide to purchase a new piece of laboratory equipment with the capability of completing multiple blood analyses electronically and much more rapidly than currently available technology. The purchase price of this equipment is $55,000. It is anticipated that the equipment has a useful life of 5 years; that is, ongoing technological enhancements will make this equipment essentially obsolete in 5 years, when it will need to be replaced. The original vendor has agreed to pay $5,000 to buy back the equipment at the time of replacement. This $5,000 is known as the salvage value or salvage price. During its 5 years of operation, it is estimated that the equipment will generate revenue through charges associated with its use. Table 12-1 displays estimated net revenue for the equipment.

Net cash flow takes into account both cash inflows and cash outflows, both of which are actual cash flows. However, some items recognized as an expense by generally accepted accounting principles are not cash flows. The most noteworthy example of this is depreciation. Depreciation expense is an accounting convention that is used to reflect the gradual erosion of an asset's value as a result of its use over time. It does not involve any actual flow of cash, however, and thus does not enter into this type of project analysis.

Table 12-1. Estimated revenues from blood analysis equipment

Time period	Net cash flow from operations at end of period (in dollars)
1	9,500
2	9,500
3	9,500
4	9,500
5	9,500 + 5,000 (salvage value)

Consider the case of a private, taxpaying nursing facility. The facility's income statement and statement of cash flows are shown in Table 12-2. According to accounting convention, net income is calculated including depreciation as an expense. Depreciation, however, is not a cash expense. It is not included in the statement of cash flows. As a result, net income for the facility is $540,000 while the net cash flow for the same period of time is $640,000. The difference between the two, $100,000, is depreciation. The relationship between net income and cash flows is shown in the following equation:

$$\text{Net income} + \text{Depreciation} = \text{Net cash flow} \qquad \text{(Eq. 12-1)}$$

Which Cash Flows Should Be Included in Analyzing Projects?

One fundamental approach to evaluating the attractiveness of a project is to analyze the cash flow implications associated with it. Certainly, from a financial perspective, projects that generate larger positive net cash flows are more attractive than projects with lower positive (or negative) net cash flows.

Only those cash flows directly related to the project are included in the assessment of project opportunities. These include:

1. Revenues and expenses other than depreciation that are directly related to the project.
2. The impact of the project on areas of the organization apart from the project itself. For example, a hospital opening a free-standing ambulatory surgery center may experience changes in demand for its existing inpatient or hospital-based outpatient surgical services, most likely reduction in demand for these services as a result of implementing the new center. Thus, for the entire organization (in this example, the hospital), some of the revenue realized by the new program will not represent "new" revenue; rather, it will be a shift in revenue brought about by patients using the new center instead of previously existing services. Only the "new" or incremental revenue associated with the new venture should be considered in the analysis. In calculating the cash inflows and outflows associated with the project, estimates of the actual incremental impact of the program would need to be made. This estimating process requires competence in forecasting methods as well.

Table 12-2.   Nursing facility income and cash flow statements (in dollars)

Income statement	
Service revenues (net of allowances)	8,300,000
Total expenses (except depreciation)	7,300,000
Depreciation expense	100,000
Taxable income	900,000
Taxes (at 40%)	360,000
Net income	540,000
Cash flow statement	
Service revenues (net of allowances)	8,300,000
Total expenses (except depreciation)	7,300,000
Pretax cash flows	1,000,000
Taxes (at 40%)	360,000
Net cash flow	640,000

Sunk costs (i.e., a cost that has already been incurred or has been committed) are not included in the cash flow analysis. For example, prior to deciding to proceed with the development of a free-standing ambulatory care surgery center, the hospital may have retained a consulting firm to analyze its feasibility. This cost is a sunk cost; whether or not the hospital proceeds with the project, this money has already been spent. Therefore, the expenditure does not represent a relevant cash flow for the analysis.

NET PRESENT VALUE

A key analysis completed by managers is an assessment of the net cash flows of a project, taking into account the timing of these cash flows. The timing of cash flows builds on the concept of the time value of money presented in Chapter 5. For example, a manager may determine that the project being analyzed is projected to generate a series of small negative cash flows, followed by a large positive cash flow. This cash flow pattern is not uncommon for a new product or service that builds market share over a period of several years. Figure 12-1 displays such a cash flow for a planned health screening program.

The initial investment in the project is $10,000, shown as a negative cash flow in time period 0. Operations in years 1–4 each generate a negative cash flow of $3,000. Finally, in year 5, a positive cash flow of $25,000 is realized. It is assumed that year 5 is the final year of the project; that is, no cash flows related to this project, positive or negative occur after this point. The question facing the manager is, "Is this a good financial investment?" One way to formulate a response to this question is to assess the project's cash flows.

It might seem intuitive to sum up the positive cash flows (cash inflows) and negative cash flows (cash outflows) associated with the project and make a decision based on whether the resulting net figure is positive or negative. After all, this approach does recognize the importance of cash flows. This approach is not adequate, however, because it ignores the time value of money.

Alternatively, a manager might calculate what is known as the payback period. This is the length of time it takes to recoup the project's investment. In this example, the project's investment is recovered in the fifth year of the project. Based on this knowledge, a decision on whether or not to proceed with the project would be made. Although used relatively frequently, calculation of the payback period is an incomplete approach because it does not directly take into account the time value of money. Therefore, the approach is overly simplistic, and its use is discouraged.

Taking into consideration the information on compounding and discounting presented in Chapter 5, it should be apparent that "adjustments" must be made to account for the timing of the anticipated cash flows. To assess the financial value of

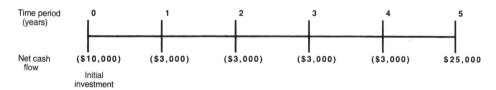

Figure 12-1. Cash flow for a health screening program that must build market share over several years.

the project, the present value of cash flows associated with the project should be computed. Recall that, in computing this present value, cash flows that are more distant in the future are discounted over more time periods. Cash flows received earlier are thus worth more than those received later.

This process of calculating the present value of future cash flows is known as calculating a discounted cash flow. The goal of computing a discounted cash flow is to derive the present value of a project's cash flows. The present value provides a measure of the project's value at the current time (time = 0), so that managers can compare the present values of various projects. The sum of the present value of the project's cash flows is known as the net present value of the project.

Determining a net present value requires discounting and involves three steps:

1. Select an appropriate discount rate, and use it to discount all future cash flows to the current time.
2. Calculate the net present value of these discounted cash flows.
3. Compare the calculated net present value with a previously stated criterion or compare the net present values of various projects against one another.

In general, the management decision rule is that projects with a positive net present value are attractive, and that projects with larger positive net present values are more attractive than those with smaller net present values. Strictly from a financial perspective, projects with a negative net present value are not attractive.

Virtually all projects entail an initial investment, so it is essential that these funds be available at the time they are needed for the project. Regardless of the net present value, if the initial investment required for the project is not available, then the project may not be feasible. It may be possible for the organization to obtain financing (short or long term) to meet the initial investment requirement. The financial impact (in terms of cash flows, ability to take on additional debt, etc.) would need to be woven into the cash flow analysis as well.

Recall that an important component of discounting is determining the appropriate discount rate. This topic is considered in greater depth later in this chapter. Assume that, after careful research, the manager determines that the $10,000 available for investment could be used to purchase a corporate bond for 5 years at an interest rate of 7.5%. Assuming an essentially equivalent level of risk between the corporate bond and a new project opportunity, 7.5% would be an appropriate discount rate to use in calculating net present value. This calculation is depicted in Figure 12-2, showing the present value of each future cash flow. The net present value of the potential project is −$2,634, not an attractive outcome from a financial perspective. Based on this analysis, then, investing in the corporate bond would be more attractive financially.

This simple example is useful for illustrating several concepts regarding net present value as a decision tool. For example, although the project is not financially viable under current conditions, what initial investment would make the project attractive? If the project's net present value can be increased to a positive value, then it becomes a viable project. In effect, if any of the cash flows can be modified to result in a positive present value of at least $2,634, then the project becomes financially viable. For example, management can determine that, if its initial investment (cash outflow in time = 0) can be reduced to less than $7,366, the project becomes financially attractive. At an initial investment of exactly $7,366, the net present

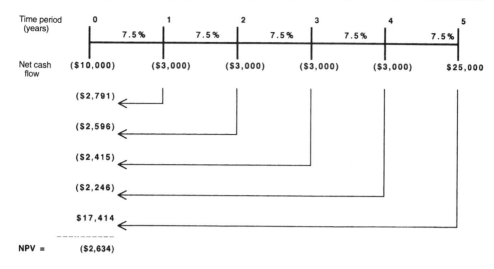

Figure 12-2.   Present values of future cash flows for project shown in Figure 12-1 and net present value of project, using a 7.5% discount rate.

value is equal to zero. If management has defined a philosophy to accept break-even projects in some circumstances, this project would then be acceptable.

Alternatively, using the cash flows and the discount rate, it is possible to compute other changes that would generate a positive net present value. Management can then assess various strategic and tactical options (e.g., pricing, marketing, distribution) to assess whether any such changes are possible. For example, what positive cash flow must be generated in year 5 to result in a positive net present value? That is, what cash flow, discounted for 5 years at 7.5%, results in a present value of at least $20,048 (the negative discounted net cash flow, excluding year 5)? Using Equation 5-2:

$$FV_{yr\ 5} = PV(1+i)^5$$
$$= \$20{,}048(1.075)^5$$
$$= \$28{,}782$$

where $FV_{yr\ 5}$ = future value in year 5
  P = present value
  i = discount rate (in this example, 7.5%)
If the project is able to generate a positive net annual cash flow for year 5 of at least $28,782, then the net present value is greater than or equal to zero.

The impact of the discount rate selected can also be illustrated by this example. Suppose the discount rate used was 5% instead of 7.5%. With the new discount rate (Figure 12-3), the net present value is −$1,050. If the discount rate were to increase to 10%, the net present value would become −$3,987.

Example 1 (below) is a summary example of comparison of net present value of two alternative projects of equal risk:

Discount rate = 6%

Project cash flows

Time period	Investment option A	Investment option B
0	($10,000)	($10,000)
1	2,000	000
2	2,000	250
3	2,000	250
4	2,000	250
5	8,000	15,000
Net present value	$2,908	$1,839

Option A has a higher net present value and represents a more attractive investment opportunity from a financial perspective.

DETERMINING THE DISCOUNT RATE AND A DISCUSSION OF RISK

Determination of an appropriate discount rate (alternatively known as the cost of capital, or opportunity cost) is an important element of financial evaluation of projects. Choosing a rate that is either unrealistically high or low may result in poor management decisions (e.g., missed opportunities or poor returns on projects).

Determining the discount rate is not a precise science; rather, it is an excellent example of a manager's use of reasoned judgment. As described earlier, probably the most appropriate approach is to use the rate of return of an alternative investment of equal risk. This is the opportunity cost.

In earlier examples, interest rates on bank savings accounts and certificates of deposit were used. A bank account interest rate is an example of a relatively risk-

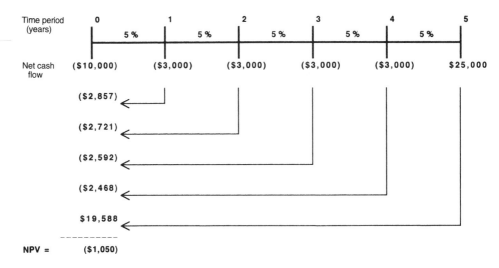

Figure 12-3. Changes in present values of future cash flows and net present value for project using a 5% discount rate.

free investment (assuming the amount of the account is less than the limit of federal deposit insurance). In the context of finance, risk refers to the probability that actual future returns will be less than expected returns. For a bank savings account, in most cases, the depositor is guaranteed the stated interest rate (i.e., the risk is low). Various investment offerings of the federal government are also examples of virtually risk-free investments (e.g., treasury bills, notes, and bonds). In fact, government treasury bonds, long-term investment vehicles requiring investments of over $1,000, are often considered the benchmark for risk-free investments. All other investments have some level of risk, however minimal.

Different types of risk exist, some associated with business uncertainty (e.g., the level of variation between actual and forecast utilization levels of a new project) and some associated with changes in the broader economy (e.g., the effect of inflation). For example, suppose in the planned health screening program discussed earlier in the chapter, utilization levels do not meet forecasts. As shown in Example 2 (below), the net present value of the project is negatively affected by the lower cash flows associated with lower utilization. Many theoretical approaches have been developed to attempt to estimate levels of risk. For a more thorough discussion of elements associated with risk and approaches to estimate it, the reader is encouraged to review any of the general finance texts cited in the Suggested Readings at the end of this book. For the purposes of this book, readers must be aware that risk is a factor in all projects, that levels of risk may vary among projects, and that it is incumbent on the manager to take the relevant risk into account when evaluating projects.

This example illustrates the impact of business risk (reflected by actual utilization lower than forecast resulting in a less attractive cash flow) on net present value of project:

Discount rate = 7.5%

Project cash flows

Time period	Cash flow forecast	Actual cash flow
0	($10,000)	($10,000)
1	(3,000)	(5,000)
2	(3,000)	(4,000)
3	(3,000)	(3,000)
4	(3,000)	(3,000)
5	25,000	25,000
Net present value	($2,634)	($5,360)

ANNUITIES: A PARTICULAR SERIES OF CASH FLOWS

Cash flows may occur in a variety of patterns. As in the health screening project example presented earlier, the initial investment can be followed by a series of uneven cash flows (i.e., the net annual cash flows differ each year). When this is the case, calculating the discounted present value of these cash flows involves a discounting calculation for each time period.

Other projects may generate equal cash flows. Table 12-1 shows the financial data for a project that generated net annual cash flows of $9,500 for each of 5 years. A pattern of even cash flows occurring over time at equal intervals is known as an annuity. In this example, $9,500 is received every year; both the amount and the timing of the cash flow are fixed and equal. The cash flows involved with an annuity can be either cash inflows or cash outflows. Common examples of annuities are a home mortgage or a car loan, both of which typically involve a series of equal payments.

By convention, and for use with business or financial calculators or spreadsheet applications, cash flows associated with annuities are known as payments. Many standard calculators have a "PMT" key that enables the user to enter the amount of the annual payment once along with the number of time periods of the annuity, rather than having to enter the same cash flow amount (the payment) for each year of the annuity. This computational function is convenient and protects against entering data incorrectly.

Ordinary Annuities

There are two types of annuities, which differ only in the timing of when the payment takes place. If the payment occurs at the end of the time period specified, the annuity is referred to as an ordinary annuity. If the payment takes place at the beginning of the time period specified, the annuity is an annuity due. The majority of annuities are ordinary annuities.

Figure 12-4 is an example of a 5-year ordinary annuity in which the purchaser will receive a series of $500 payments after each of the next 5 years. The first payment of $500 is received at the end of year 1, the second payment at the end of year 2, and so on for 5 years. How much should an individual be willing to pay now for this annuity?

It should be clear that this question is a variant of the present value computations already discussed. To begin, an appropriate discount rate, or cost of capital, must be selected. Suppose an alternative investment is identified (e.g., a 5-year CD with an interest rate of 6%). This problem becomes one of discounting each annual cash flow of $500 at the rate of 6% to determine the present value.

The calculated present value of $2,106 is the purchase price at which the individual should be indifferent between the two investments; that is, at that price there is no financial advantage in investing in one over the other. Obviously, if the annuity is priced at less than $2,106, it becomes a more attractive investment; if the annuity is priced at more than $2,106, it becomes less attractive.

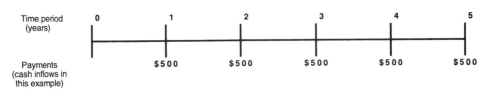

Figure 12-4.   An ordinary annuity of $500 per year.

Embedded Annuities

Often, situations arise in which there is an annuity embedded within a series of annual cash flows (Figure 12-5). This cash flow has a series of six payments of $750 each from years 3–8 of the project. Assuming a discount rate of 7%, what is the present value of this project (i.e., what is the most that should be invested in this project)? There are two ways to go about solving this problem. One way is to calculate the discounted present value of each annual cash flow and determine the net present value. This approach requires that each cash flow be entered individually.

A second, somewhat shorter, way to solve this problem is to utilize the fact that there is an annuity embedded in the cash flow stream. In effect, the cash flow stream is divided into multiple parts, those included in the annuity and those separate from it. The steps to solve this problem using the embedded annuity are described below and illustrated in Figure 12-6.

1. Calculate the present value of the discounted cash flow for those periods not included in the annuity (i.e., years 1, 2, 9, and 10):

Year 1:	$934.58
Year 2:	$436.72
Year 9:	$271.97
Year 10:	$50.83

2. Calculate the present value of the embedded annuity. For this computation, the payment is $750, the interest rate is 7%, and the number of periods is six (the length of the annuity). This calculation yields a present value for the annuity of $3,574.89. The annuity cash flows, however, have been discounted only to the end of time period 2, not time period 0. Therefore, this calculated value must be discounted for an additional two periods to arrive at a present value at time = 0. The calculated value of the embedded annuity portion of the cash flow stream at time = 0 is $3,122.45.
3. Sum the calculated present values to arrive at the net present value for the project. This amount equals $4,816.55 for this example.

Based on these calculations, the organization should be willing to invest no more than $4,816.55 in this project.

INTERNAL RATE OF RETURN

The net present value measures the present value of discounted cash flows for a project, assuming a particular discount rate. This is useful input for organizational decision making. In contrast, the manager might be interested in knowing what rate of financial return is, in fact, generated by the project. This rate is known as the internal rate of return (IRR).

Figure 12-5.   An embedded annuity of $750 per year in a 10-year project.

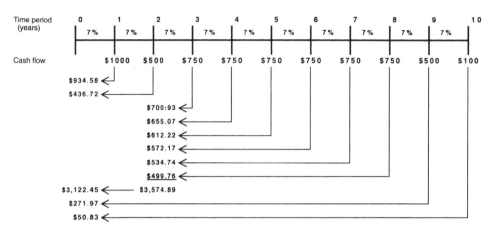

Figure 12-6.   Calculation of the present value of the project shown in Figure 12-5.

Figure 12-7 displays the anticipated cash flows for a large respite care program planned by a nursing facility. Management of the facility has determined that an appropriate discount rate for this project is 6%. The net present value of the project is $5,103, as shown in Table 12-3. The net present value is positive, so the organization decides to pursue the project.

Management may also be interested in calculating the actual rate of return (i.e., the IRR) for this project—that is, determining what discount rate generates a net present value of zero. A financial calculator with an IRR key can easily accomplish this computation; the IRR is 9.9%. As a check, the net present value is computed using a discount rate of 9.9%. As shown in Figure 12-8, the net present value using these data is −$2, a value essentially equivalent to zero; this indicates that the calculated IRR is correct.

Managers, particularly in industries other than health care, speak of something known as the "hurdle rate," which refers to the minimum rate of return required for a project to be pursued by the organization. Hurdle rates may be established formally by boards, committees, or management teams, or they may be informal expectations of an organization. If the formally established hurdle rate of the nursing facility is 12%, it is willing to invest only in projects with an IRR equal to or greater than 12% (i.e., 12% is the financial return hurdle that must be "cleared" by the project).

Based on the information presented, the proposed respite care program would not be pursued because the IRR is less than the approved hurdle rate. If the IRR exceeds the hurdle rate, then the project exceeds the required minimum return, and, all other things being equal, it is financially acceptable to the organiza-

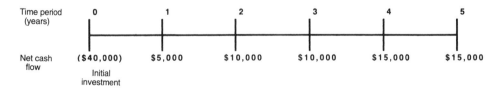

Figure 12-7.   Cash flows for a respite care program in a nursing facility.

Table 12-3. Present values and net present value for respite care program

Year	Net cash flow (in dollars)	Present value (discounted at 6%) (in dollars)
0 (initial investment)	(40,000)	(40,000)
1	5,000	4,717
2	10,000	8,900
3	10,000	8,396
4	15,000	11,881
5	15,000	11,209
Net present value	5,103	

tion. Nonfinancial factors, such as community need and impact on health status, must then be considered before making a final decision on health services projects.

Adjusted Internal Rate of Return

It should be apparent that, calculating the IRR involves compounding each future cash flow at the IRR rate. In the respite care example, this amounts to compounding at a rate of 9.9%. That is, an assumption is being made that funds could be invested and generate a return of 9.9%. This IRR rate may or may not be an appropriate (or available) interest rate. That is, this rate may be higher or lower than the actual financial rate of return that could be obtained. To reflect this discrepancy, the IRR is frequently modified or adjusted to take into account any disparity between the IRR and the rate of financial return actually available in the financial market. This new measure can be referred to as the adjusted, or modified, IRR.

Determining the adjusted IRR involves what is known as the terminal value. The terminal value is the value (taken at the final, or terminal, year of the project) of all cash flows compounded to this terminal year at an appropriate cost of capital. The specific steps to determine the adjusted IRR are:

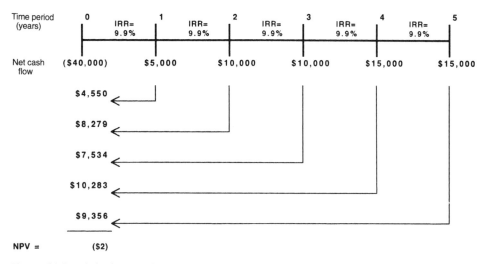

Figure 12-8. Calculation of net present value of the project shown in Figure 12-7.

1. Determine an appropriate cost of capital or discount rate.
2. Compound all net cash outflows forward to the terminal year using this cost of capital. (This compounded value is known as the terminal value.) Compute the sum of the terminal values in the terminal year.
3. Use the cost of capital to discount all cash outflows back to year 0 of the project. Frequently, there may be only one cash outflow—the initial investment. (This outflow takes place in year 0, so no discounting is required.)

The adjusted IRR is the discount rate that equates the present value of the terminal value to the present value of cash outflows.

Figure 12-9 displays the discounted and compounded cash flow values for the respite care project. For this example, management has determined that 7% is an appropriate cost of capital (step 1). The terminal value of each cash flow is computed by compounding each cash flow by the cost of capital (7%). For example, the terminal value of the $5,000 cash flow projected for year 1 is the future value of this amount compounded for 4 years at 7%, or $6,554. The sum of terminal values for the project is $51,303. The only cash outflow in this example is the initial investment of $40,000, which takes place at time 0, so it need not be discounted.

The adjusted IRR is the discount rate that equates the present value of the terminal value to the present value of the cash outflows. In this example, the adjusted IRR is the discount rate that "equates" $51,303 with $40,000. Taken another way, it is the compounding factor that grows an investment of $40,000 to a value of $51,303 in 5 years. The adjusted IRR is 5.1033%.

To illustrate with another example, suppose a group of hospitals and several physicians are considering developing a state-of-the-art mammography center. To participate, hospital A must contribute $25,000 now. Its anticipated net cash flows over the next 3 years are $7,000, $10,000, and $20,000, respectively. The board of trustees of hospital A has identified 14% as the organization's hurdle rate for this type of project. The chief financial officer has identified an opportunity cost of 7%. Based only on financial factors, should hospital A participate in the project?

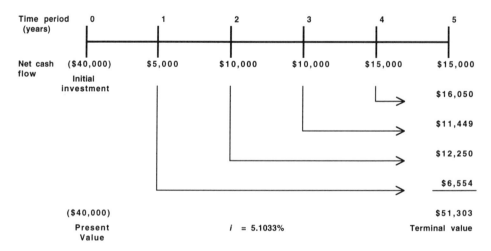

Figure 12-9.   Calculation of adjusted internal rate of return on the project shown in Figure 12-7.

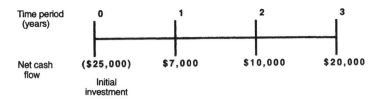

Figure 12-10.   Timeline for hospital A's participation in a mammography center project.

Figure 12-10 displays the timeline for this project. Using a present value or initial investment of $25,000, with the net cash flows anticipated, an IRR of 18.6% is computed. Using 7% as the discount rate, or cost of capital, yields an adjusted IRR of 15.7%. Both the IRR and the adjusted IRR exceed the hurdle rate of 14%, so hospital A should pursue the mammography center project.

CONCLUSION

In this chapter, three tools have been presented to assist in analyzing projects: 1) the net present value, 2) the internal rate of return, and 3) the adjusted, or modified, rate of return. In practice, the IRR is the most frequently used tool. Discussions regarding hurdle rates are not uncommon in finance and executive management meetings. Although the adjusted or modified IRR is, in some respects, a more accurate assessment of the return of a project, it is rarely encountered in management suites or boardrooms. Net present value falls somewhere in between in terms of frequency of use. Capable health care managers should be equally competent in the use of all three tools, and it may be useful to compare the outcomes of the three approaches in arriving at a final determination regarding a potential project.

EXERCISES

12-1. A representative of a reputable financial services company has approached you as manager of a four-person group of anesthesiologists with an opportunity to purchase a 10-year annuity due for each member of the group. The annuity due would pay $40,000 each year beginning 5 years from now (i.e., at time = 5). What is the most you would be willing to pay now, per physician, for this investment? Assume a discount rate of 7%.

12-2. The hospital's marketing and finance departments have just provided you, as chief financial officer, with pro forma income statements for your proposed sonogram center (see Table 12-4). What is the project's IRR? Assume an initial investment of $175,000 and a discount rate of 6%. The hospital is operated as a not-for-profit facility.

12-3. The chief operating officer of a small, not-for-profit community hospital must make a recommendation to the board of trustees on choosing among three project options for an unrestricted gift of $250,000 that has just been received. The board has established a time horizon of 5 years on this project. The options are:

1. Purchase a 5-year treasury note at an annual interest rate of 7%.
2. Purchase the practice of a young physician (the hospital's third highest admitter). Estimates of projected cash flows for the practice (postpurchase) are shown in Table 12-5.
3. Purchase an upgraded analyzer for the laboratory. Based on forecasts of laboratory utilization, the net cash flows for this project are:

Time	Net cash flow
$t + 1$	$75,000
$t + 2$	$75,000
$t + 3$	$50,000
$t + 4$	$50,000
$t + 5$	$50,000

Which investment should the chief operating officer recommend, and why?

Table 12-4.   Pro forma income statement for proposed sonogram center (Exercise 12-3) (amounts in dollars)

	Time			
	$t + 1$	$t + 2$	$t + 3$	$t + 4$
Service revenues (net)	425,000	500,000	580,000	700,000
Expenses	400,000	450,000	525,000	600,000
Depreciation expense	35,000	35,000	35,000	35,000
Net income	(10,000)	15,000	20,000	65,000

Table 12-5.   Probability of cash flow for physician practice (Exercise 12-3) (amounts in dollars)

Time	60%	20%	20%
$t + 1$	40,000	20,000	60,000
$t + 2$	60,000	30,000	80,000
$t + 3$	75,000	40,000	100,000
$t + 4$	100,000	50,000	125,000
$t + 5$	100,000	50,000	125,000

12-4.   What are some of the factors that can influence the riskiness of projects (investments) in health care organizations?

IV

DESIGNING AND ANALYZING SYSTEMS

A hospital, a nursing home, a multispecialty group practice—all are examples of systems. This section provides methods for evaluating systems with respect to their clients and their capacity and provides a format to report management recommendations involving the redesign of systems.

Chapter 13, "Analyzing Waiting Lines," presents methods to analyze and manage arrival rates and service times associated with lines. If arrivals are too close together, clients may wait a long time. This may have service and economic consequences to the organization if potential clients decide to go elsewhere or if the organization cannot serve all the clients demanding service. It may also have consequences for the patient, client, or resident served by the specific system. Conversely, designing a specific system to minimize wait in a line during peak periods of demand may have negative economic consequences for the organization because too many resources may be left idle during periods of off-peak demand. Given these types of considerations, this chapter provides methods to design and analyze line-based systems.

Chapter 14, "Analyzing Capacity and Resources," provides methods to determine the capacity of specific systems and subsystems within the organization. Knowing the current capacity of a system enables the manager to estimate the current level of productivity as well as identify specific changes that must be implemented to change the capacity of a specific system.

Chapter 15, "The Business Plan," presents questions and issues managers consider when analyzing and designing systems and modifications to existing systems. Frequently, a formal report—a business plan—is authored by managers to answer these specific questions and provide decision makers with the information needed to evaluate the proposed new modification to existing systems. This chapter is the logical end to this book. Whereas previous chapters provided specific methods and techniques to analyze, design, and implement within the health care organization, this chapter provides a master framework of questions and issues a manager is expected to be able to answer as part of the process of securing organizational approval (and capital) to implement change within the organization. As a master framework, this chapter states the questions and issues any manager must consider and address when implementing change within a health care organization.

The techniques, frameworks, concepts, and methods included in the book are intended to enrich and expand the repertoire of the health services manager. As needed, each can be used by the manager to analyze, design, and implement within health care organizations. Health services management is a robust profession with few formally prescribed protocols. It is based on knowledge, skills, and reasoned judgment. Developing proficiency with the methods described in this book should assist managers in expanding their abilities to reason and, as a result, to manage well in the complex world of health care organizations. These methods also are intended to improve the efficiency and effectiveness of health care organizations, not as isolated methods, but as tools for the manager to use to improve his or her health care organization's ability to provide efficient and effective services to patient, clients, and residents.

13

Analyzing Waiting Lines

Chapter Objectives

1. To be able to describe and analyze service systems and waiting lines using queuing theory
2. To be able to use queuing theory calculations to manage the relationship between patient or client waiting and the resources needed to provide services

Key Terms and Concepts

Arrival rates	Jockeying
Balking	Multiple-channel systems
Batching	Poisson probability distribution
Exponential probability distribution	Queuing theory
	Service rates
FIFO	Single-channel systems
Idle time	Reneging

People wait in line for service. Laboratory specimens wait in line for processing. Bills wait in line for payment. Prescriptions wait in line for filling. X-rays wait in line for development and interpretation. This chapter examines waiting lines and service systems and presents models that can be used to analyze these lines and balance waiting time with the resources used to provide services. Throughout this chapter, anything or anyone waiting in a line is referred to as a unit. The service provided to the unit is referred to as a unit of service.

GENERAL CONCEPTS

A Waiting Line as a Demand for Service

Most people find waiting lines, especially waiting lines they consider too long, to be an irritating but unavoidable factor of contemporary life. People generally do not like to wait. From a people perspective, waiting is idle and nonproductive time. From a service system perspective, however, a line represents a demand for service.

As long as a line of units is present, the server has the ability to engage in productive activity, such as serving the unit (patient, resident, or client). In situations that use lines, when no line exists, the server is idle. Idle servers are not productive elements of the organizations. Having units, such as people, waiting in a line for service ensures that a server is productive. If no unit is on line, the server is idle, just waiting for a unit to enter the line and proceed to be served.

Providing a service requires and consumes resources. For example, filling a prescription requires the time of a pharmacist as well as the supplies necessary to satisfy the demand represented by the prescription. It also requires adequate space and, in some instances, specialized equipment. How long a specific unit, such as a specific prescription, waits in a line for service depends on the number of pharmacists on duty to fill prescriptions as well as the time it takes the pharmacist to fill prescriptions that arrived earlier. In principle, the time a unit waits in line can be cut by adding more pharmacists and/or other resources. Being able to process more units should lower the time any one unit must wait in line for service. However, if demand fluctuates and too many pharmacists are hired, some will be idle and not engaged in productive activity.

Capacity of Service Systems

Any service system has a finite processing capacity. If one professor can grade five short papers per hour, then 12 minutes per paper, or five papers per hour, would be the service rate of a system that relied on one professor to grade short papers. Therefore, faced with a stack of 40 papers, it would take one professor 8 hours to grade them all. Two professors should be able to complete the same task in 4 hours each. Although the total amount of service time (8 hours) did not change, the time any one paper had to wait in line was shortened. With one professor, the last paper in the stack had to wait 8 hours minus the 12 minutes necessary to grade any one paper, or 7 hours and 48 minutes, to be processed. With two professors, the last papers only had to wait 4 hours minus the 12 minutes, or 3 hours and 48 minutes. In an ambulatory care clinic, one physical therapist can treat three patients per hour. At this rate, if one additional therapist was added, six patients could be treated per hour. The general point is that, by adding resources to the service system, such as adding an additional professor, the speed at which the service system can process units can be increased.

Service systems, however, have a finite, not an infinite, capacity to provide a unit of service. In some instances, the limitation of the service system is a physical limit. A hospital with three surgical suites can perform only three surgical operations at any one time. If the demand for surgery is more than three patients at any one time, some patients must wait. Machines also have limitations. For example, a CT scanner may be technically capable of doing no more than 100 individual scans per hour, regardless of the staffing used to support the machine. In still other instances, management establishes a limitation of a service system based on the number and type of servers assigned to the service system. By assigning one, in contrast to more than one, pharmacist to the pharmacy, management has defined the service capacity of the pharmacy. If one pharmacist is able to fill 10 prescriptions per hour, assigning only one pharmacist to the pharmacy limits the pharmacy's ability to service prescriptions to no more than 10 prescriptions per hour.

Most service systems are designed with a ceiling productivity of 80%. This means that up to 80% of a worker's time is expected to be devoted to service activities, leaving 20% of the available time for nonservice activities.

The Balance Between Waiting Time and Resources

Management must balance waiting time with the resources used to provide a service. Health administrators face a dual and potentially conflicting concern. On the one hand, health administrators are concerned about efficiency and worker productivity. Idle staff, machines, and surgical suites benefit neither the organization, the organization's financial position, nor its potential patients or clients. On the other hand, health administrators want their organization and its staff to be able to provide a quality service when it is needed. Health administrators want to minimize, for example, the amount of time a patient must wait for surgery, a laboratory test, or a specific treatment. Delay in providing a service is never therapeutic. Long delays may lead to a change or deterioration in the condition of the patient or a laboratory specimen awaiting a test. Although short delays are usually acceptable from a clinical perspective, the definition of what constitutes a long or short delay depends on specific circumstances. Twenty minutes may constitute too long a delay for a special medical test or procedure, given the condition of the patient. However, 20 minutes may be a short delay for a patient to be seen by a physician in an ambulatory care clinic. The clinical acceptability or unacceptability of the delay in the service system in providing the demanded service varies based on the specific service in question as well as other clinical and medical considerations. The client's acceptance of a delay also may affect patient participation in the service. Too long a wait may decrease clientele.

To have an efficient organization as well as efficient service systems and subsystems, managers must balance acceptable waiting times with the input resources used to provide the service. This balancing can be referred to as managing the service system.

In some instances, service systems are managed by advising units when to arrive. For example, physicians in private practice schedule patient appointments. Most patient admissions to a hospital are scheduled by providing an appointment for a given day. Surgeons are given schedules for using a specific surgical suite in the hospital. Scheduling attempts to minimize the wait for service by establishing a constant demand over time for a service that can be met within existing resource levels.

In still other situations, special procedures are used to manage service systems. For example, in hospitals, a physician can order stat (from the Latin *statim*, or immediately) processing of a medical test, meaning that the test will be rushed to the laboratory and processed ahead of any other tests awaiting service. In hospital emergency rooms, patients are seen and evaluated, and then placed in the service line based on their medical needs, not the order in which they arrive for service. This type of service system is referred to as medical triaging. The order of units in the line is continually redetermined every time another patient arrives based on the new patient's medical need. Thus, in a hospital emergency room, a patient will remain last in line as long as patients with more pressing medical needs continue to arrive and demand service.

Many analytical models exist to assist the manager in analyzing service systems and balancing the capacity of the system to provide a unit of service with the time a unit must wait for service. Some of these models can be found in queuing theory, the formal study of waiting lines.

DEFINING CHARACTERISTICS OF WAITING LINES

Random Arrivals

Random arrivals refers to unscheduled arrivals that are not influenced by when previous units arrived or left. If the average number of units that arrive in 1 hour is six, this does not mean that a unit arrives every 10 minutes. It means that, in any 1 hour, six units on average will arrive. There is some probability that all six units will arrive at one time during the hour, just as there is a probability that one unit will arrive every 10 minutes. Random arrivals means that probabilities govern when units will arrive in the specified time period.

FIFO Line Behavior

FIFO means first in, first out. In a FIFO situation, the order of service is determined by the order of arrival. Hospital emergency rooms do not use FIFO; here, the need for stat servicing of some units can change any FIFO system for one specific case or situation. Where the order of arrival determines the order in which the service system services the unit, such as in a walk-in ambulatory care clinic, a FIFO system is in effect.

Channels and Servers

Channels are servers. The number of channels refers to the number of servers available to arriving units. Some systems are designed to have a single channel, and other systems are designed to have multiple channels. Supermarkets usually have many servers equal to the checkout stations, with one line for each, i.e., parallel single-channel systems. Some banks use one line to feed multiple service windows or tellers, i.e., a multiple-channel system.

Servers provide the service. The checkout clerk in the supermarket is a server. The bank teller is a server. The physician in the walk-in ambulatory care clinic is a server. The pharmacist is a server. Some systems have one server and other systems have multiple servers. Common situations are one line, one server and one line, many servers.

Waiting

Wait is defined as the amount of time between the time a unit arrives and enters the line and the time the unit begins to receive service. The fact that units wait does not mean that every unit waits. It means that every unit, when it arrives for service, has some probability of waiting. Depending on the situation, some or many units may wait.

Other Terms and Concepts

Other important terms and concepts with reference to waiting lines are:

Balking: When a unit, seeing the length of the line, decides the line is too long and refuses to enter the queue.

Reneging: When a unit waits in line for awhile, decides the wait has been too long, and leaves the queue.

Batching: When more than one unit enters service at a time (e.g., family photo, well-child clinic).

Jockeying: When a unit chooses one line, then decides another line is shorter and changes lines.

QUEUING THEORY

Queuing theory uses the Poisson probability distribution to describe arrivals to the service facility and the exponential probability distribution (the inverse of the Poisson distribution) to describe service times. Based on these data distributions and specific equations, queuing theory can be used to determine:

1. The percentage of the time that a service facility is idle
2. The probability of a specific number of units in the service system
3. The average number of units in the system
4. The average time each unit spends in the system (waiting plus service time)
5. The average number of units in the waiting line
6. The average time each unit spends in the waiting line
7. The percentage of time, or probability, that an arriving unit must wait for service

Together with additional information on the cost of providing a service and patient waiting line limitations (e.g., space), this information provides the manager with ample information to analyze and design and redesign waiting lines.

A service "system" includes the line for service (if any) and the actual service facility. For example, in a walk-in ambulatory care clinic, the "system" includes the waiting room. The service facility is the examination room used by the nurses and physicians to diagnose and treat the patient.

Basic queuing theory uses a Poisson probability distribution to estimate the pattern in which units arrive for service. The Poisson distribution is considered a more appropriate estimate of random arrival patterns than the standard normal probability distribution. Unlike the standard normal probability distribution, which is symmetrical and bell shaped, the Poisson distribution has a long tail (on the right) and the distribution is not symmetrical. Unlike the standard normal distribution, which gives equal probabilities to values on either side of a mean, the Poisson distribution recognizes that random arrival rates cluster about the mean, cannot be less than zero, and have a low probability of being much higher than the mean. The queuing theory models presented in this chapter are based on the use of the Poisson distribution to estimate the random arrival pattern.

Queuing theory also uses an exponential probability distribution to describe service times. A service time probability distribution is needed to estimate how long it takes to provide a unit of service. Unlike the standard normal data distribution, the exponential probability distribution suggests that service times will be greater than zero and more frequently short than long.

Although the Poisson probability distribution and the exponential probability distribution are considered most appropriate for modeling and analyzing waiting lines, in some instances they may fail to capture the essence of arrivals and service times. In such situations, other probability distributions are used or waiting line models are developed using computer simulations. These types of applications and issues are reserved for advanced study.

For the purposes of this chapter, it is assumed that:

1. The Poisson probability distribution is considered an appropriate representation of arrivals.
2. The exponential probability distribution is considered an appropriate representation of service times.
3. The lines to be analyzed are governed by FIFO.
4. There is no balking, reneging, or jockeying.
5. There are no batch services.
6. The client population is infinite.

Based on these assumptions, queuing models are available to describe waiting lines based on the number of channels (lines) and the number of servers. In general, as the arrival rate gets numerically closer to the service rate, the line will get longer while the idle time in the system will decrease. As the arrival rate gets numerically farther away from (and less than) the service rate, the line will get shorter, but the idle time in the system will increase.

If for some reason the arrival rate is greater than the service rate, the queue will be infinitely long. In other words, all systems must be designed with the service rate (per hour) greater than the arrival rate (per hour). Queuing theory can describe waiting lines only when the service rate is higher than the arrival rate.

Single-Server, Single-Line Model

The single-server, single-line model has one server and one line. To use this model requires estimating:

λ = the expected number of arrivals per time period (mean arrival rate)
μ = the expected number of services possible per time period (mean service rate)

(*Note:* For any system to work, λ must be less than μ.) For example, if λ = 3 per hour and μ = 4 per hour, the following equations can be used to calculate various probabilities and averages describing a waiting line. Managers can use these performance measures to analyze the relationship between waiting lines and resources.

1. The probability that the service facility is idle (p_0) (i.e., no units are in the system)

$$p_0 = 1 - (\lambda/\mu)$$
$$= 1 - (3/4)$$
$$= .25, \text{ or } 25\%$$

2. The average number of units in the system (L)

$$L = \lambda/(\mu - \lambda)$$
$$= 3 (4 - 3)$$
$$= 3 \text{ units}$$

3. The average time a unit spends in the system (W) (i.e., waiting + service time)

$$W = L/\lambda$$
$$= 3/3$$
$$= 1 \text{ hour}$$

4. The average number of units in the queue waiting for service (L_q)

$$L_q = \lambda^2/[\mu(\mu - \lambda)]$$
$$= 3^2/[4(4-3)]$$
$$= 2.25 \text{ units}$$

5. The average time a unit spends in the queue waiting (W_q).

$$W_q = L_q/\lambda$$
$$= 2.25/3$$
$$= 0.75 \text{ hour}$$

6. The probability that a unit must wait (p_w)

$$p_w = \lambda/\mu$$
$$= 3/4$$
$$= .75, \text{ or } 75\%$$

p_w is $1 - p_0$ because a unit waits for service only if the server is busy. In a single-channel, single-server system, an idle system means an idle server (no wait for service), and a busy system means a unit must wait for service.

Given this model, additional estimates can be made based on different values for λ, the rate of arrivals per hour, and μ, the service rate per hour (see Table 13-1). It is interesting to note that, based on these calculations:

As the service rate (μ) increases 25% (from 4 to 5 service units per hour), the estimated time a unit spends in the system (W) decreases 50% (from 1 hour to 0.5 hours).

As the rate of arrivals (λ) increases 33% (from 3 to 4 per hour) and the service rate (μ) increases 100% (from 3 to 6 per hour), the estimated time a unit spends in the system (W) decreases 50% (from 1.00 hours to 0.50 hours).

The closer μ is to λ, the higher W will be.

These types of calculations and observations highlight the Poisson and exponential probability distributions at work and the types of trade-offs managers can consider.

Economic Analysis for Single-Server Systems

Any service system can (usually) increase its service rate by adding servers plus space, equipment, and other items needed to provide an additional service facility. Each of these costs can be estimated:

Hourly wage rates can be used to estimate the cost of a service team.

Table 13-1. Sample performance measures for single-server, single-channel model

Service rate per hour	4	5	6	7	8
Arrival rate per hour	3	3	4	4	4
p_0	25.00%	40.00%	33.33%	42.86%	50.00%
L (units)	3.00	1.50	2.00	1.33	1.00
W (hours)	1.00	0.50	0.50	0.33	0.25
L_q (units)	2.25	0.90	1.33	0.76	0.50
W_q (hours)	0.75	0.30	0.33	0.19	0.12
p_w	75.00%	60.00%	66.67%	57.14%	50.00%

The cost of equipment can be estimated based on its useful life expressed in units of service and purchase plus operational or rental costs.

The cost of space can be estimated based on operational and capital costs expressed on a square-foot basis or by the market rental cost.

In the preceding example, a single-server system was analyzed using different service rates (e.g., μ = 4, 5, 6, 7, and 8 units per hour). Increasing the service rate requires additional input resources. The critical managerial issue is the *value* associated with adding additional resources to the service system given the characteristics of the service system.

For example, the cost per hour of a one-physician plus one-nurse service team for an ambulatory care clinic is $80. This service team can serve on average up to four patients per hour. If a physician assistant is added to the team for an additional $12 per hour, the service team (i.e., one physician, one nurse, and one physician assistant) can serve on average up to six patients per hour. If an additional nurse is added to the team for an additional $20 per hour, the service team (i.e., one physician and two nurses) can serve on average up to eight patients per hour. The arrival rate is estimated to be three patients per hour.

Consider the calculations shown in Table 13-2. Is it worth an additional $12 per hour or $20 per hour to alter this system? To answer this question requires managerial judgment. The queuing theory model plus some basic cost estimates provide the manager with the information necessary to evaluate the situation and make an insightful decision based on the circumstances.

Multiple-Server, Single-Line Models

Multiple-server systems have more than one server available to the waiting line. When a unit gets to the head of the line, the unit is served by the next available server. In multiple-server queuing models:

s = the number of servers
λ = mean arrival rate for the system
μ = mean service rate for the system

The equations for this model are especially complex when s is greater than 2. These equations are provided in Appendix B. A table of the values for p_0, the probability that the service facility is idle, for the multiple-server model may be found at the end of this chapter (Table 13-7). This table also provides the calculations for L_q, the average number of units waiting for service. Table 13-7 uses two inputs: 1) the ratio of λ/μ, and 2) the number of servers. For example, if the arrival rate is 8 clients

Table 13-2.   Performance measures for ambulatory care clinic with single-server model

Service rate per hour	4	5	6	7	8
Service teams	1	1	1	1	1
Arrival rate per hour	3	3	3	3	3
Staff cost per hour ($)	80	92	92	100	100
p_0	25.00%	40.00%	50.00%	57.14%	62.50%
L (units)	3	1.5	1	0.75	0.60
W (hours)	1	0.5	0.33	0.25	0.20
L_q (units)	2.25	0.9	0.5	0.32	0.22
W_q (hours)	0.75	0.3	0.17	0.11	0.07
p_w	75.00%	60.00%	50.00%	42.86%	37.50%

per day and the service rate is 10 clients per day, the ratio λ/μ is 0.80. If three servers are present, the cell values in the row for 0.8 and the column for 3 in Table 13-7 are:

$$p_0 = 0.4472$$
$$L_q = 0.0189$$

Thus, on average, the system is idle (empty) 44.72% of the time, and the number of units waiting for service is 0.0189—much less than 1 unit.

All other measures of performance can be calculated from these two values. For example, if $\lambda = 3$, $\mu = 4$, and $s = 2$, Table 13-7 provides values of $p_0 = 0.4545$ and $L_q = $ approximately 0.125 (interpolating between 0.7 and 0.8 for 3/4). Thus, we can calculate:

1. The average number of units in the system (L), both waiting and being served.

$$L = L_q + (\lambda/\mu)$$
$$= 0.125 + 0.75$$
$$= 0.875 \text{ unit}$$

2. The average time a unit spends in the system (W).

$$W = L/\mu$$
$$= 0.875/3$$
$$= 0.29 \text{ hr}$$
$$= 0.29 \text{ hr} \times 60 \text{ min/hr}$$
$$= 17.5 \text{ min}$$

Another formula for W is:

$$W = W_q + (1/\mu)$$

3. The average time a unit spends in the queue waiting for service (W_q).

$$W_q = L_q/\lambda$$
$$= 0.125/3$$
$$= 0.041 \text{ hr}$$

The probability that an arriving unit must wait for service (p_w) is equal to the probability that all servers are busy when a unit arrives. This means that the number (n) of units in the system is equal to or greater than the number of servers (s). This probability can be obtained from the last table in this chapter (Table 13-8). In our example, the ratio $\lambda/\mu = 3/4 = 0.7500$ and $s = 2$. Thus, p_w is found to be 0.2045. That is, over 20% of the time, a unit must wait to be served. If the arrival rate is 8 clients per day and the service rate is 10 clients per day, the ratio $\lambda/\mu = 0.8$. With three servers ($s = 3$) the value of p_w is 0.0520; that is, 5% of the time a unit must wait for service.

Economic Analysis of Multiple-Server Systems

Using the multiple-server queuing theory model, we can extend the economic analysis of the ambulatory care clinic described in the previous section. In this case, the option is to establish additional service teams, not just add resources to an existing single-service team. In the previous section, it was stated that the cost per hour of a one-physician plus one-nurse service team for the ambulatory care clinic is $80 and that this team can serve on average up to four patients per hour. Therefore, two such teams could be expected to serve up to eight patients per hour. If a physician assistant is added to the team (i.e., one physician plus one nurse plus one physician assistant) for an additional $12 per hour, each service team can service on average up to six patients per hour. If an additional nurse is added to the original team (one physician plus two nurses) for an additional $20 per hour, the service team can service on average up to eight patients per hour. The arrival rate is estimated to be three patients per hour.

The costs associated with adding a service team include expenses associated with the physical plant and equipment. For example, an additional service team may need additional offices, examination rooms, and/or treatment rooms. Additional equipment will be required so that the new service team need not borrow from the original service team. The cost of adding an additional service team may be significantly different from adding salaries. For our example, the estimate of these other costs is $5 per hour.

The economic implications of different staffing levels for a single-server model can be compared with the economic implications of using two ($s = 2$) service teams. Table 13-3 contains performance estimates for both types of service systems. These queuing theory calculations and cost estimates provide the manager with the ability to examine line and system characteristics and, by adding cost estimates, consider different configurations of the service system and waiting lines and the economic implications associated with these configurations.

For example, if the manager wants to minimize the probability that a patient waits when he or she arrives at the walk-in clinic, given the parameters cited in the example, two service teams would be used. The probability of waiting (p_w) is lowest under this option (20.45%). At $165 per hour, however, the cost of this option is the highest. If the manager wants to minimize costs, the best option would be to use a single-server system with a staffing configuration of one physician and one nurse. Under this option, the cost per hour is $80. The probability of patient waiting (p_w), however, is the highest (75%).

Marginal costs and marginal benefits also can be compared using the estimates included in Table 13-3. For example, is an increased cost of $85 per hour ($165 − $80)—an increase of 106%—worth a 73% decrease (75% to 20.45%) in the probability that a patient will wait? This depends on the value placed on patient time.

Table 13-3. Performance measures for ambulatory care clinic with single-server and multiple-server models

Service rate per hour	4	5	6	7	8	8
Service teams	1	1	1	1	1	2
Arrival rate per hour	3	3	3	3	3	3
Staff cost per hour	80	92	92	100	100	165
p_0	25.00%	40.00%	50.00%	57.14%	62.50%	45.45%
L (units)	3	1.5	1	0.75	0.60	0.873
W (hours)	1	0.5	0.33	0.25	0.20	0.291
L_q (units)	2.25	0.9	0.5	0.32	0.22	0.123
W_q (hours)	0.75	0.3	0.17	0.11	0.07	0.041
p_w	75.00%	60.00%	50.00%	42.86%	37.50%	20.45%

Queuing theory models provide the manager with a rich and comprehensive tool for analyzing and designing service systems that includes the evaluation of lengths of lines and the potential for waiting. Based on the goals and objectives for the system, the manager uses this information to trade off economic considerations with service system characteristics and considerations in arriving at the preferred configuration.

Appointment-Based Systems

Most appointment-based systems used in health care resemble a single-server system. For example, a patient is given an appointment to see a specific physician, even though the physician may be one of many employed in a clinic. As a single-server system, appointment-based systems can be analyzed using the single-server queuing theory model.

Appointment systems fix the mean arrival rate but not necessarily the inter-arrival times. Therefore, the arrival rate (λ) is no longer an estimate. It is defined by the manager. An arrival rate of 2 units per hour means scheduling appointments every 30 minutes; a rate of 3 units per hour means scheduling appointments every 20 minutes; and a rate of 4 units per hour means scheduling appointment every 15 minutes.

The service rate (μ) is estimated as is done for the single-server queuing models. Table 13-4 shows performance measures for $\lambda = 2, 3$, and 4 at various service rates (i.e., $\mu = 3, 4, 5$, and 6).

Using Queuing Theory for Staffing Determinations

A critical rule in queuing theory is that, on average, the arrival rate must be less than the system service rate. The system service rate is the rate at which the entire system, potentially made up of many servers, can provide services. In a single-server system, the service rate is equal to the service rate of the one server. In a multiple-server system, the service rate of the system is equal to the service rate of each server times the number of servers. Consider a clinic in which, on average, 280 patients arrive during the 7 hours the clinic is open. This would be calculated as an arrival rate of 40 patients per hour. Service time is estimated to average 12 minutes per patient per service team or server. This is a service rate of five patients per hour per server. If this system were designed as a single-server system, with an arrival rate of 40 patients per hour and a service rate of 5 patients per hour, the system would create very long lines. To avoid this problem, a multiple-server system should be used.

To calculate the minimum number of servers needed so that the arrival rate, on average, is less than the system service rate, the arrival rate (40 patients per

Table 13-4. Performance measures for an ambulatory care clinic with an appointment-based system

Service rate per hour	3	4	4	5	5	6
Arrival rate per hour	2	2	3	3	4	4
p_0	33.33%	50.00%	25.00%	40.00%	20.00%	33.33%
L (units)	2.00	1.00	3	1.50	4.00	2.00
W (hours)	1.00	0.50	1.00	0.50	1.00	0.50
L_q (units)	1.33	0.50	2.25	0.90	3.20	1.33
W_q (hours)	0.67	0.25	0.75	0.30	0.80	0.33
p_w	66.67%	50.00%	75.00%	60.00%	80.00%	66.67%

hour) is divided by the service rate per server (5 patients per hour). This yields the number of servers (eight) at which the arrival rate (40 patients per hour) would equal the system service rate. To be an efficient system, however, the service rate must be larger than (not just equal to) the arrival rate. In this example, the service rate must be increased by adding a ninth server. With nine servers, the service rate is 45 patients per hour. Appropriate calculations can be made to examine the characteristics of this new system to determine, for example, whether a 10th server would be desirable. This is a general way to estimate the number of servers needed to staff a service system.

In situations in which arrival rates vary dramatically, such as by time of day or day of the week, the manager must analyze the system at peak and slow times using the standard queuing theory calculations to determine appropriate staffing.

CONCLUSION

Table 13-5 summarizes the equations and analytical approaches for waiting lines described in this chapter. If the Poisson probability distribution or the exponential probability distribution or both are found to be inappropriate, other models and approaches must be used. In some instances, a computer simulation must be used to develop and then use an appropriate probability distribution that best fits the circumstances. Analytical models such as these can be used to analyze the operation of the line and assist the manager in making decisions concerning the line and the service system. However, making the actual decision is the prerogative and role of the manager, not the analytical model or technique. At best, the model will inform the manager and clarify alternatives and implications.

Table 13-5. Queuing theory equations and analytical approaches

Parameter	Single channel	Multiple channel
P_0	$1 - \lambda/\mu$	See Table 13-7
L_q	$\lambda^2/\mu(\mu - \lambda)$	See Table 13-7
L	$L_q + (\lambda/\mu)$	$L_q + (\lambda/\mu)$
W_q	L_q/λ	L_q/λ
W	L/λ	L/λ
	or $W_q + (1/\mu)$	or $W_q + (1/\mu)$
P_w	λ/μ	See Table 13-8

EXERCISES

13-1. Consider the data in Table 13-6 concerning an outpatient medical laboratory. Analyze and report your findings. Make recommendations as appropriate.

13-2. The following data have been collected for a hospital pharmacy as a single-server system for each of the three shifts used in hospital operations. What are the trade-offs between system idle time and waiting time for prescriptions?

	Days	Evenings	Nights
Service rate per hour	200	100	50
Arrival rate per hour	60	50	40

The service rate can be increased or decreased in increments of 50 prescriptions per hour. The expense associated with each increment is $100. In other words, to be able to process 50 additional prescriptions will cost an additional $100 per hour. If the current rate of processing or service is lowered by 50 prescriptions per hour, the savings are $100 per hour.

13-3. A woman arrives at a birth center on average every 12 hours. On average each woman uses a birthing suite for 18 hours. How many suites should there be? Why? Assume one waiting area in the center, and use days as the unit of time.

Table 13-6. Data on outpatient medical laboratory

Day	7 A.M.–11 A.M.	11 A.M.–3 P.M.	3 P.M.–7 P.M.	7 P.M.–7 A.M.
1	156	105	44	305
2	155	110	48	313
3	160	121	59	340
4	154	127	32	313
5	180	127	50	357
6	170	120	32	322
7	155	126	30	311
8	167	129	30	326
9	148	130	40	318
10	155	105	35	295
Average per time period	160 40	120 30	40 10	320 26.67
Service rate per hour	60	60	20	46.67

Table 13-7. Probability of an empty system (p_0) and expected number of units in the queue (L_q) for queuing systems with Poisson arrivals and exponential arrival times

λ/μ^a	Number of servers in queuing system									
	1	2	3	4	5	6	7	8	9	10
0.1	0.9000[b]	0.9048	0.9048	0.9048	0.9048	0.9048	0.9048	0.9048	0.9048	0.9048
	0.0111[b]	0.0003	0.0000	0.0000	0.0000	0.0000	0.0000	0.0000	0.0000	0.0000
0.2	0.8000	0.8182	0.8187	0.8187	0.8187	0.8187	0.8187	0.8187	0.8187	0.8187
	0.0500	0.0020	0.0001	0.0000	0.0000	0.0000	0.0000	0.0000	0.0000	0.0000
0.3	0.7000	0.7391	0.7407	0.7408	0.7408	0.7408	0.7408	0.7408	0.7408	0.7408
	0.1286	0.0069	0.0004	0.0000	0.0000	0.0000	0.0000	0.0000	0.0000	0.0000
0.4	0.6000	0.6667	0.6701	0.6703	0.6703	0.6703	0.6703	0.6703	0.6703	0.6703
	0.2667	0.0167	0.0013	0.0001	0.0000	0.0000	0.0000	0.0000	0.0000	0.0000
0.5	0.5000	0.6000	0.6061	0.6065	0.6065	0.6065	0.6065	0.6065	0.6065	0.6065
	0.5000	0.0333	0.0030	0.0003	0.0000	0.0000	0.0000	0.0000	0.0000	0.0000
0.6	0.4000	0.5385	0.5479	0.5487	0.5488	0.5488	0.5488	0.5488	0.5488	0.5488
	0.9000	0.0593	0.0062	0.0006	0.0001	0.0000	0.0000	0.0000	0.0000	0.0000
0.7	0.3000	0.4815	0.4952	0.4965	0.4966	0.4966	0.4966	0.4966	0.4966	0.4966
	1.6333	0.0977	0.0112	0.0013	0.0001	0.0000	0.0000	0.0000	0.0000	0.0000
0.8	0.2000	0.4286	0.4472	0.4491	0.4493	0.4493	0.4493	0.4493	0.4493	0.4493
	3.2000	0.1524	0.0189	0.0024	0.0003	0.0000	0.0000	0.0000	0.0000	0.0000
0.9	0.1000	0.3793	0.4035	0.4062	0.4065	0.4066	0.4066	0.4066	0.4066	0.4066
	8.1000	0.2285	0.0300	0.0042	0.0005	0.0001	0.0000	0.0000	0.0000	0.0000
1.0	******	0.3333	0.3636	0.3673	0.3678	0.3679	0.3679	0.3679	0.3679	0.3679
	******	0.3333	0.0455	0.0068	0.0010	0.0001	0.0000	0.0000	0.0000	0.0000
1.1	******	0.2903	0.3273	0.3321	0.3328	0.3329	0.3329	0.3329	0.3329	0.3329
	******	0.4771	0.0664	0.0106	0.0016	0.0002	0.0000	0.0000	0.0000	0.0000
1.2	******	0.2500	0.2941	0.3002	0.3011	0.3012	0.3012	0.3012	0.3012	0.3012
	******	0.6750	0.0941	0.0159	0.0026	0.0004	0.0001	0.0000	0.0000	0.0000
1.3	******	0.2121	0.2638	0.2712	0.2723	0.2725	0.2725	0.2725	0.2725	0.2725
	******	0.9511	0.1303	0.0230	0.0040	0.0006	0.0001	0.0000	0.0000	0.0000
1.4	******	0.1795	0.2360	0.2449	0.2463	0.2466	0.2466	0.2466	0.2466	0.2466
	******	1.3451	0.1771	0.0325	0.0060	0.0010	0.0002	0.0000	0.0000	0.0000

1.5	******	0.1429	0.2105	0.2210	0.2228	0.2231	0.2231	0.2231	0.2231
	******	1.9286	0.2368	0.0448	0.0086	0.0016	0.0003	0.0000	0.0000
1.6	******	0.1111	0.1872	0.1993	0.2014	0.2018	0.2019	0.2019	0.2019
	******	2.8444	0.3129	0.0605	0.0122	0.0023	0.0004	0.0001	0.0000
1.7	******	0.0811	0.1657	0.1796	0.1821	0.1826	0.1827	0.1827	0.1827
	******	4.4261	0.4095	0.0803	0.0168	0.0034	0.0006	0.0001	0.0000
1.8	******	0.0526	0.1460	0.1616	0.1646	0.1652	0.1653	0.1653	0.1653
	******	7.6737	0.5321	0.1052	0.0288	0.0048	0.0009	0.0002	0.0000
1.9	******	0.0256	0.1278	0.1453	0.1487	0.1494	0.1495	0.1496	0.1496
	******	17.587	0.6884	0.1360	0.0303	0.0066	0.0014	0.0003	0.0000
2.0	******	******	0.1111	0.1304	0.1343	0.1351	0.1353	0.1353	0.1353
	******	******	0.8889	0.1739	0.0398	0.0090	0.0019	0.0004	0.0001
2.1	******	******	0.0957	0.1169	0.1213	0.1222	0.1224	0.1224	0.1225
	******	******	1.1488	0.2204	0.0515	0.0121	0.0027	0.0006	0.0001
2.2	******	******	0.0815	0.1046	0.1094	0.1105	0.1107	0.1108	0.1108
	******	******	1.4909	0.2772	0.0659	0.0159	0.0037	0.0008	0.0002
2.3	******	******	0.0683	0.0933	0.0987	0.0999	0.1002	0.1002	0.1003
	******	******	1.9511	0.3464	0.0835	0.0207	0.0049	0.0011	0.0002
2.4	******	******	0.0562	0.0831	0.0889	0.0903	0.0906	0.0907	0.0907
	******	******	2.5888	0.4306	0.1048	0.0266	0.0065	0.0015	0.0003
2.5	******	******	0.0449	0.0737	0.0801	0.0816	0.0820	0.0821	0.0821
	******	******	3.5112	0.5331	0.1304	0.0339	0.0086	0.0021	0.0005
2.6	******	******	0.0345	0.0651	0.0721	0.0737	0.0742	0.0742	0.0743
	******	******	4.9328	0.6582	0.1610	0.0427	0.0111	0.0027	0.0006
2.7	******	******	0.0249	0.0573	0.0648	0.0666	0.0671	0.0672	0.0672
	******	******	7.3535	0.8115	0.1976	0.0533	0.0142	0.0036	0.0009
2.8	******	******	0.0160	0.0502	0.0581	0.0601	0.0606	0.0608	0.0608
	******	******	12.2735	1.0002	0.2412	0.0660	0.0180	0.0047	0.0012
2.9	******	******	0.0077	0.0437	0.0521	0.0543	0.0548	0.0550	0.0550
	******	******	27.1927	1.2345	0.2929	0.0812	0.0227	0.0061	0.0015
3.0	******	******	******	0.0377	0.0466	0.0490	0.0496	0.0497	0.0498
	******	******	******	1.5283	0.3542	0.0991	0.0282	0.0078	0.0020

(continued)

Table 13-7. *continued*

λ/μ[a]	Number of servers in queuing system									
	1	2	3	4	5	6	7	8	9	10
3.1	******	******	******	0.0323	0.0417	0.0441	0.0448	0.0450	0.0450	0.0450
	******	******	******	1.9019	0.4269	0.1203	0.0349	0.0098	0.0026	0.0007
3.2	******	******	******	0.0273	0.0372	0.0398	0.0405	0.0407	0.0407	0.0408
	******	******	******	2.3857	0.5130	0.1453	0.0428	0.0123	0.0034	0.0009
3.3	******	******	******	0.0227	0.0330	0.0358	0.0366	0.0368	0.0369	0.0369
	******	******	******	3.0273	0.6152	0.1745	0.0522	0.0153	0.0043	0.0011
3.4	******	******	******	0.0186	0.0293	0.0322	0.0331	0.0333	0.0334	0.0334
	******	******	******	3.9061	0.7367	0.2086	0.0633	0.0190	0.0054	0.0015
3.5	******	******	******	0.0148	0.0259	0.0290	0.0298	0.0301	0.0302	0.0302
	******	******	******	5.1650	0.8816	0.2485	0.0762	0.0232	0.0068	0.0019
3.6	******	******	******	0.0113	0.0228	0.0260	0.0269	0.0272	0.0273	0.0273
	******	******	******	7.0898	1.0553	02948	0.0913	0.0283	0.0085	0.0024
3.7	******	******	******	0.0081	0.0200	0.0233	0.0243	0.0246	0.0247	0.0247
	******	******	******	10.3471	1.2646	0.3488	0.1089	0.0343	0.0105	0.0031
3.8	******	******	******	0.0051	0.0174	0.0209	0.0219	0.0222	0.0223	0.0224
	******	******	******	16.9370	1.5187	0.4116	0.1293	0.0413	0.0129	0.0038
3.9	******	******	******	0.0025	0.0151	0.0187	0.0198	0.0201	0.0202	0.0202
	******	******	******	36.8595	1.8302	0.4846	0.1529	0.0495	0.0157	0.0048
4.0	******	******	******	******	0.0130	0.0167	0.0178	0.0182	0.0183	0.0183
	******	******	******	******	2.2165	0.5695	0.1801	0.0590	0.0190	0.0059
4.1	******	******	******	******	0.0111	0.0149	0.0160	0.0164	0.0165	0.0166
	******	******	******	******	2.7029	0.6685	0.2115	0.0701	0.0229	0.0072
4.2	******	******	******	******	0.0093	0.0132	0.0144	0.0148	0.0149	0.0150
	******	******	******	******	3.3273	0.7839	0.2476	0.0828	0.0275	0.0088
4.3	******	******	******	******	0.0077	0.0117	0.0130	0.0134	0.0135	0.0136
	******	******	******	******	4.1493	0.9191	0.2890	0.0975	0.0328	0.0107
4.4	******	******	******	******	0.0063	0.0104	0.0117	0.0121	0.0122	0.0123
	******	******	******	******	5.2682	1.0778	0.3365	0.1143	0.0389	0.0129

4.5	******	******	0.0050	0.0091	0.0105	0.0109	0.0110	0.0111
	******	******	6.8624	1.2650	0.3910	0.1336	0.0460	0.0155
4.6	******	******	0.0038	0.0080	0.0094	0.0098	0.0100	0.0100
	******	******	9.2893	1.4869	0.4535	0.1556	0.0542	0.0185
4.7	******	******	0.0027	0.0070	0.0084	0.0089	0.0090	0.0091
	******	******	13.3821	1.7520	0.5251	0.1807	0.0636	0.0220
4.8	******	******	0.0017	0.0061	0.0075	0.0080	0.0081	0.0082
	******	******	21.6408	2.0711	0.6073	0.2093	0.0744	0.0261
4.9	******	******	0.0008	0.0053	0.0067	0.0072	0.0074	0.0074
	******	******	46.5655	2.4593	0.7017	0.2418	0.0867	0.0307
5.0	******	******	******	0.0045	0.0060	0.0065	0.0066	0.0067
	******	******	******	2.9376	0.8104	0.2788	0.1006	0.0361
5.1	******	******	******	0.0038	0.0053	0.0058	0.0060	0.0061
	******	******	******	3.5363	0.9357	0.3207	0.1165	0.0423
5.2	******	******	******	0.0032	0.0047	0.0052	0.0054	0.0055
	******	******	******	4.3009	1.0805	0.3683	0.1345	0.0493
5.3	******	******	******	0.0027	0.0042	0.0047	0.0049	0.0050
	******	******	******	5.3028	1.2486	0.4222	0.1549	0.0573
5.4	******	******	******	0.0021	0.0037	0.0042	0.0044	0.0045
	******	******	******	6.6611	1.4444	0.4833	0.1779	0.0664
5.5	******	******	******	0.0017	0.0032	0.0038	0.0040	0.0040
	******	******	******	8.5902	1.6736	0.5527	0.2039	0.0767
5.6	******	******	******	0.0013	0.0028	0.0034	0.0036	0.0037
	******	******	******	11.5185	1.9438	0.6314	0.2332	0.0884
5.7	******	******	******	0.0009	0.0025	0.0030	0.0032	0.0033
	******	******	******	16.4462	2.2643	0.7208	0.2662	0.1016
5.8	******	******	******	0.0006	0.0021	0.0027	0.0029	0.0030
	******	******	******	26.3732	2.6482	0.8226	0.3033	0.1165
5.9	******	******	******	0.0003	0.0018	0.0024	0.0026	0.0027
	******	******	******	56.2996	3.1130	0.9385	0.3451	0.1332
6.0	******	******	******	******	0.0016	0.0021	0.0024	0.0024
	******	******	******	******	3.6830	1.0709	0.3920	0.1519

(continued)

Table 13-7. *continued*

					Number of servers in queuing system					
λ/μ^a	1	2	3	4	5	6	7	8	9	10
6.1	******	******	******	******	******	******	0.0013	0.0019	0.0021	0.0022
	******	******	******	******	******	******	4.3937	1.2226	0.4447	0.1730
6.2	******	******	******	******	******	******	0.0011	0.0017	0.0019	0.0020
	******	******	******	******	******	******	5.2981	1.3968	0.5039	0.1966
6.3	******	******	******	******	******	******	0.0009	0.0015	0.0017	0.0018
	******	******	******	******	******	******	6.4796	1.5977	0.5705	0.2230
6.4	******	******	******	******	******	******	0.0007	0.0013	0.0015	0.0016
	******	******	******	******	******	******	8.0771	1.8306	0.6455	0.2525
6.5	******	******	******	******	******	******	0.0006	0.0012	0.0014	0.0015
	******	******	******	******	******	******	10.3406	2.1019	0.7298	0.2855
6.6	******	******	******	******	******	******	0.0004	0.0010	0.0012	0.0013
	******	******	******	******	******	******	13.7701	2.4200	0.8249	0.3223
6.7	******	******	******	******	******	******	0.0003	0.0009	0.0011	0.0012
	******	******	******	******	******	******	19.5323	2.7960	0.9323	0.3634
6.8	******	******	******	******	******	******	0.0002	0.0008	0.0010	0.0011
	******	******	******	******	******	******	31.1272	3.2446	1.0536	0.4092
6.9	******	******	******	******	******	******	0.0001	0.0007	0.0009	0.0010
	******	******	******	******	******	******	66.0548	3.7856	1.1911	0.4603
7.0	******	******	******	******	******	******	******	0.0006	0.0008	0.0009
	******	******	******	******	******	******	******	4.4472	1.3473	0.5174
7.1	******	******	******	******	******	******	******	0.0007	0.0007	0.0008
	******	******	******	******	******	******	******	5.2697	1.5253	0.5810
7.2	******	******	******	******	******	******	******	0.0004	0.0006	0.0007
	******	******	******	******	******	******	******	6.3138	1.7289	0.6521
7.3	******	******	******	******	******	******	******	0.0003	0.0005	0.0006
	******	******	******	******	******	******	******	7.6747	1.9627	0.7315
7.4	******	******	******	******	******	******	******	0.0003	0.0004	0.0006
	******	******	******	******	******	******	******	9.5111	2.2325	0.8204

7.5	******	******	******	******	******	******	0.0002 / 12.1088	0.0004 / 2.5457	0.0005 / 0.9198
7.6	******	******	******	******	******	******	0.0002 / 16.0392	0.0004 / 2.9118	0.0004 / 1.0314
7.7	******	******	******	******	******	******	0.0001 / 22.6357	0.0003 / 3.3432	0.0004 / 1.1566
7.8	******	******	******	******	******	******	0.0001 / 35.8982	0.0003 / 3.8563	0.0004 / 1.2976
7.9	******	******	******	******	******	******	0.0000 / 75.8269	0.0002 / 4.4736	0.0003 / 1.4567
8.0	******	******	******	******	******	******	******	0.0002 / 5.2226	0.0003 / 1.6367
8.1	******	******	******	******	******	******	******	0.0002 / 6.1608	0.0002 / 1.8411
8.2	******	******	******	******	******	******	******	0.0001 / 7.3444	0.0002 / 2.0740
8.3	******	******	******	******	******	******	******	0.0001 / 8.8845	0.0002 / 2.3406
8.4	******	******	******	******	******	******	******	0.0001 / 10.9597	0.0002 / 2.6474
8.5	******	******	******	******	******	******	******	0.0001 / 13.8914	0.0001 / 3.0025
8.6	******	******	******	******	******	******	******	0.0001 / 18.3226	0.0001 / 3.4166
8.7	******	******	******	******	******	******	******	0.0000 / 25.7532	0.0001 / 3.9032
8.8	******	******	******	******	******	******	******	0.0000 / 40.6832	0.0001 / 4.4807
8.9	******	******	******	******	******	******	******	0.0000 / 85.6127	0.0001 / 5.1742
9.0	******	******	******	******	******	******	******	******	0.0001 / 6.0186

(continued)

Table 13-7. *continued*

	Number of servers in queuing system									
λ/μ^a	1	2	3	4	5	6	7	8	9	10
9.1	******	******	******	******	******	******	******	******	******	0.0001
	******	******	******	******	******	******	******	******	******	7.0644
9.2	******	******	******	******	******	******	******	******	******	0.0000
	******	******	******	******	******	******	******	******	******	8.3873
9.3	******	******	******	******	******	******	******	******	******	0.0000
	******	******	******	******	******	******	******	******	******	10.1066
9.4	******	******	******	******	******	******	******	******	******	0.0000
	******	******	******	******	******	******	******	******	******	12.4204
9.5	******	******	******	******	******	******	******	******	******	0.0000
	******	******	******	******	******	******	******	******	******	15.6861
9.6	******	******	******	******	******	******	******	******	******	0.0000
	******	******	******	******	******	******	******	******	******	20.6179
9.7	******	******	******	******	******	******	******	******	******	0.0000
	******	******	******	******	******	******	******	******	******	28.8825
9.8	******	******	******	******	******	******	******	******	******	0.0000
	******	******	******	******	******	******	******	******	******	45.4799
9.9	******	******	******	******	******	******	******	******	******	0.0000
	******	******	******	******	******	******	******	******	******	95.4101

Note: See Appendix B for the equations from which the values in this table were derived.

[a] In the relationship λ/μ, λ = arrival rate to the queuing system and μ = service rate for each server.

[b] Cells show the values for p_0 (top value) and L_q (bottom value) for each λ/μ and number of servers. For example, if $\lambda = 3$ and $\mu = 2$, then $\lambda/\mu = 3/2 = 1.5$. With the number of servers = 2, $p_0 = 0.1429$ and $L_q = 1.9286$. That is, the system with these characteristics is empty of units less than 15% of the time and, on average, there are almost two units waiting for service.

Table 13-8.   Probability that a unit must wait for service (p_w) in queuing systems with Poisson arrivals and exponential service times

	Number of servers in the queuing system									
$\lambda\mu^a$	1	2	3	4	5	6	7	8	9	10
.1	.1000	******	******	******	******	******	******	******	******	******
.15	.1500	.0104	******	******	******	******	******	******	******	******
.2	.2000	.0181	******	******	******	******	******	******	******	******
.25	.2500	.0277	******	******	******	******	******	******	******	******
.3	.3000	.0391	******	******	******	******	******	******	******	******
.35	.3500	.0521	******	******	******	******	******	******	******	******
.4	.4000	.0666	******	******	******	******	******	******	******	******
.45	.4500	.0826	.0113	******	******	******	******	******	******	******
.5	.5000	.1000	.0151	******	******	******	******	******	******	******
.55	.5500	.1186	.0195	******	******	******	******	******	******	******
.6	.6000	.1384	.0246	******	******	******	******	******	******	******
.65	.6500	.1594	.0304	******	******	******	******	******	******	******
.7	.7000	.1814	.0369	******	******	******	******	******	******	******
.75	.7500	.2045	.0441	******	******	******	******	******	******	******
.8	.8000	.2285	.0520	******	******	******	******	******	******	******
.85	.8500	.2535	.0606	.0117	******	******	******	******	******	******
.9	.9000	.2793	.0700	.0143	******	******	******	******	******	******
.95	.9500	.3059	.0801	.0171	******	******	******	******	******	******
1.0	******	.3333	.0909	.0204	******	******	******	******	******	******
1.2	******	.4499	.1411	.0370	******	******	******	******	******	******
1.4	******	.5764	.2033	.0603	.0153	******	******	******	******	******
1.6	******	.7111	.2737	.0906	.0258	******	******	******	******	******
1.8	******	.8526	.3547	.1285	.0404	.0111	******	******	******	******
2.0	******	******	.4444	.1739	.0597	.0180	******	******	******	******
2.2	******	******	.5421	.2267	.0839	.0274	******	******	******	******
2.4	******	******	.6471	.2870	.1135	.0399	.0125	******	******	******
2.6	******	******	.7588	.3544	.1486	.0558	.0187	******	******	******
2.8	******	******	.8766	.4286	.1895	.0754	.0270	******	******	******
3.0	******	******	******	.5094	.2361	.0991	.0376	.0129	******	******
3.2	******	******	******	.5964	.2885	.1271	.0508	.0184	******	******
3.4	******	******	******	.6893	.3466	.1595	.0669	.0256	******	******

3.6	******	******	.7877	.4103	.1965	.0862	.0346	.0127	******
3.8	******	******	.8914	.4795	.2382	.1088	.0456	.0175	******
4.0	******	******	******	.5541	.2847	.1351	.0590	.0237	******
4.2	******	******	******	.6337	.3359	.1650	.0749	.0313	.0121
4.4	******	******	******	.7183	.3919	.1988	.0935	.0407	.0164
4.6	******	******	******	.8077	.4525	.2365	.1150	.0518	.0217
4.8	******	******	******	.9016	.5177	.2783	.1395	.0650	.0282
5.0	******	******	******	******	.5875	.3241	.1672	.0805	.0361
5.2	******	******	******	******	.6616	.3740	.1982	.0983	.0455
5.4	******	******	******	******	.7401	.4279	.2287	.1186	.0565
5.6	******	******	******	******	.8227	.4859	.2706	.1415	.0694
5.8	******	******	******	******	.9094	.5479	.3120	.1673	.0843
6.0	******	******	******	******	******	.6138	.3569	.1959	.1012
6.2	******	******	******	******	******	.6836	.4055	.2275	.1204
6.4	******	******	******	******	******	.7572	.4576	.2622	.1420
6.6	******	******	******	******	******	.8345	.5133	.2999	.1660
6.8	******	******	******	******	******	.9155	.5725	.3408	.1925
7.0	******	******	******	******	******	******	.6353	.3849	.2217
7.2	******	******	******	******	******	******	.7015	.4322	.2536
7.4	******	******	******	******	******	******	.7711	.4827	.2882
7.6	******	******	******	******	******	******	.8441	.5363	.3256
7.8	******	******	******	******	******	******	.9204	.5932	.3659
8.0	******	******	******	******	******	******	******	.6533	.4091
8.2	******	******	******	******	******	******	******	.7165	.4552
8.4	******	******	******	******	******	******	******	.7828	.5042
8.6	******	******	******	******	******	******	******	.8522	.5561
8.8	******	******	******	******	******	******	******	.9246	.6110
9.0	******	******	******	******	******	******	******	******	.6687
9.2	******	******	******	******	******	******	******	******	.7293
9.4	******	******	******	******	******	******	******	******	.7927
9.6	******	******	******	******	******	******	******	******	.8590
9.8	******	******	******	******	******	******	******	******	.9281

Note: See Appendix B for the equations from which the values for this table were derived. Calculations assume that the number of units in the system is equal to or greater than the number of servers in the system.

[a] In the relationship λ/μ, λ = arrival rate to the queuing system and μ = service rate for each server. For example, if λ = 6 and μ = 5, then λ/μ = 6/5 = 1.2. With the number of servers = 2, P_w = 0.4499. That is, the system with these characteristics has all servers busy almost 45% of the time, so there is a 45% probability that a unit must wait for service.

14

Analyzing Capacity and Resources

Chapter Objectives

1. To understand the relationship between the capacity of a system and its resources
2. To be able to estimate the production capability of a specific system

Key Terms and Concepts

Capacity analysis   Fixed costs
Break-even analysis   Variable costs

The purpose of this chapter is to focus attention on the relationship between the maximum capacity of a system or subsystem and the resources needed to establish a particular level of capacity. Managers, especially health administrators, must monitor systems to ensure that system capacity is close to actual or forecast demand. If capacity is significantly above actual or forecast demand, then some resources may need to be subtracted to increase the efficiency of the system. If capacity is below actual or forecast demand, then resources may need to be added to ensure that an adequate capacity exists to provide an effective as well as efficient service. In either case, to achieve reasonable levels of efficiency, the manager must know when, where, and how to act and what resources either to add or subtract.

Health administrators manage service-oriented systems in health care organizations. These systems have specific properties that influence how they can be analyzed and the options available to a manager for resource allocation.

CHARACTERISTICS OF HEALTH CARE SERVICE SYSTEMS

Service systems used to provide medical care are usually very complex. They are multistep processes, with each step governed by procedures and protocols, and involve many service stations or servers. Even expressed in its simplest form, a typical stay at a hospital is a coordinated multistep process, as shown in Figure 14-1.

Each of these steps, or phases, in the multistep process is complex. Admitting a patient requires the coordinated actions of many individuals and service stations in the hospital, some of which deal directly with the patient and others of which respond to patient-oriented actions. The admitting process may be significantly different for different types of patients. For example, routine admissions are different from emergency admissions.

Treatment is also highly complex. People come to a hospital for a medical treatment they need (as determined by the admitting physician) and expect the needed treatment to be provided in a professional manner. Treatment is a multistep process involving many servers, or service stations, in a hospital. The plan for the treatment also may change along the way as a physician alters the treatment plan given a change or modification in diagnosis, patient condition, or both. The service systems in the hospital are expected to respond to patient needs even if these needs change. If the hospital lacks the capacity to respond to patient needs, it must transfer the patient to another hospital with the needed capability. Discharge is also a complex action. It requires decisions and actions to be made by many individuals and service stations in the hospital.

Producing medical care is a complex production process involving many steps and the coordinated interplay of many individuals and servers or service stations. Health care is not unique in this regard. Manufacturing an automobile requires the coordinated interplay of many individual service stations (e.g., molding, assembly, painting) and servers along the production line. It is also a phased process that requires that some operations precede others (e.g., assembly precedes painting). Procedures and protocols are used to govern the actions of individual service stations. Although manufacturing processes used in the automobile industry resemble production processes used in hospitals, nursing homes, and clinics, production processes used in health and medical care are different. These differences make service systems in health and medical care even more complex.

Service systems used in medical care must be able to adjust and modify their actions based on a patient's needs—needs that may change during the production process. To see how this process is fundamentally different from the process of manufacturing other types of goods, we can consider the process of manufacturing

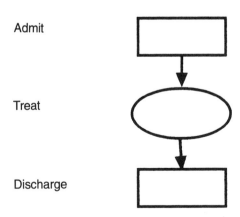

Admit

Treat

Discharge

Figure 14-1.   Flow of patients through hospital to produce output.

an automobile. Every automobile that passes through the production line requires four regular tires and one spare tire. When the manufacturing process is started, four, and only four, regular tires must be available to complete the production process. Machines and workers are needed to install only these four tires on the automobile. In health and medical care, as patients pass through the process of receiving medical care, however, their needs can change. A patient admitted to a hospital for routine abdominal surgery requiring two units of plasma may develop a complication during surgery that necessitates the use of two additional units of plasma. The hospital must have the capability to respond as needed to these changes.

If each wheel requires five lug nuts to install the wheels and tires on the car, the total number of lugs nuts needed per car would be 20. The analogous situation in health and medical care is much more difficult to estimate. How many laboratory tests per patient will be required? How many x-rays or CT scans will be required for each patient? How many meals will be required per patient? Each of these are questions that cannot be answered with the same amount of certainty associated with answering the question of how many lug nuts per car will be required.

The central point of the analogy between automobile production and medical care production is that medical care service systems must be able to respond to change during the production process and must plan for unanticipated needs. Service systems in medical care must reserve some of their capacity for these unanticipated needs. This requires that the capacity of a medical service system be established based on anticipated as well as unanticipated needs.

People use many of the service systems provided by a health care organization. People have wants, as well as needs and demands, and different people have different wants, as well as different needs and demands. People expect that their wants, as well as their needs, will be met by the medical service systems. For example, most people want to be referred to by their name, not by their medical condition (e.g., the gallbladder in room 224). People want treatment to be professional, and they define professional to include knowing what is happening to them and why. Some people may want more information than others. Giving a CT scan to a patient for the first time may require extra time. The experienced patient may know the appropriate routine and behaviors, may be better able to cooperate with the technician, and may not be frightened by the machine. The amount of increased time necessary to scan a first-time patient effectively has nothing to do with the scan per se; it reflects the human dynamic associated with administering medical care to people. Similarly, younger patients may have different wants than do more mature patients, even though they are in a hospital for the same service.

People evaluate their medical care and the systems used to provide the needed services based on the outcome associated with their treatment as well as how well the service met their wants. Therefore, the services offered by a hospital, nursing home, or clinic must be able to respond to the wants of their patients as well as their needs. Again, this is different from the production processes used to produce and manufacture automobiles.

As will be examined, the output of a medical service system is a unit of service as well as information. Examples of service units are: 1) a specific medical test, x-ray, or scan; 2) a meal; 3) a prescription; and 4) a specific surgical operation. Service systems produce these service units. They also produce information that records the action in a medical record and/or management information system. Service systems are expected to produce information as well as service units.

A final characteristic of medical service systems involves their capacity—the ability to produce service units based on the capability and productivity of the servers as well as on the machines and other resources used to produce a service unit.

CAPACITY IN HEALTH CARE SERVICE SYSTEMS

Examining and determining the capacity of a system or subsystem is as much an art as a science, especially in health care organizations. It is difficult to define the boundaries of a specific health care service system, as well as to assess the current capacity level, given the multiple demands the systems and servers are expected to fulfill. To examine this point requires a basic review of systems theory.

Systems can be examined as processes. These processes convert input resources into outputs. The process of converting inputs into outputs adds value. Systems feed back information to adjust, as necessary, the conversion of inputs into outputs. Systems adjust the way in which they convert resources by changing the processes used to convert inputs into outputs, by changing the conversion process to be able to produce either fewer or more outputs, or both. Feedback, usually in the form of information, is the primary stimulus for managerial change in the resource input mix. Feedback is also the primary stimulus for a redefinition of the processes used to convert resources into outputs. Systems are directed by goals and objectives. Managers design, control, and modify systems in order to meet these goals and objectives. Any specific system is another system's subsystem. A typical system is shown in Figure 14-2.

These central points of the systems model as an analytical framework, especially when examined from the perspective of a health care organization, demonstrate the rationale for the assertion that determining capacity is a managerial art— it requires judgment to do well. Although determining capacity and matching resources to intended and required levels of capacity must be done in a systematic manner—often using tools and approaches developed in the field of industrial engineering and cost analysis—the decisions that must be made are judgmental, not scientific.

In system terms, the health administrator creates capacity by assigning resources to a specific service station. The service station converts these resources into services. The capacity of a service station is created by the amount and type of

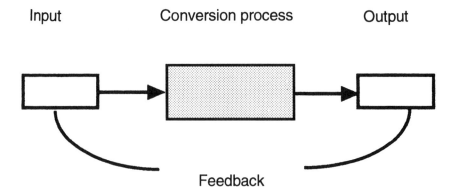

Figure 14-2.   Components of a typical system.

input resources assigned to the service station. The health administrator as manager must ensure that the capacity created by the mix of input resources is appropriate. If the capacity of a service station is too high, the service system may be inefficient. If the capacity of a service station is too low, the goals and objectives of the organization that depend on the service station are jeopardized.

Service stations create feedback. One type of feedback is the quantity of outputs generated by specific service stations. Management must judge whether the amount of resources assigned to all service stations is justified, given past output performance and anticipated future requirements. In some instances, the capacity of a service station may need to be lowered to return the service station to a reasonable level of efficiency.

Fixed Costs versus Variable Costs

Costs behave differently in relation to volume of service provided. A fixed cost is a cost that does not change as the volume of service provided changes. Salaries and benefits are fixed costs. The vast majority of expenses associated with physical structures are fixed costs. Equipment represents fixed costs. Interest on debt and taxes (if any) represent fixed costs. In contrast, a variable cost changes as the volume of service provided changes. A unit of variable cost is added when an additional unit of service is provided. Similarly, a unit of a variable cost is avoided when a unit of service is not provided. Parts and supplies are typically variable costs.

The total cost of a system or subsystem is equal to total fixed costs plus the variable costs associated with the volume of service provided (i.e., output level). In other words:

$$TC = FC + (VC \times U) \qquad \text{(Eq. 14-1)}$$

where TC = total costs
FC = total fixed costs
VC = variable cost per unit
U = units

This relationship has special relevance to the health services administrator. In general, health service administrators manage organizations and systems that are dominated by fixed costs. Although some variable costs do exist, the vast majority of the costs associated with providing a personal health care service in a hospital, nursing home, or clinic setting are fixed. To manage a health care organization successfully requires the ability to manage fixed costs. Other industrial sectors that face the same challenge include schools and colleges and airlines.

When the concept of fixed costs and variable costs are added to the relationships between volume and revenue production, the classical break-even, or cost–volume–profit, relationship emerges. Figure 14-3 illustrates this relationship. It should be noted that:

1. At the break-even point in volume, total costs equal total revenue.
2. Below the break-even point in volume, the contribution margin is contributed to paying for the fixed costs.
3. Above the break-even point, the contribution margin is contributed to profits (excess revenue left after all costs have been paid).

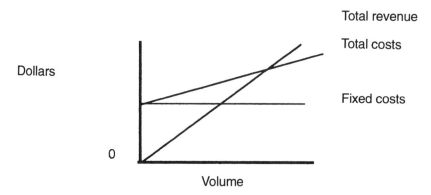

Figure 14-3.   The cost–volume–profit relationship.

It is important that features and characteristics of the break-even, or cost–volume–profit, relationship be appreciated in this context. Given these relationships, the manager faced with the challenge of managing an organization or system dominated by fixed costs efficiently and effectively has few choices.

Variable costs are managed by ensuring that the unit of variable cost is the lowest possible. For example, different supplies are used to produce a patient day or to treat a patient in a clinic. The dual challenge of efficiency and effectiveness demands that the manager ensure that the organization uses technically appropriate supplies (i.e., quality) and secures these supplies at the lowest unit cost possible, sometimes by purchasing supplies in bulk. To manage a variable cost, the manager strives to minimize the cost per unit.

Managing fixed costs is different. To manage a system or subsystem dominated by fixed costs effectively requires that the actual or forecast volume of services corresponds to the capacity created by the fixed costs. To accomplish this, managers have some options.

Managers can change fixed costs into variable costs by redefining certain practices. For example, changing personnel expenses from a fixed salary to a per-patient fee paid to each employee changes a fixed cost to a variable cost. This option lowers total fixed costs and reduces the break-even point. In health care, however, most professionals are compensated based on a guaranteed salary or an hourly rate guaranteed for 37.5 or 40 hours per week. Changing the basis of compensating employees from a fixed cost to a variable cost is rarely accepted well by employees.

Another option is to lower fixed costs. Paying lower salaries, providing less comprehensive benefits, lowering staffing levels, changing the staffing mix to include lower paid workers, refinancing a capital debt to lower debt payments based on lower interest charges, reducing energy costs through a conservation program, borrowing money at the lowest possible interest rates, and other related actions can be used to lower fixed costs. Because a significant majority of all fixed costs found in health care organizations lie in the area of personnel, lowering staffing levels and changing the staffing mix are options that usually attract most managerial interest when fixed costs must be reduced. This option also lowers the break-even point.

Another related option is to change a fixed cost into a semifixed cost. Unlike a fixed cost, which does not vary or change based on the volume of service rendered, and a variable cost, which does change based on the volume of service rendered, a cost that is semifixed changes in increments or steps. It is when considering this option that managers become especially interested in the capacity associated with specific levels of resources.

When combined, these last two options present an interesting approach. Staffing could be held at one level when the volume is or is expected to be between *x* and *y* units of service and increased to a higher level when volume exceeds or is expected to exceed *y* units of service. This type of approach, for example, changes salary from a fixed to a semifixed cost. The cost of personnel increases or decreases only when the volume exceeds the threshold established (e.g., *y* units of service). This last option establishes a different break-even point in volume depending on the fixed or semifixed costs used to create the needed capacity.

In general, the challenge of fixed costs must be met with volume. Actions must be taken to ensure that capacity and output are reasonably close and that capacity is lowered when output is expected to fall. The capacity created by the fixed costs must be used for productive purposes. Having the capacity and not using it is highly inefficient.

As noted in Chapter 13, however, if volume is too close to capacity, it is likely that a patient or unit will have to wait an unacceptably long time. One can never have volume equal capacity and maintain an effective health care delivery system.

Capacity and Output in Relation to Efficiency

The relationship between capacity and output is a measure of efficiency and is best explored using an analogy from the airline industry. Airlines measure their capacity by counting the number of seats in their airplanes. The capacity of a particular flight depends on the number of seats in the airplane assigned to that flight. A larger airplane may have 250 seats, a smaller airplane only 100 seats. The capacity of the larger airplane is 250 passengers, the capacity of the smaller airplane is 100 passengers. If an airline assigned a 250-seat airplane to a specific flight, no more than 250 passengers could be accommodated. If the airline assigned a 100-seat airplane to a specific flight, no more than 100 passengers could be accommodated.

As resources are increased, more service units are possible. As the size of an airplane assigned to a specific flight increases, the number of service units that can be generated increases. If the 250-seat airplane is substituted for the 100-seat airplane on a specific flight, capacity shifts from 100 passengers to 250 passengers.

The finite capacity of an airplane establishes a limit that cannot be exceeded. This "production frontier" is the upper limit of capacity. For the 250-seat airplane, it is 250 passengers; for the 100-seat airplane, it is 100 passengers. Anytime actual usage is less than the production frontier, inefficiency exists, as shown in Figure 14-4.

The line in Figure 14-4 represents the maximum level of production associated with a specific level of resources. This line establishes the boundary between the possible and impossible, or the production frontier. At any specific level of resources, the production frontier cannot be crossed. The 100-seat airplane cannot fly more than 100 passengers; 101 passengers is impossible. The 250-seat airplane cannot fly more than 250 passengers; 251 passengers is impossible. However, 250 or fewer passengers is possible. The only way capacity can be increased along the production frontier, in this case, is by substituting a larger airplane with more seats. The concept of a production frontier establishes a quantitative measure of the upper limit of production capability at a set level of resources.

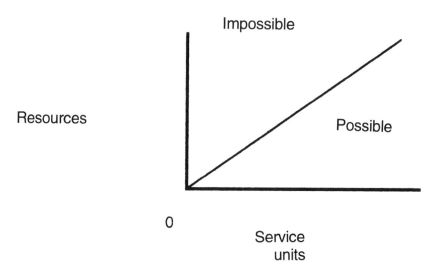

Figure 14-4.   A production frontier.

Airlines measure their output based on passenger miles. Each mile one passenger flies is one passenger mile. Flying 100 passengers 400 miles generates 40,000
passenger miles, for example. Knowing the production frontier associated with specific levels of resources (e.g., a 100- vs. a 250-seat airplane) establishes the upper
limit of output.

The upper limit of output can be used to compare actual output with potential
upper limit capability in order to assess and manage the relationship between input
resources and output. For example, if 100 passengers flew on the 250-seat airplane
for the 400-mile trip, 40,000 of the potential 100,000 passenger miles were used,
and 60,000 of the passenger miles were not used. In this example, only 40% of the
capacity was being used. If the same airplane and load factors were experienced on
a flight of 200 miles, 5,000 passenger miles would be possible, but only 40%, or
2,000 passenger miles, would be produced.

Switching to health care organizations and systems, patient days are a measure
of a hospital's output. A 100-bed hospital can produce no more than 36,500 patient
days in any 1 year (365 days × 100 beds). Resident days are used to express the output of a nursing home. Visits are used to express the output of a clinic or a home
health service. Most other measures of output (and capacity) used in health care
organizations and systems are production rates, such as the number of procedures
per unit of time (e.g., minute, hour, day, week, or year). The number of procedures
possible is the system's capacity. The number of procedures performed is the system's output. Greater degrees of efficiency are achieved when the ratio measure of
output to capacity approaches 1. If 100 procedures per hour are possible, performing 80 procedures per hour indicates a higher level of efficiency than performing
30 procedures per hour.

ANALYZING COMPLEX SYSTEMS

The process of designing and analyzing service systems can be accomplished using
a multistep process:

1. Identify the system or subsystem in question, and identify the process and the individual steps in the process. Typically, general systems flow charting is used to accomplish this step.
2. Determine who or what does what. General systems flow charting is a useful tool to accomplish this step.
3. Determine the system's current capacity. This can be done by determining the capacity of each component in the overall production process.
4. Compare system capacity with the system's output.
5. Change the resource mix of the system as necessary to enhance the system's efficiency.

The critical step in this process is the determination of a system's capacity.

In some instances the best way to determine capacity is to ask professionals to estimate how many service units they can produce in a specific time period. Capacity can also be measured. The time it takes staff to do a specific procedure or task can be measured. Repeated measures can be taken to ensure reliability and validity. Industrial engineering provides numerous approaches to measure the capacity of systems. Most involve observing a system and timing different steps.

Measuring and estimating the capacity of service systems should focus on the components of the service system. Sometimes categories of activities must be used. For example, a typical radiology department in a hospital can do in excess of 200 different x-ray procedures. The time and resources it takes to do each type of procedure can be estimated. Grouping specific procedures into resource-based categories facilitates analysis. In radiology, x-rays can be grouped into those that require one film versus those that require multiple films. Once categorized the resources needed by each step in the production process can be measured and estimated by the type of procedure.

If capacity cannot be measured, the capacity of the system can be set at the level of peak volume. If a radiology department is able to process 150 x-rays in an 8-hour shift with a specific resource mix, then this system or subsystem has demonstrated it has this level of capacity. Although not as precise as capacity established based on formal study, using peak levels of performance to estimate capacity does provide the manager with a usable surrogate to estimate capacity.

USING THE CAPACITY ANALYSIS MODEL

The capacity analysis model is a quantitative model that can be used to establish the optimal or best level of resources needed to achieve a certain level of output. It is used when:

1. The same resources can be used to produce two or more types of services.
2. The problem is one of "mix"—that is, a problem that requires the most efficient optimal mix of at least two resources to produce the products or services.
3. The problem requires an optimal or best solution. A best solution is different than a good solution or an acceptable solution.
4. There are constraints on the solution, so that certain solutions are outside the range of usable answers—they are infeasible solutions. A production frontier is an example of a constraint. These constraints are limited resources.
5. A linear relationship exists between the variables (i.e., when one variable changes, the others change in direct proportion, regardless of production level).

Two methods for using the capacity analysis model exist: 1) the graphical method and 2) the algebraic method.

Graphical Method

The graphical method of capacity analysis establishes a graphical representation of two variables. For example, a hospital operates its nursing service under the following constraints:

1. The budget is $5,000 per day to support nursing salaries.
2. Registered nurses are paid $200 per day, and licensed practical nurses are paid $100 per day.

The manager's task is to determine:

1. The nursing mix that will: a) ensure at least one registered nurse and b) maximize the number of nurses in the hospital.
2. The nursing mix that will: a) maximize the educational level of the nurses in the hospital and b) ensure at least 10 registered and 10 licensed practical nurses.

In this case, the problem is one of "mix." To solve this problem, a graphical model is developed that is based on the constraints and issues in the task.

First consider the constraints: budget and salary. With $5000, 25 registered nurses ($5,000 ÷ $200 per day) or 50 licensed practical nurses ($5,000 ÷ $100 per day) can be hired. These constraints are shown graphically in Figure 14-5. Neither of these mixes of resources (25 registered nurses and no licensed practical nurses, or 50 licensed practical nurses and no registered nurses) satisfies all the parameters associated with the task, however. Some other mix is necessary.

The first part of the task is to determine the nursing mix that will ensure at least one registered nurse and maximize the number of nurses in the hospital. One registered nurse costs $200 per day, leaving $4,800 to support licensed practical nurses. For $4,800, at $100 per day, 48 licensed practical nurses can be retained. Thus, the solution to the first part of the task is to hire one registered nurse and 48 licensed practical nurses (Figure 14-6).

The second part of the task is to determine the nursing mix that will maximize the educational level of the nurses in the hospital and ensure at least 10 registered and 10 licensed practical nurses. Registered nurses have more education than licensed practical nurses. Ten licensed practical nurses cost $1,000 per day, leaving $4,000 to support registered nurses. For this amount, at $200 per day, 20 registered nurses can be retained. Thus, the solution to the second part of the task is to hire 10 licensed practical and 20 registered nurses (Figure 14-7).

The graphical method of capacity analysis demonstrates the concept of the capacity analysis model when the problem involves mixing two variables or resources with known constraints. Figures 14-5, 14-6, and 14-7 also demonstrate that some combinations of the two variables lie outside the realm of feasibility. They are infeasible solutions as long as the constraints and parameters established for the problem remain as given. For example, given the constraints, it is infeasible to hire 35 registered nurses and 55 licensed practical nurses. Such a solution would violate the budgetary constraint used in this example. Solutions that are infeasible are beyond the production frontier associated with the constraints established for the specific situation.

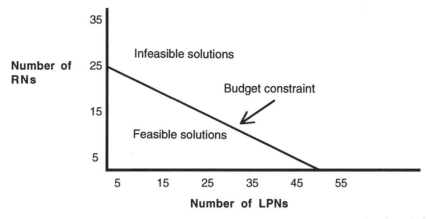

Figure 14-5.   Graphical representation of the mix of nursing resources in a hospital.

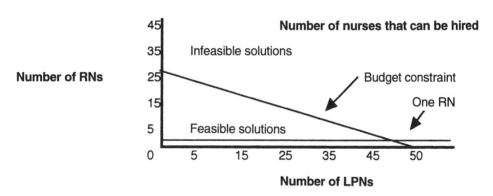

Figure 14-6.   Graphical solution to first part of the nursing mix task.

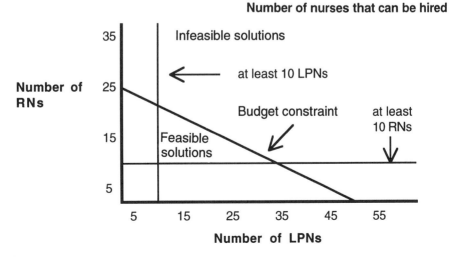

Figure 14-7.   Graphical solution to second part of the nursing mix task.

Algebraic Method

The graphical approach is simple to use when only two resources must be mixed and sufficient constraints and parameters are known to determine the "best" mix of resources. The algebraic method of capacity analysis provides the same type of problem-solving approach but is able to determine the best mix of more than two variables or resources. Similar to the graphical method, this method is based on determining the production frontier and then determining the best mix of resources given specific constraints and parameters.

For example, analysis has determined that the radiology department uses a four-step process in handling x-rays:

1. The x-ray is imaged. The patient is escorted to a room with appropriate machines and the x-ray is taken. At the end of imaging, the patient leaves.
2. The x-ray is developed. The exposed x-ray is processed through a machine. After it is processed, it is usable.
3. The x-ray is read by a radiologist. The physician reads the x-ray, makes a clinical finding, and dictates a report.
4. The x-ray is reported. The report dictated by the radiologist is typed. One copy is placed in the patient's medical record, one copy is filed in the radiology department, and one copy is sent to the physician who ordered the x-ray.

Analysis indicates that, over the next 3-month period, each of these steps in the process has a finite capacity. Each service station in the radiology department has a finite or limited number of work hours (assuming 80% productivity levels for all workers):

1. Imaging: 630 work hours available
2. Developing: 600 work hours available
3. Reading: 708 work hours available
4. Reporting: 135 work hours available

The radiology department does two types of x-rays:

1. General x-rays: simple procedures often only requiring one film
2. Special x-rays: complex procedures that often require multiple films over a period of time

Each step in the production process requires a different amount of time for each type of x-ray. Table 14-1 provides the time data for these steps.

The manager's task is to find the mix of general and special x-rays that maximizes contribution to either profit or fixed costs. Analysis has also determined that:

1. Each general x-ray contributes $10 to profit or fixed costs.
2. Each special x-ray contributes $9 to profit or fixed costs.

Table 14-1.   X-ray processing time data (in hours) by type of x-ray

Stage	General x-rays	Special x-rays
Imaging	0.70	1.00
Developing	0.50	0.83
Reading	1.00	0.67
Reporting	0.10	0.25

The relationship between total profit (P) and the contribution to profit of each type of radiograph can be expressed as:

$$P = \$10 \times GXR + \$9 \times SXR$$

where GXR = the number of general x-rays
SXR = the number of special x-rays

Fulfilling the task requires maximizing profit of 10 general plus 9 special x-rays, subject to the following constraints. (Note that work time estimates for each step in the process are coefficients for GXR and SXR in the equation.)

X-ray imaging cannot exceed 630 staff hours, so ($0.70\ GXR + 1.00\ SXR$) $\leq$ 630 hours. (*Note:* This should be read that the sum of the length of time it takes to image each general x-ray (7/10ths of an hour) times the number of general x-rays provided *plus* the time it takes to image each special x-ray (1 hour) times the number of special x-rays provided must (in the next 3 months) be equal to or less than 630 work hours. If it were more, a constraint would be violated.)

X-ray developing cannot exceed 600 staff hours, so ($0.50\ GXR + 0.83\ SXR$) $\leq$ 600 hours.

X-ray reading cannot exceed 708 staff hours, so ($1.00\ GXR + 0.67\ SXR$) $\leq$ 708 hours.

X-ray reporting cannot exceed 135 staff hours, so ($0.10\ GXR + 0.25\ SXR$) $\leq$ 135 hours.

Both GXR and SXR must be numbers equal to or greater than zero.

Based on these relationships and constraints, the production function for the multistep process can be determined. For example, 630 hours are available for imaging. Therefore,

At 0.70 hour for each general x-ray, GXR can equal 900 as long as SXR equals 0.
At 1 hour for each special x-ray, SXR can equal 630 as long as GXR equals 0.

Using this approach to calculate maximum production possibilities by production step yields the data in Table 14-2. This table indicates that only 708 general x-rays can be produced because, even though 900 general x-rays can be imaged, 1,200 developed, and 1,350 reported, only 708 can be read. Therefore, the overall production process is limited to a maximum of 708 general x-rays. Similarly, only 540 special x-rays can be produced because, even though 630 special x-rays can be imaged, 720 developed, and 1,072 read, only 540 can be reported. Therefore, the overall production process is limited to a maximum of 708 general, or 540 special, x-rays.

Using this information, the range of possible maximum profits can be calculated:

Table 14-2. Limits on capacity of radiology department

Stage	Maximum number of general x-rays	Maximum number of special x-rays
Imaging	900	630
Developing	1,200	720
Reading	708	1,072
Reporting	1,350	540

Table 14-3.   Maximum use of resources in radiology department

Stage	Hours used	Slack	Total hours
Imaging	630	0	630
Developing	480	120	600
Reading	708	0	708
Reporting	117	18	135

If 708 general x-rays are produced (and 0 special x-rays), profit will be 708 times $10 per x-ray, or $7,080.

If 540 special x-rays are produced (and 0 general x-rays), profit will be 540 times $9 per x-ray, or $4,860.

Determining the exact mix of special and general x-rays that will maximize profits given the production constraints and parameters requires using a computer program that performs linear programming.

The next step in developing the model is to include the concept of slack (S). Slack refers to resources not used. In this example, slack would be the unused staff time or excess capacity. In each of the following equations, slack will take on the value necessary to establish the equality relationship:

Imaging: $0.70\ GXR + 1.00\ SXR + S_1 = 630$
Developing: $0.50\ GXR + 0.83\ SXR + S_2 = 600$
Reading: $1.00\ GXR + 0.67\ SXR + S_3 = 708$
Reporting: $0.10\ GXR + 0.25\ SXR + S_4 = 135$

All slack variables must be zero or greater than zero. Table 14-3 provides a summary of excess capacity (slack) at these levels of production.

Effects of Changes in Capacity

The data from the radiology department capacity analysis model can be used to assess the effects of changes in capacity. If, during the next 3 months, demand is expected to exceed a stated production frontier, then this model indicates which step in the production process should receive additional resources. It also indicates where capacity could be reduced to increase efficiency at the stated production frontier. Using the maximum ranges (708 general x-rays or 540 special x-rays), slack can be estimated (see Table 14-4). The data in Table 14-4 indicate that reducing

Table 14-4.   Excess capacity (slack) in radiology department

Stage	Production capability (number of x-rays)	Production limit (number of x-rays)	Slack (hours)[a]
General x-rays			
Imaging	900	708	192
Developing	1,200	708	492
Reading	708	708	0
Reporting	1,350	708	642
Special x-rays			
Imaging	630	540	**90**
Developing	720	540	**180**
Reading	1,072	540	532
Reporting	540	540	0

[a]The numbers in bold type represent excess capacity that could be eliminated without changing the mix of x-rays that could be produced in the next 3 months.

imaging by up to 90 hours and developing by 180 hours would enhance efficiency and not affect any mix of x-rays that could be produced during the future 3-month period. If only general x-rays are needed, reducing imaging hours by 90 would still leave an excess capacity of 102 hours. Slack would be 102 (i.e., $192 - 90 = 102$). If the radiology department was called on to produce only special x-rays, reducing imaging by 90 staff hours would leave zero slack. The situation with the developing step is similar. If only general x-rays were produced, reducing staffing by 180 hours over the next 3 months would still leave 312 excess hours (i.e., $492 - 180 = 312$). Reducing the developing step by 180 staff hours would leave zero excess if only special x-rays were produced.

As demonstrated by this example, the capacity analysis model identifies the production frontier associated with multistep production processes and can be used to develop strategies to increase or reduce resources so that capacity and output are an efficient aspect of the operation of the system or subsystem. It is important to note that different services require different resources. The example classified x-rays into either general or special types and stated different resource requirements for each at each step in the production process. More often than not, service stations in medical care production systems provide more than one type of service. The capacity analysis models are designed to assist when two or more variables are present. These models provide the ability to estimate production frontiers when faced with this type of situation.

EXERCISES

14-1. Two types of visits are provided by the Durham Health Clinic: first time visits and return visits. Table 14-5 provides the processing time for each work station and the available staff hours per week. Determine the production frontiers for this clinic and indicate which station should be expanded to increase the overall capacity of the clinic. Which service station could be reduced?

14-2. Durham Health Clinic has a contribution margin of $35 per visit. Calculate the break-even point in visits with fixed costs at $4,000, $6,500, and $8,500 per week. Given this analysis, what would you recommend and why?

14-3. Durham Health Clinic is considering signing a contract to perform 50 preemployment physicals per week for a specific corporation. In terms of staff time, a preemployment physical requires 0.20 hour in reception/discharge, 0.45 hour in nursing and testing, and 0.20 hour in examination. By work station, determine how many work hours per week will be needed to perform these physicals.

Table 14-5. Processing time and staff hours data for Durham Health Clinic (Exercise 14-1)

Work station	Time estimates (hours)	
	First visit	Return visit
Reception/discharge	0.25	0.12
Nursing and testing	0.40	0.38
Medical exam and treatment	0.50	0.25

Currently the clinic receives 250 visits per week, with 50% of all visits as return visits. Each employee (physician, nurse, receptionist) is scheduled to work 35 hours per week.

a. How many employees, by type, does the clinic currently need?
b. How many employees, by type, will the clinic need if it signs the contract for preemployment physicals?
c. If return visits shift to 10% of all regular visits, how many employees by type will the clinic need with and without the contract for preemployment physicals?
d. How will the answers to (b) and (c) change if the number of physicals is modified to 35 preemployment physicals per week?

Throughout these analyses, specify all assumptions, including assumptions concerning worker productivity.

15

The Business Plan

Chapter Objectives

1. To understand the function of the business plan in health services management
2. To be able to prepare a business plan for a specific project

Key Terms and Concepts

Business plans as formal reports   Pro forma financial statements
The business plan as a methodo-
    logy

Every health care organization is an ongoing, active system. From the perspective of such a system, a project is a change or alteration. Managers make changes in health care organizations for many reasons, including the enhancement of the organization's operational efficiency. This chapter presents the business plan as both a formal document prepared by managers as part of the process of altering ongoing systems and a methodology used by managers to design alternatives for health care organizations.

A business plan is a way of thinking about change within the organization. It is intended to present the consequences associated with a change. Within the organization, a business plan is used to present to decision makers a proposed change as well as its purpose, the plan to accomplish it, and the consequences associated with it.

Business plans also are considered by decision makers from outside the organization. For example, securing external capital to finance a project is usually based on the comprehensive review of a business plan by banks and other external sources of capital. Regulatory agencies also consider business plans and frequently have specific questions and issues that must be addressed.

Business plans used outside the organization are presented in written reports. Some are very detailed, others are short. When used as the basis for internal decision making, different organizations have different traditions and cultures involving business plans. Frequently, a business plan is presented orally in order to highlight major points to decision makers. Whether a detailed written report is presented or not, the business plan contains the analytical results and intended actions to design or redesign features of the organization. It also addresses implementation.

The methods and techniques covered in previous chapters are relevant to the health services manager only insofar as they contribute to the manager's ability to develop business plans and address the questions contained in the business plans. Managers learn to use quantitative methods as a means to produce accurate and comprehensive business plans. Some parts of business plans require expertise in other areas, including such fields as marketing, epidemiology, and finance.

THE ROLE AND FUNCTION OF THE BUSINESS PLAN

Every change has consequences. Some changes affect the economic position of the organization. Other changes expand or redefine the organization's mission and the organization's ability to meet its mission. Some changes have direct consequences on some employees and indirect consequences on others. A change in one part of the organization may affect many parts of the organization. Some changes, such as a new or modified building, are so major that they require decision makers from outside the organization to approve their financing or grant regulatory approval (e.g., Certificate of Need). Some changes may affect the market position of the organization and its ability to meet the health needs, demands, and wants in the community it serves. Many changes require the coordinated actions of many individuals to design and implement. All changes require that many decision makers understand the proposed change and the consequences associated with it.

Analyzing a system is intended to reveal some operative feature of the system, such as the average amount of time a patient waits for service or the capacity of the laboratory to process medical tests. Designing or redesigning systems is intended to identify aspects of a system that must be altered in order to change the system's ability to meet specific goals and objectives (e.g., on average, no patient should wait more than 20 minutes in the walk-in ambulatory care clinic). Analyzing and designing or redesigning systems are core competencies of a manager. Health services managers are expected to be able to analyze ongoing systems and design changes as needed. The business plan is the framework used by the manager to secure approval for the change.

To accomplish this task, the business plan must include sufficient information for decision makers to make an informed and reasoned decision. It also must be presented in a manner that facilitates understanding of the issues, the plans, and the positive and negative consequences of the proposed change. It must inform decision makers and facilitate their reasoned judgment concerning the change. Sometimes decision makers face the unenviable situation of having to choose between two or more proposals to do different things. The business plan provides the information that decision makers should use to evaluate competing proposals.

Generally, most discussions of business plans emphasize their role in making decisions concerning new business ventures. In these discussions, the business plan is the document that is used to transform the new venture from an idea (a concept) to a reality (an implemented program). The business plan describes the proposed new business venture as a package and then indicates the impact associated with adding this package to the organization. Given this focus, most discussions emphasize the market and financial impact associated with the proposed new business venture. Other discussions of the business plan emphasize the need for a formal document written specifically to secure external capital that concisely describes and analyzes the proposed new business venture.

The business plan as a methodology is not limited to new business ventures or ventures that require external approval or capital. The questions that must be answered in a business plan are equally valid for changes to existing services and changes that can be approved and implemented without external approval or resources. The business plan requires clear and precise answers to important questions that typically must be addressed before any significant organizational change is approved or implemented. Considering and answering the questions is good management practice. In other words, the analysis and systems design done using many of the techniques and approaches addressed in this book are the basis for much of the information contained in a business plan.

Business plans for health care organizations must include all the information used in the commercial sector as well as information specific to health and medical care delivery. The following section examines the core elements of any business plan, with specific questions added to make the business plan relevant to organizations that provide health and medical care services.

ELEMENTS OF A BUSINESS PLAN

Numerous approaches can be used to organize a business plan. The approach used in this chapter focuses on key questions organized into specific sections. Sections are organized to provide a broad overview of the proposed change or project, backed up with specific plans.

Description of the Project

The business plan begins by indicating the name and location of the organization and giving a description of the proposed project. This projected change could be a new service or a significant modification to an existing service. The description is short and concise and indicates the nature and scope of the change. This section of the business plan also describes how the proposed change fits with the mission and goals of the organization. Key questions that must be addressed are:

- What is proposed?
- Is this a new capability or an expansion of an existing capability?
- Why is the change being recommended?
- How does the proposed change fit with the mission and goals of the organization?

Some managers choose to begin this section with a brief history of the organization and a general discussion of the organization's mission. For this section to be complete, it must state exactly what is being proposed and why.

A free-standing occupational health clinic adjacent to the hospital and located on the campus of the hospital is proposed. The facility will be a newly constructed 24,000-square foot facility with ample parking located on 1 acre. It will provide diagnostic and treatment services to occupational health clients 12 hours per weekday and 6 hours on Saturdays.

This is a new capability that will improve the existing ability to serve occupational health clients. Currently, occupational health clients are treated in the emergency department and by diagnostic and treatment services located in the hospital.

Emergency department prices and practices are not competitive with those of other providers of occupational health services. Unless a new service is developed, more employers will establish internal clinics. Using the hospital's emergency department is not convenient for most worker injuries for which urgent but non-emergency care is needed. Employers have expressed dissatisfaction at the waiting time many employees experience before they are served and discharged from the emergency department.

The mission of the hospital is to meet the health needs and demands of people living and working in the surrounding communities with cost-effective services. The proposed occupational health clinic will provide high-quality services to workers and provide employers with consulting services to prevent worker injuries. Both are within the scope of the hospital's existing mission statement.

Market and Competitor Analysis

A market and competitor analysis is used to inform decision makers about how the proposed project will affect the market position of the organization. It generally describes the competition and provides a statement of how the organization will be able to secure and retain market share. Other information can include: 1) current and anticipated market trends, 2) growth potential by market segment, and 3) estimated sales. (Details on marketing are provided in the section on the marketing plan.) Often this section includes a SWOT analysis of the organization that indicates and discusses the organization's *s*trengths, *w*eaknesses, *o*pportunities, and *t*hreats and examines how the proposed project fits into this framework. It also identifies the target market for the new or changed service and analyzes the competition faced in the market place. The market and competitor analysis must be sensitive to regional as well as national trends and issues, so that organizational action positions the organization to meet its overall goals and objectives in the local market as well as in keeping with national industry trends and issues. Key questions that must be addressed are:

- What is the current market served by the organization?
- Who else provides this service?
- How will this change affect the current market position of the organization?
- What is the target market for this new service?

The hospital is the sole provider of acute care services for 32,450 people living within 25 miles of the hospital. No other hospital within 50 miles has an occupational health clinic. Currently, injured workers are served by the hospital emergency department, by physicians in private practice, and by one walk-in urgent care center located 24 miles from the hospital. Six area corporations within 5 miles of the hospital employ physicians and nurses in on-site clinics. Two of these corporations have indicated that they will close their clinics if the hospital provides occupational health services. Two others have indicated that they may close their clinics if the hospital is able to provide equally convenient service at a lower cost. Free-standing, hospital-owned occupational health clinics are common throughout the region, even though no other provider in this hospital's market offers this service. The first entrant into this market niche should be able to achieve and retain market position. Employers in this area are currently looking for one of the hospitals to bring this service to them. No other area hospital has announced any plans to develop such a service.

The development of a free-standing occupational health clinic will increase the market position of the hospital in occupational medicine and occupational health and may help the hospital maintain market position in other areas. Success with the clinic will help the hospital maintain its market position as the leading provider of organized outpatient and inpatient services in the county. Occupational health services will increase the demand for hospital-based physical and occupational therapy and medical testing. Imaging will be done at the occupational health clinic. The clinic will make referrals to the medical staff for specialized care and care requiring an inpatient admission. Over time, local employers will come to depend on the hospital to provide medical care, which may be the basis for additional services. Using the occupational health clinic will educate more potential patients about the hospital. The existing strategic plan for the hospital lists the development of a free-standing occupational health clinic as a strategy to develop a more formal service linkage with area employers.

The target market is composed of 1) employees of area corporations located within 10 miles of the hospital who need nonurgent and urgent medical care during the period from 7:00 A.M. to 7:00 P.M. on weekdays and from 7:00 A.M. to 1:00 P.M. on Saturdays, 2) employees and potential employees who need work-related physical examinations, 3) employees who need outpatient physical and occupational therapy as part of an approved treatment plan, and 4) employers who need specific consultation regarding the prevention of worker injuries. Services will be covered by direct payment from employers and/or workers' compensation. Patients needing emergency care will be sent directly to the hospital's emergency department. After hours, patients needing nonurgent and urgent care will be served by the hospital's emergency department, with follow-up provided by the occupational health clinic.

Community Health Analysis

A community health analysis is specific to business plans for health care organizations. It addresses the rationale for the change from the perspective of the regional health care system and the patient. It can include epidemiological information as well as demographic and economic information on the community. Much of the information in the community health analysis is drawn from an economic analysis. Key questions that must be addressed are:

- Why is the proposed change needed?
- What impact will this change have on the health status of the community?
- Who needs this service?
- Will this new or modified service make any other existing services obsolete?
- Why has this need gone unfilled in the past?

The rate of worker injury in the hospital's service area is 12% higher than the national average. Approximately 24,500 lost work days per year are experienced by employers as a result of worker injury. Workers' compensation cases filed over the last 5 years indicate that worker injuries in this service area lead to longer periods of recovery and more permanent disability than in other areas of the state. These conclusions are based on an analysis that controlled for worker age and work type. Excess morbidity exists in all phases of employee health.

Studies indicate that a worksite evaluation program conducted by the occupational health clinic should be able to lower the rate of worker injuries and shorten the length of time that an injured worker is away from work. Non–work-related health problems could be detected by annual physicals, enabling early intervention. Referrals can be made to a worker's physician or, if the worker does not have a primary care physician, to a member of the hospital's medical staff. Annual physicals also provide the employer with the ability to match job requirements with employee capabilities. Finally, timely treatment of worker injuries in conjunction with needed therapies should also decrease the amount of time a worker is unable to work.

Employees need this service and the occupational health expertise it will provide. Employers also need this service. Area employers report spending $450 more per employee per year than their regional and national competition on workers' compensation. Unless aggressive action is undertaken, local employers may conclude that relocation is needed to regain a position of cost competitiveness.

The occupational health clinic will replace the hospital's emergency department as a service provider during the time period that corresponds with most worker injuries. The clinic will operate a satellite imaging (i.e., x-ray) operation, replacing the need for the hospital to perform routine x-rays.

Until recently, larger employers believed it was more cost-effective to develop and offer occupational health services on site. The six largest area employers currently provide on-site services. Smaller employers use the hospital's emergency department and other ambulatory medical services. Recently, two of the large corporations have indicated their willingness to close their on-site clinics and sign a service contract with the hospital for this service. This, coupled with demand from smaller employers, now makes it possible to provide an organized occupational health service. Low long-term rates for borrowing coupled with existing prices and forecast utilization now make this a reasonable business venture.

Service Development Plan

Any significant modification, such as a project to add a free-standing occupational health clinic, requires time and resources to design and implement. The service development section of the business plan describes this process. It indicates what financial, human, physical, and information resources are necessary to develop the new or modified service. Typically a business plan is developed during the definition phase of development. In the earlier conceptual phase, many ideas and options have been considered. During the definition phase, one specific plan is developed. The business plan contains the information needed to move the proposed project into the last phase, the implementation phase. The service development plan is used to describe the developmental (or one-time) activities that must be completed prior to the service becoming operational. Key questions that must be addressed are:

- What resources are necessary to bring this project on line?
- Who will be the project manager?
- Who else will be on the project team?
- What external approvals are needed?

A 24,000-square-foot free-standing facility will be constructed. The estimated construction cost for this facility is $1,800,000. This cost includes all design and site development costs. Equipment is estimated to cost $400,000. This project will require a total of $2,200,000 to complete. Details on the building plan and equipment list are located in Appendix X. This project will use 1 acre of hospital land on the southeastern side of the hospital. Ample parking will be provided.

The vice president for operations will manage this project. She has previous experience in developing a similar service with another hospital. A fixed price contract will be awarded to a construction corporation to construct the facility. The contract will contain incentives and penalties to ensure timely completion.

All other vice presidents will serve on the project team. The vice president for facility services will develop the building specifications and provide direct coordination with the construction company. The vice president for human resources will manage the process of acquiring needed staff. The vice president for marketing will manage the advertising and promotional campaign. Three months before the clinic is opened, the hospital will hire a full-time physician as medical director and a supervising occupational health nurse. Both will join the project team. Under the direction of the medical director, other staff will be hired, policies and procedures will be written, and supplies will be ordered. Both will also work with the vice president of marketing to develop the client base for this service.

Because of a special exception, a Certificate of Need is not required. The occupational health clinic will be a department in the hospital. Therefore, action will be taken to ensure a compliance with all accreditation requirements. Local zoning regulations grant a blanket permission within the hospital zone for the hospital to construct any facility needed to fulfill its mission. Construction will adhere to all building codes.

Development Schedule

The development schedule provides a summary and detailed schedule for the completion of the proposed project. The project schedule is used to indicate when the project must be begun and when it will be complete. If possible, a summary program evaluation review technique (PERT) network diagram is included. Key questions that must be addressed are:

- How long will it take to complete this project?
- Are there any special time considerations?

After project approval, the facility can be ready for occupancy in 8 months. Services will be offered as soon as the facility is ready.

Construction of the foundation for this structure cannot be done during the period from December through February. Therefore, project approval is needed prior to September 1 to ensure that the foundation is completed prior to the wintertime period. If approved by September 1, the facility will be ready in 8 months. If approved after September 1, a revised date for project completion will need to be determined.

Organizational Plan

The organizational plan describes the impact the project will have on the organization and the existing systems the organization uses to manage its fiscal, information, human, and physical assets. This section is sometimes call an impact statement because it indicates the impact the proposed change will have on the existing organization. The organizational plan considers all impacts of the proposed change and notes where additional resources will be needed or saved. Key questions that must be addressed are:

- How will this change affect the structure of the organization?
- How will this change affect the fiscal management systems in the organization?
- How will this change affect the information management systems in the organization?
- How will this change affect the human resources management systems in the organization?
- How will this change affect the physical asset management systems in the organization?
- How will this change affect other services provided by the organization?

The occupational health clinic will be an organized outpatient department. It will report to the vice president of operations. Its medical director will be a department head in the hospital as well as a member of the medical staff in the department of emergency medicine. The medical director will attend all department head meetings.

The clinic will be a new revenue and expense center in the hospital with an appropriate chart of accounts. The hospital's accounting system will accumulate expenses and revenues and provide periodic reports. The clinic's receptionist will issue all bills. The hospital's business office will process all payments received and reconcile billing actions with the receptionist. Within its budget, the occupational health clinic will be authorized to voucher expenses for subsequent payment by the hospital's business office. No new staff are needed in the business office to perform these activities.

The existing hospital-wide computer system will be expanded to include the occupational health clinic as an organized outpatient department. This system will provide patient registration and patient tracking as well as expense and revenue information. The upgrade to accomplish this will require $25,000 to acquire a computer monitor and train the receptionist. The occupational health clinic will maintain its own medical records in accordance with hospital standards and policy. The clinic will have no impact on the department of medical records.

In total, this project will add six full-time and three part-time employees. Existing human resource systems will be used to acquire and manage these employees. Existing resources are able to accommodate this increase.

Housekeeping will provide custodial service to clean the new facility. To accomplish this, 0.5 full-time equivalent staff will be needed. This project will require that the staffing authorization in the department of housekeeping be expanded by this amount. The facility to be constructed will have a self-contained heating and ventilation system that will not affect any existing system in the hospital. Supplies to support the operation of the clinic will be drawn from existing inventories maintained by the department of materials management. No new supplies will be needed. Materials management has agreed to deliver supplies as needed to the clinic. The department of maintenance will provide services as needed. The hospital's consulting physicist will calibrate all x-ray equipment. All equipment will be purchased with service contracts. Except for the need to increase the number of custodians, no other impacts are anticipated.

The occupational health clinic will increase the utilization in the departments of physical therapy by 15% and occupational therapy by 4%. Patients will be referred to these departments for service under the direction of the clinic's medical director as case manager. Space will be provided for each of these departments in the new facility. The equipment list contained in the project estimate includes equipment to support the services of these two departments. The operational budget for the occupational health clinic includes resources to purchase needed staff time for the clinic from these departments. Both departments indicate that they will be able to provide needed services for at least the initial year of operation without changing the number of employed therapists. The department of marketing will develop and implement a promotional plan focused on area employers. The occupational health clinic will be featured in special publications.

Operational Plan

As implied by its name, the operational plan describes how the proposed project will operate in the existing organization once it is implemented. It must include any special or unique operational provisions associated with the change. It addresses staffing as well as staff responsibilities. It also indicates the services to be offered. Key questions that must be addressed are:

- How many and what type of employees will be used?
- How will this department operate?

On weekdays, staffing will be one physician, two occupational health nurses, and one receptionist. All employees will work a 12-hour shift. On Saturday, staffing will be one physician, one occupational health nurse, and one receptionist. In total, six full-time and three part-time employees will be used. One physician will be the director of the clinic and medical director. One of the full-time occupational health nurses will be a supervisor. The medical director will supervise all employees, provide services to patients, be responsible for service marketing and conducting on-site consultations with area employers, and approve all contracts with area corporations. As necessary, the supervising occupational health nurse will also conduct on-site evaluations. The clinic will be a department in the hospital and adhere to all existing policies except that the clinic will be closed on major business holidays.

Marketing Plan

The marketing plan includes the detailed plan for acquiring and retaining market share to sustain the project or change in service. It indicates the projected utilization for the new or revised service. New services rarely acquire a high percentage of market share when they are first introduced. Marketing is the strategy to acquire an initial market as well as to increase market share over time. Typically a 5-year market share/utilization projection is included. This section of the business plan also indicates the prices to be charged and how these prices relate to the pricing practices of competitors and substitute services. It also indicates how the new or revised service will be target marketed as well as the costs of promotion.

In health care, it is important that the marketing plan specifically describe and analyze the sources of funds that patients or clients will use to pay for the service. Often the prices for health and medical services are set by the buyer or the buyer's agent, such as an insurance company. In these situations, the marketing plan must indicate the revenue the organization can expect, given forecast utilization, by type of payer.

Overall, the marketing plan is the basis for estimating the revenue impact associated with a new or revised service. It includes the projected utilization, which reflects the fact that new services build market share over time. Unlike other sections of the business plan, the marketing section requires specialized expertise. Key questions to be addressed are:

- What is the projected utilization of the new or revised service?
- What is the total market for this service?
- What percentage of market share will be acquired within the first 6 months, in the first year, and after 5 years?
- What prices will be charged for services?
- Will total revenue depend on payer mix? If so, how?
- What will affect utilization?
- How will this service be promoted? What are the 5-year costs associated with promotion?

Utilization is projected to be 20 patients per day during the first 12 months of operation, increasing 25% in years 2 and 3 and 15% in years 4 and 5. Currently, within our market area, an average of 45 workers (standard deviation = 5.7) are referred by their employers for medical care per workday. Within 6 months, a 10% market share will be acquired. At the end of 12 months, a 35% market share will be acquired. By the end of 5 years, a 50% market share will be acquired and retained.

A basic visit will be priced at $45.00. No discounts will be provided. A detailed listing of all prices is included in Appendix A. Total revenue does not depend on payer mix. Employer satisfaction with services will affect utilization.

Promotional costs of 5% of anticipated new revenue are budgeted. These funds will be used to provide employers with descriptive information and underwrite a direct sales approach.

Financial Plan

It is somewhat ironic that the last section of a business plan is usually read first. The financial plan provides decision makers with a detailed assessment of the costs associated with developing and implementing the project and a realistic estimate of the financial consequences associated with the change. This comprehensive financial analysis is presented in three parts. The first part estimates the total cost of the project—the cost associated with developing the operational capability. The total project cost includes the costs associated with internal or external borrowing. The source of funds for project development is indicated. Project costs are one-time, nonrecurring costs, such as the cost of constructing a new building or modifying a building.

The second part of the financial plan indicates the operating costs and revenues of the project given projected utilization and service level. Operating costs and revenues are estimated for at least 5 years. Operating costs include all costs needed to provide the service. A break-even analysis is included.

The last part of the financial plan is an assessment of the short- and long-term financial impact of the proposal. Forecast or pro forma financial statements (i.e., the balance sheet and the statement of expenses and revenue) for the organization are prepared. Two sets of pro forma statements are prepared. One set indicates the forecast financial position of the organization for at least 5 years with the project, and the other set the forecast financial position for at least 5 years without the project. The decision maker is able to compare the two sets of pro forma statements to discern the financial impact of the project. Also included in this section of the financial plan is a 5-year analysis of the impact the project will have on cash flow and the source of funds to be used by the project.

Special expertise in financial analysis and financial management is needed to prepare the financial plan. Key questions to be addressed are:

- How much will the project cost to develop?
- What funds will be used?
- Under what conditions will these funds be acquired and paid back?
- What are the forecast annual expenses and revenue for this project for each of the next 5 years?
- What is the forecast financial position of the organization over the next 5 years without this change?
- What is the forecast financial position of the organization over the next 5 years with this change?
- How will this project affect cash flow?
- Overall, how will this project affect the financial condition of the organization?

Executive Summary

A formal business plan is written with an executive summary. This section, prepared for senior decision makers, reports the essence of the proposed project and the information contained in the detailed chapters of the business plan. Again, no specific convention exists for all business plans. The following topic list is provided as a guide:

- Name of the business
- Location
- Description of existing services and proposed new service
- Distinctive characteristics of the business
- Market overview
- Threats to success
- Business goals and objectives
- Projected financial statements

CONCLUSION

Any business plan is filled with assumptions and estimates. All sections of the plan must identify the assumptions made and explain why the assumptions are appropriate. The purpose of the business plan is to present decision makers with the information needed to make the decision to implement a specific change.

Business plans call attention to some very important questions. In preparing a business plan for a new or revised service, these questions require the manager to design the project in keeping with the goals and objectives of the organization. These questions also require that the manager explicitly indicate the positive and negative consequences associated with the proposed project.

A business plan is different from a project plan. A project plan merely describes the proposed project. A business plan describes the project in the context of the organization. The business plan estimates the impact the project or change will have on the organization.

Appendix A

Management Communications

Effective management communications are a management competency. Being able to communicate effectively the results of using quantitative methods is an allied competency associated with the professional use of these methods. Health services managers communicate in many ways, some formal and some very informal. They must have well-developed abilities to communicate, in writing as well as in front of or as part of small or large groups. The intent of this appendix is not to review communications as a field of study but to share general and specific professional conventions associated with management communication.

Health services managers communicate with many different types of individuals and organizations: health services professionals such as physicians, nurses, therapists, and technicians as well as paraprofessional and nonprofessional workers; patients, clients, and the general public; and board members, owners, government officials, other stakeholders, and managers in other organizations. To ensure that their messages are conveyed effectively, health services managers must design their communications for the intended audience. Senders generally assume that the message they send is the message that is received (and understood) by the receiver. However, this may not always be the case. People receiving a message or communication can interpret it in ways not intended by the sender. For example, a common mistake is assuming that the receiver is familiar with the jargon and abbreviations common to health services management (e.g., average length of stay, CON). People receive and interpret messages from their own individualistic, and sometimes idiosyncratic, perspective.

When the characteristics of the receiver are unknown, the appropriate approach is to adhere to dominant conventions. Generally, the effectiveness and appropriateness of the communication will be enhanced if these conventions are used. Adhering to professional conventions is one way to increase the probability that a receiver will treat the communication seriously and respond in accordance with the intent of the sender. Adhering to professional conventions also makes the receiver's task easier because the information or request is furnished in a usual or comfortable style. When a communication is well executed, no one notices its form. When the form is unclear or incorrect, the receiver is distracted and may never get to the substance of the intended message.

WRITTEN COMMUNICATIONS

Three types of written communications merit consideration: 1)the business letter, 2)the memorandum, and 3)the formal or technical report. Each fulfills a specific purpose.

The Business Letter

The business letter is an official communication used to conduct the formal business of the organization. Business letters are used whenever the communication extends beyond the organization, the nature of the communication is official business, or both. When the organization wishes to convey a message to an employee officially, a business letter is written, even though the message remains within the organization. For example, if an official grievance is filed with an employer, the employer will answer in letter form. Changes in job description or compensation are communicated to employees using a letter, even though the correspondence remains within the organization. When an employee is disciplined or fired, the action is communicated in letter form because the action represents an official action of the organization. Business letters are considered official correspondence, with copies retained in the organization's records.

Convention dictates that a business letter must be answered with a business letter, even if the communication remains within the organization. A business letter must also be used to respond to all communications from individuals or groups outside the organization.

Many formal guides have been published to help managers write effective business letters. Sometimes specific organizations have certain protocols involving business letters that supersede general professional conventions. General conventions are exactly that—general rules of thumb that can be used to guide practice. Aside from adhering to the basic conventions and ensuring an appropriate appearance, the primary challenge in composing a business letter is to deliver the intended message. If the intent is to convey information, then the letter must contain the information. If the letter is intended to establish a request, the request must be explicit, the general reasons for the request must be indicated, and the receiver must be furnished with sufficient information to meet the request.

The Memorandum

In contrast to the business letter, the memorandum, or memo, is a written communication intended to remain within the organization. The memo transmits information and should not be used to convey official organizational business. As for the business letter, general conventions exist for the structure and content of memos. Many formal guides on business memos are available for additional reference. Most organizations have protocols that must be learned by new employees.

The Formal or Technical Report

Formal or technical reports are used to communicate and record detailed analysis and recommendations. After the analysis has been completed, it is often useful to write the recommendations first, then the findings to support the recommendations, then the methodology used to construct the findings, and finally the introduction and purpose. Even before beginning the work requested, it is useful to construct "dummy" tables that will be used in data presentation; this will ensure that appropriate data are collected and used.

Generally, a report should be thought of as a pyramid-shaped layer cake intended to communicate a large amount of information in increasing detail. To be effective, it must be well organized, with each layer having a specific purpose. One conventional approach is to present a report in the following sequence:

Transmittal letter
Executive summary
Detailed report
    Section I: Statement of purpose
    Section II: Methods used
    Section III: Results
    Section IV: Recommendation and implications
Appendices (as needed)

The transmittal letter is addressed to the receiver of the report. It complies with all standards of the business letter even though it (and the report) may remain within the organization. In professional language it says, "Here is the report requested," and "I am prepared to discuss this report with you or to provide additional information as per your request." Some managers include the report's primary conclusion and/or recommendation in this letter. Although somewhat pro forma, the transmittal letter is the official cover of the report.

The report itself has multiple parts. The title page includes the title of the report, the date the report was completed, and the name and title of the person or persons who prepared the report. If not self-evident, the author's organization and address are included. If the report contains sensitive information, the title page is marked "Confidential" or "For Internal Release Only" or "Not for Citation."

The executive summary is usually no longer than five pages. It is written specifically for the chief executive officer or senior management. It states in succinct style the purpose of the report, the sources of data used in the report, the analytical methodology used, the primary findings, and the primary recommendations and implications. The purpose of the executive summary is to obviate the need for senior managers and other senior officials, such as board members, to read the entire report in order to glean its primary findings.

The executive summary provides a summation of the entire report specifically related to the purpose of the report. All information in the executive summary is backed by the information contained in the detailed report. Often, major findings and recommendations are highlighted in the executive summary so that they can be found easily and read quickly. Highlighting can involve bold print, underlining, or other techniques. Short reports may omit the executive summary.

Most written reports contain an introduction, a statement of methodology, and findings and recommendations. The introduction or statement of purpose states the intent of the report (e.g., "This report identifies and analyzes characteristics of area hospitals to determine which hospital is the most efficient"). The statement of methodology presents information on how the data were analyzed. Sources of data as well as the analytical approach are explained.

The findings and recommendations can be included as one section or as two parts in the report. Important charts, graphs, and tables are usually found in this part of the report. Supporting tables, charts, calculations, and graphs are included in appendices and referenced in this section (e.g., "see Chart A-3, included in Appendix A, for additional information," or "Appendix B includes additional information on this subject," or "Appendix C contains the calculations for these results").

Recommendations must be stated clearly and be easy to find. A reader should not have to search for the recommendations. The rationale for each and every recommendation must be clearly presented and can appear as a paragraph below each recommendation. Recommendations with rationales are the primary conclusions of the report, conclusions that have been logically established by all the previous work covered in the report. Findings are the rationales for the recommendations. Therefore, findings must be linked logically to the recommendations.

Appendices are used to report background data and detailed analyses. Often a written report may have many appendices, each separately labeled with a specific letter or number designation. When a table or chart is included in an appendix, it is numbered sequentially with a number that includes the letter or number designation of the appendix (e.g., Table A-4). Pages of appendices are numbered using this same type of system (e.g., A-1, A-2, A-3). Some consider appendices to be mini-reports, with each appendix containing the detailed data and calculations used to construct the overall report. Often the appendices are developed before the primary report is prepared.

ORAL PRESENTATIONS

Managers are frequently required to communicate information to small or large groups by giving an oral presentation. Although the substance of the oral presentation may be very similar to the information included in a written report, the oral presentation relies on somewhat different conventions. In the oral presentation, the presenter provides the voice track designed to complement the 35-mm slides, overhead transparencies, or posters shown to the audience.

Visual Aids

Overhead transparencies or 35-mm slides are the essence of the oral presentation. They tell the primary story associated with the presentation. They also serve as note cards for the presenter. Transparencies or slides are used to:

- Create the agenda for the presentation
- Report information
- Draw attention to critical findings
- Focus attention on primary recommendations

All slides must be simple and easily read and understood by the audience. Generally, slides contain main points, findings, and recommendations. Unlike tables of data, which leave the responsibility of finding key data points to the reader, slides used in oral presentations present only the key data points. To be effective, slides must include the intended information and be presented so that the intended purpose is visually perceived and understood by the receiver.

Slides are subject to the same professional conventions associated with a written report. In addition, every slide should have a title, and consecutive numbering, either in the title or at the bottom of the slide, can be helpful. Data sources should be included on any slide that reports data. All slides must be checked carefully; errors in mathematics, spelling, or grammar reduce the effectiveness of an oral presentation.

The type or print used on slides must be large enough to be read by the audience. The wording used on slides should be as succinct and direct as possible. Text slides should be presented in bulleted or numbered outline form. Charts or graphs tend to be more effective for presenting data on a slide than are tables.

Every slide should have a purpose, and no slide should take more than 1 minute to understand. The following seven guidelines for visual aids are helpful in preparing slides:

1. Write the paper or speech and trim it to the allotted time before designing visual aids so that there will be no more visual aids than are needed.
2. Keep visual aids simple; simplicity is more effective in a presentation. A visual aid that uses one color for emphasis is most effective.
3. Reduce the number of plot points to those needed to show trends or peaks and valleys. The audience cannot extract data from a graph on a screen. Rather, they will be trying to visualize what the presenter is saying and verifying that the data support those statements.
4. Try not to present more than two or three variables on one chart, graph, or table. Break complex correlations down into a series of simple components and "walk the audience through." The audience is less familiar with the data than is the presenter, and more time is required for them to comprehend a complex graphic.
5. Limit the amount of material presented on a visual aid by using the "five words/five lines" rule (no more than five words per line or five lines per slide). The more material included, the smaller it must be, and the harder it will be to read. Show only selected data or present only a few columns or lines at a time. Use key words.
6. Trim footnotes and titles where possible. The more space these take, the less remains for the data.
7. Use type and other elements that are large and bold enough to be readable. A good rule of thumb is to imagine typing with a conventional typewriter on a 3 inches by 5 inches card. If the material does not fit, it needs trimming. More material can usually be included on an overhead transparency than on a 35-mm slide because overhead transparencies often project larger than slides.

Consider the examples shown in Figures A-1 and A-2. These slides provide succinct statements. They include important information. They are clear and simple. They create an effective visual reception.

Frequently, paper copies (handouts) of slides are provided to the audience to use in conjunction with the presentation. Paper copies of slides allow the audience to write notes about the slides and to have a record of the presentation. Paper copies of slides may also be furnished at the end of the oral presentation or upon request.

Being an Effective Presenter

Being an effective presenter begins with the design of the oral presentation. For example, some presenters consider it more effective to give the audience the primary findings and recommendation before presenting the detailed rationale. This method establishes a context for the detailed information that will be presented in the main part of the presentation. Others believe waiting to the end of the presentation is more effective. This is a decision that must be made by the individual presenter.

Primary conclusions

1. Emergency Room visits have declined for the last 6 months.
2. All area hospitals have experienced this same trend.
3. Staffing in the Emergency Room should be reduced.

Figure A-1.   Sample slide 44 for an oral presentation.

Staffing reductions should include:

1. 1.0 FTE RN on weekday day shift.
2. 2.3 FTE EMTs on the weekday evening shift.
3. 1.0 FTE EMT on all weekend shifts.
4. No change on the weekday night shift.
5. No change is needed in medical or clerical staff.

Figure A-2.   Sample slide 45 for an oral presentation.

The presentation must be organized to meet the objectives and stay within the time constraints established for the presentation. A common mistake is to squeeze too much into too little time. Novice presenters tend to over present, and in the process create confusion instead of understanding.

The effective organization of an oral presentation starts with establishing its agenda and a statement of the purpose of the oral presentation. Aside from indicating to the audience what is to come, this information enables the audience to anticipate the content of the presentation. The first slides in every oral presentation should include the title, agenda, and purpose of the presentation and the names and titles of all presenters.

Most effective presentations—especially those that cover many related topics—are organized into individual sections much like reports. Each section can have a subobjective and subagenda. Like an effective story, an oral presentation has an introduction, which establishes what the presentation is about; a middle, in which the primary story line or lines are developed; and an end, in which conclusions are stated or restated for purposes of emphasis. Effective oral presentations exclude any information that is not directly related to the primary story line or objective of the presentation. Effective presenters do not attempt to incorporate responses to all possible questions; they present the core information knowing that questions are natural. An effective oral presentation focuses on the essence of the material.

Being an effective presenter requires practice. Novice presenters are usually nervous until they realize that audiences are more interested in examining the slides than in examining them. Every presenter is, to some degree, nervous. Experienced presenters know what they need to do to channel this nervousness into useful energy. Experienced presenters know that they are merely voice tracks that establish the logical bridges between the slides and that answer questions.

When an audience member asks a question, two types of responses are generally acceptable. If the answer is known, it should be supplied. If the answer is not known, the presenter should restate the question so that the questioner knows that it is understood, and should indicate that the answer will be furnished after the presentation.

In addition to the above conventions and suggestions, the effective presenter should:

1. Practice the presentation. Presentation skills can be assessed using videotapes if possible. As necessary, add emphasis to the substance of the presentation. A thorough knowledge of the material in a presentation, combined with practice, is necessary for success.
2. Always introduce himself or herself and any other presenters at the beginning of the presentation, and acknowledge any colleagues who are not present but contributed to the report.
3. Indicate his or her preference concerning when questions should be asked—either during or at the end of the presentation.
4. Try to start on time, and always attempt to finish on time, even if the presentation started late. Generally, if a presentation runs over the scheduled time, the audience becomes distracted and pays little attention to what is being presented.
5. Focus the attention on the audience, and tell them when something is really important.
6. Throughout the presentation, create and recreate the sense of agenda and purpose. Refer back to the agenda and purpose often.
7. As in written reports, use language that is appropriate for the intended audience.
8. Speak clearly and loudly enough to be heard by all audience members.
9. Always remain civil, even in the face of an obnoxious question or questioner.
10. At the end, thank the audience for their attention, and ensure that all questions have been asked and addressed. Inform the audience of any next steps in the project.
11. After the presentation, follow up on any unresolved questions.

Effective oral presentations are an essential managerial tool. They are very useful for communicating complex material to large groups of people. They facilitate decision making at all levels of the organization. Designed and presented well, they are effective. Poorly designed, poorly organized, and/or poorly presented presentations are unpleasant experiences for all and make the presenter look incompetent.

HINTS FOR EFFECTIVE WRITING

Managers must be able to write effectively in order to communicate effectively. Effective writing is a skill that must be learned and practiced. The following are general conventions intended to help develop this skill.

1. Simplicity, clarity, and grace should characterize writing. The tone of the writing should be courteous, even if the topic seems simplistic, self-evident, or boring.
2. The text of reports should be written in an appropriate style. Use of first or second person or questions in the text should be avoided.
3. Flawless spelling and grammar are expected. It must be remembered that spelling check programs on computers merely verify that a word is in the dictionary, not whether it is the appropriate word.
4. Contractions (e.g., don't), jargon (e.g., service units), and slang (e.g., a lot) should be avoided. Abbreviations should be spelled out at the first usage (e.g., "average length of stay [ALOS]").
5. Contractions and possessives must not be interchanged (e.g., "it's" means "it is"; the possessive form of it is "its").
6. "Data" is a *plural* word (e.g., "Data were collected from . . .").
7. A sentence should never begin with the conjunctions "and," "or," and "but."
8. Verbs should *not* be split with multiple adjectives:
   Poor: "Order *has* only recently *been established*."
   Better: "Order *has been* established only recently."
9. When using numbers, the Arabic number should be used for ten or above (i.e., 10), unless it is the first word in a sentence; then it should be spelled out (i.e., "Ten . . ."). Numbers below 10 should be spelled out.
10. The percent symbol should be used for percentages in the text (e.g., 9%, not 9 percent), except at the beginning of a sentence (e.g., "Nine percent of . . .").
11. The present tense should be used to report literature, even if the literature is old (e.g., "Smith [1929] concludes . . .").
12. The future tense should not be used to refer to subsequent developments or sections in a report:
    Incorrect: "This report will discuss. . . ."
    Correct: "This report discusses. . . ."
13. Sexist language should be avoided.
14. Strong verbs and the active (not passive) tense should be used. For example, use verbs such as:

acknowledges	credits	observes
addresses	defines	predicts
admits	demands	presents
advocates	demonstrates	proposes
argues	develops	recognizes

asserts	directs	recommends
believes	discusses	rejects
challenges	emphasizes	reports
claims	endorses	speculates
concludes	explains	suggests
concurs	examines	states
contends	illustrates	supports
contrasts	implies	urges
creates	maintains	writes

15. Data should not be criticized if they fail to support a specific conclusion. The report should state what the data do indicate and should use them appropriately.
16. Notes or comments should be used to explain specific points about the data. Notes can include references as well as comments for the reader.
17. The work and ideas of others should be credited with appropriate references. An accepted reference style, such as that recommended by the American Psychological Association, should be used.
18. The report should look professional and be easy to read and understand. It is important to design and present a report that the receiver will want to read as well as understand. If possible, the draft copy of the report should be reviewed by a colleague before a final version is submitted. Beauty is in the eye of the beholder; the audience's preferences, needs, and eccentricities must be considered.

CONCLUSION

Being an effective communicator is a skill that must be incorporated into the repertoire of any effective manager. The communication method selected by the manager must be appropriate to the material and the audience and used within the conventions and rules associated with the method. Managers with limited abilities to communicate effectively handicap themselves as well as their employers.

EXERCISES

A-1. Write a business letter to a hospital requesting a copy of their most recent annual report. Use the *AHA Annual Guides* for addresses.
A-2. Prepare an oral presentation with no more than five slides that indicates your background and interests in the field of health services management. Indicate your educational background and your professional objective(s).
A-3. Present a written report that analyzes the 20-year history of the hospital you were born in. Use *AHA Annual Guides* as data sources. Report current services and whether these services have changed over the last 20 years. Using *Hospital Statistics* (published by the American Hospital Association) as a data source, indicate whether, over the last 20 years, "your" hospital has been similar or dissimilar to other similar hospitals. Select one or more groups of similar hospitals for purposes of comparison (e.g., size, ownership, location, type). Report trends involving utilization and other measures included in American Hospital Association data.

Appendix B
Probability Distributions Used in Queuing Theory

Queuing theory relies on the Poisson and exponential probability distributions. This appendix provides additional information on these distributions as well as the equations used in queuing theory.

STANDARD NORMAL PROBABILITY DISTRIBUTION

The standard normal probability distribution, represented by the bell-shaped curve, is a fundamental concept of statistics. Operations researchers, however, warn that the standard normal probability distribution may be inappropriate for modeling waiting lines and service times because the distribution of time in such systems is more variable than in the standard normal distribution. That is, it is not symmetrical and truncated at zero. Therefore, this distribution should be used only when there is little or no variance demonstrated in the arrival and service rates.

USING THE POISSON AND EXPONENTIAL DISTRIBUTIONS

Using the Poisson Distribution

The following example illustrates how the Poisson distribution is used to estimate arrival rates. If the expected arrival rate (λ) at a walk-in clinic is three patients per hour ($\lambda = 3$), the Poisson probability distribution estimates that:

0 or no arrivals per hour would occur 4.98% of the time
1 arrival per hour would occur 14.99% of the time
2 arrivals per hour would occur 22.41% of the time
3 arrivals per hour would occur 22.41% of the time
4 arrivals per hour would occur 16.81% of the time
9 or more arrivals per hour would occur 0.038% of the time

These estimates were calculated using standard statistical tables.
The equation for the Poisson distribution is:

$$P(x) = \frac{\lambda^x e^{-\lambda}}{x!}$$

(Eq. B-1)

239

where $P(x)$ = probability of exactly x arrivals
$\quad\quad\quad x$ = actual number of arrivals in a specific time period
$\quad\quad\quad \lambda$ = arrival rate for a specific period of time
$\quad\quad\quad e$ = the constant 2.71828
$\quad\quad\quad x!$ = x factorial (e.g., $3! = 3 \times 2 \times 1$)

The probabilities associated with $\lambda = 3$ as listed above, when graphed, illustrate the general shape (not a bell shape) of the Poisson probability distribution.

Using the Exponential Distribution

The following example shows how the exponential distribution is used to estimate waiting time. The average service rate (μ) in a walk-in clinic is 4 patients per hour. (This average rate also could be the expected average rate of service, a design parameter.) Using an exponential distribution to describe service times and basing the calculation on this average service rate, the probability of a patient being served within a specified time period (t) can be estimated using the following equation:

$$P(t) = 1 - e^{-\mu t} \quad\quad\quad\quad \text{(Eq. B-2)}$$

where P = probability of serving 1, 2, 3, or any number of patients within a time t
$\quad\quad\quad t$ = service time
$\quad\quad\quad e$ = the constant 2.71828. . .
$\quad\quad\quad \mu$ = average or expected service rate

According to this model, if μ (the average or expected service rate) was four patients per hour:

32.97% of all patients would be served in 6 min or less (i.e., $t = 0.1$ hour)
69.88% of all patients would be served in 18 min or less (i.e., $t = 0.3$ hour)
86.4% of all patients would be served in 30 min or less (i.e., $t = 0.5$ hour)
93.92% of all patients would be served in 42 min or less (i.e., $t = 0.7$ hour)

The pattern of service times is affected by a change in the expected service rate. When the expected service rate drops to three patients per hour, using Equation B-2, we find that:

25.92% of all patients would be served in 6 min or less (i.e., $t = 0.1$ hour)
59.34% of all patients would be served in 18 min or less (i.e., $t = 0.3$ hour)
77.69% of all patients would be served in 30 min or less (i.e., $t = 0.5$ hour)
87.75% of all patients would be served in 42 min or less (i.e., t 4 0.7 hour)

USING MULTIPLE-SERVER QUEUING THEORY MODELS

In multiple-server queuing theory models:

s is the number of servers
λ is the mean arrival rate for the system
μ is the mean service rate for the system

The examples in this section use the following values for these variables: s = two servers, λ = three patients per hour, and μ = four patients per hour.

Estimating the Probability that All Channels are Idle

The probability that all channels are idle (the system is empty of units) is represented by the equation:

$$P_0 = \frac{1}{\left[\sum_{n=0}^{n=s-1} \frac{1}{n!}\left(\frac{\lambda}{\mu}\right)^n\right] + \left(\frac{1}{s!}\right)\left(\frac{\lambda}{\mu}\right)^s\left[\frac{s\mu}{(s\mu) - \lambda}\right]} \qquad \text{(Eq. B-3)}$$

where λ = arrival rate to the queueing system
   μ = service rate for each server
   s = number of servers in the system
   $x!$ = x factorial

Note that 0! and 1! = 1.
   For example, if λ = 3 and μ = 4 with s = 2, then n = 1 and

$$P_0 = \frac{1}{\left(1 + \frac{3}{4}\right) + \frac{1}{2}\left(\frac{3}{4}\right)^2\left[\frac{2 \times 4}{(2 \times 4) - 3}\right]}$$

Thus, P_0 = 0.4545 = 45.45%.

Estimating the Average Number of Units in the Queue (L_q)

The expected number of units in the queue—that is, the length of the queue—is represented by the following equation:

$$L_q = \frac{\left(\frac{\lambda}{\mu}\right)^{s+1}}{s \times s! \times \left[\frac{(s\mu) - \lambda}{s\mu}\right]^2} \times P_0 \qquad \text{(Eq. B-4)}$$

where λ = arrival rate to the queueing system
   μ = service rate for each server
   s = number of servers in the system
   $x!$ = x factorial

For example, if λ = 3 and μ = 4 with c = 2, then

$$L_q = \frac{\left(\frac{3}{4}\right)^3}{2 \times 2! \times \left[\frac{(2 \times 4) - 3}{2 \times 4}\right]^2} \times 0.4545$$

Thus, L_q = 0.1227.

Estimating the Probability that an Arriving Unit Must Wait (P_w)

The probability that an arriving unit must wait for service—that is, the probability that all servers are busy—is represented by the following equation:

$$P_w = \frac{1}{s!}\left(\frac{\lambda}{\mu}\right)^s\left[\frac{s\mu}{(s\mu) - \lambda}\right] \times P_0 \qquad \text{(Eq. B-5)}$$

where λ = arrival rate to the queueing system

μ = service rate for each server

s = number of servers in the system

$x!$ = x factorial

For example, if $\lambda = 3$ and $\mu = 4$ with $c = 2$, then

$$P_w = \frac{1}{2} \left(\frac{3}{4} \right)^2 \left[\frac{2 \times 4}{(2 \times 4) - 3} \right] \times 0.4545$$

Thus, $P_w = 0.2045 = 20.45\%$.

Suggested Readings

Analyzing Capacity

Hillier, F.S., & Lieberman, G.I. (1990). *Introduction to operations research* (5th ed.). New York: McGraw-Hill.

Analyzing Waiting Lines

Hillier, F.S., & Lieberman, G.I. (1990). *Introduction to operations research* (5th ed.). New York: McGraw-Hill.

The Business Plan

O'Hara, P.D. (1990). *The total business plan: How to write, rewrite and revise.* New York: John Wiley & Sons.

Decision Analysis

Hillier, F.S., & Lieberman, G.I. (1990). *Introduction to operations research* (5th ed.). New York: McGraw-Hill.

Economic Analysis

Teutsch, S.M., & Haddix, A.C. (Eds.). (1995). *A practical guide to prevention effectiveness: Decision and economic analysis.* New York: Oxford University Press.

Financial Evaluation of Projects

Brigham, E.F. (1995). *Fundamentals of financial management* (7th ed.). Fort Worth, TX: Dryden Press.
Gapenski, L.C. (1993). *Understanding health care financial management.* Ann Arbor, MI: AUPHA Press/Health Administration Press.

Forecasting

Hillier, F.S., & Lieberman, G.I. (1990). *Introduction to operations research* (5th ed.). New York: McGraw-Hill.
Sanders, N.R., & Manrodt, K.B. (1994). Forecasting practices in U.S. corporations: Survey results. *Interfaces, 24,* 2.

General System Flow Charting

Bae, H.M. (1993). Process flow modeling and analysis: A practitioner's approach. *Industrial Engineering, 25,* 4.
Betka, R.D. (1993). Managing by fact. *Healthcare Financial Management, 47,* 1.
Denton, D.K. (1992). Redesigning a job by simplifying every task and responsibility. *Industrial Engineering, 24,* 8.
Quinn, J.C. (1991). Flow chart eases planning process for hospitals. *Health Care Strategic Management, 9,* 4.

Present and Future Value of Money

Brigham, E.F. (1995). *Fundamentals of financial management* (7th ed.). Fort Worth, TX: Dryden Press.
Gapenski, L.C. (1993). *Understanding health care financial management.* Ann Arbor, MI: AUPHA Press/Health Administration Press.

Program Evaluation Review Technique

Hillier, F.S., & Lieberman, G.I. (1990). *Introduction to operations research* (5th ed.). New York: McGraw-Hill.

Kuklan, H. (1993). Effective project management: An expanded network approach. *Journal of Systems Management, 44*, 3.

Littlefield, T.K., & Randolph, P.H. (1991). PERT duration times: Mathematics or MBO. *Interfaces, 21*, 6.

Soroush, H.M. (1994). The most critical path in a PERT network. *Journal of the Operations Research Society, 45*, 3.

Working With Numbers/Presenting Data

Parson, R.J. (1992). A manager's guide to statistical methods. *Industrial Engineering, 24*, 1.

Index

Page numbers followed by "*t*" or "*f*" indicate tables or figures, respectively.